TACKLING
HATE

Library and Archives Canada Cataloguing in Publication

Tackling hate : combating antisemitism : the Ottawa protocol / edited by Scott Reid & Mario Silva.

Includes essays, testimony, and documents drawn from the work of the Canadian Parliamentary Coalition to Combat Anti-semitism (CPCCA).
Issued in print and electronic formats.
ISBN 978-1-77161-078-0 (pbk.).-- ISBN 978-1-77161-079-7 (html).--ISBN 978-1-77161-080-3 (pdf)

1. Antisemitism--Canada--Prevention. I. Reid, Scott, 1964-, editor
II. Silva, Mario, 1966-, editor III. Title: Combating antisemitism : the Ottawa protocol.

DS146.C2T33 2014   305.892'4071   C2014-903500-4
                                                 C2014-903501-2

Pubished by Mosaic Press, Oakville, Ontario, Canada, 2014.
Distributed in the United States by Bookmasters (www.bookmasters.com).
Distributed in the U.K. by Gazelle Book Services (www.gazellebookservices.co.uk).

MOSAIC PRESS, Publishers
Copyright © 2014, Scott Reid and Mario Silva
Front cover design by Joanne Howard
Book layout by Eric Normann

Printed and Bound in Canada.
ISBN   Paperback 978-1-77161-078-0
            ePub   978-1-77161-079-7
            ePDF   978-1-77161-080-3

We acknowledge the financial support of the Government of Canada through the Canada Book Fund (CBF) for this project.

Nous reconnaissons l'aide financière du gouvernement du Canada par l'entremise du Fonds du livre du Canada (FLC) pour ce projet.

 Canadian Heritage Patrimoine canadien

MOSAIC PRESS
1252 Speers Road, Units 1 & 2
Oakville, Ontario L6L 5N9
phone: (905) 825-2130

info@mosaic-press.com

www.mosaic-press.com

TACKLING
HATE

COMBATING ANTISEMITISM:
THE OTTAWA PROTOCOL

edited by SCOTT REID & MARIO SILVA

Contents

Biographies

Scott Reid

Scott Reid is the Member of Parliament for Lanark-Frontenac-Lennox & Addington and is currently the Deputy Leader of the Government in the House of Commons. He also serves as chairman of the subcommittee on International Human Rights of the Standing Committee on Foreign Affairs and International Development. Scott Reid was first elected in November 2000. In 2010 Scott Reid Chair the Steering Committee of the CPCCA.

Scott Reid has held five Constituency Referendums, in which the voters of his riding indicate how they would like him to vote on important pieces of legislation. As a result of his first referendum, his constituents advised him to opt in to the MP pay raise and then donate it to charity. Since that time, Scott has donated $140,000 to purchase Automated External Defibrillators and CPR training for his riding. Scott Reid is the author of two books - Lament for a Notion and Canada Remapped - as well as numerous articles. He has appeared before parliamentary committees, at both the provincial and federal levels as an expert witness on issues relating to national unity and democracy.

Prior to his election, Scott served as chief constitutional advisor to Preston Manning. He also taught history at the University of Western Sydney in Australia. Having grown up in the family business, Scott Reid is a member of the Board of Directors of Giant Tiger Stores Ltd.

Dr. Mario Silva

Dr. Mario Silva has had a distinguished career as an elected official in Canada between the years 1994 and 2011 as well as an author and international legal scholar. In 2010-2011, he co-chaired the Canadian Parliamentary Coalition to Combat Antisemitism. In December 2011, he was appointed by the Government of Canada to serve as the 2013 Chair of the International Holocaust Remembrance Alliance (IHRA). The IHRA is an intergovernmental body comprised of 31 member countries with a mandate to engage the support of political and social policy leaders to encourage Holocaust education, remembrance, and research both nationally and internationally.

Dr. Silva is a graduate of the University of Toronto, the University of Sorbonne in Paris and holds a Master's degree in International Law from Oxford University as well as a PhD in law from the National University of Ireland in

Galway. He has been honoured by the French President with the title of Knight of the Order of the Legion of Honour and has also been awarded the Order of Merit of Portugal, the Order of Rio Branco from Brazil. Dr. Silva is the recipient of the Bridge Builder Award by the Parliament of Canada All Party Interfaith Friendship Group and the Holocaust Education Humanitarian Award of the Hamilton Jewish Federation.

Dr. Silva has published several articles in the field of international law and has authored two books, State Legitimacy and Failure in International Law and Hanging By a Thread: Afghan Women's Rights and Security Threats, which he co-author with Dr. Massouda Jalal.

Part I: Introduction

The world today is witnessing an escalating, sophisticated, global, virulent and lethal antisemitism that has become unprecedented since the end of the Second World War. The term antisemitism evokes images of concentration camps, gas chambers, ghettos, and inexcusable human suffering, indignity, and systematic violence against an identifiable group, namely European Jewry. It has been nearly seventy years since the end of the Second World War and the creation of a Jewish State, Israel. These two facts may lead one to believe that antisemitism has faded from the international collective consciousness and that the horrors of the Holocaust have been diminished from human memory.

However, the current resurgence in antisemitism has become altered by international and domestic landscapes. In popular discourse, in media, using new tools of the internet and social media, a rise in antisemitism is real and not imagined. What has become striking and alarming has been the rise of antisemitic incidents within the OESC countries. Combating antisemitism is vitally important in upholding human rights. But the emergence of new forms of this old hatred represents a genuine threat to international security. It breeds a culture of hate and hostility against those deemed to be outside society. In many ways, antisemitism represents an original form of hatred.

The reality of a new and virulent antisemitism has led to the creation of the Inter-parliamentary Coalition for Combating Antisemitism (ICCA) and the Canadian Parliamentary Coalition to Combat Antisemitism (CPCCA). Parliamentarians—as democratically elected representatives from around the world and the embodiment of essential elements of a free and equal society—

3

have now taken up the challenges faced in tackling the blight of hatred and persecution found through the incarnation of antisemitism in all its forms.

The Inter-Parliamentary Coalition for Combating Antisemitism was created at the inaugural meeting of one hundred twenty-five legislators from over forty countries in London, United Kingdom in February 2009. These democratic representatives from around the world expressed their concerns and alarm at the evidence of a global rise in antisemitic incidents and their recognition of traditional antisemitic themes in international discourse. The principal purpose of this Coalition is to share knowledge, experience, best practice, and to make and disseminate recommendations in an attempt to deal more effectively with contemporary antisemitism.

The stated objectives of the ICCA is to promote awareness and understanding of the nature and threat of antisemitism; to establish a reliable set of indicators of antisemitism for the purpose of better identifying, monitoring, confronting and combating it; to work with scholars of antisemitism and the leading scholarly institutions for the study of antisemitism; to identify and develop a range of remedies to combat antisemitism; and to organise working groups around the indicators of antisemitism.

Most importantly, in hopes of combating the injustice of antisemitism in democratic society, the ICCA called upon participating legislators to establish inquiry panels to their countries using the All-Party Parliamentary Inquiry Into Antisemitism in the UK as a model template for other national assemblies to follow. The conference produced "The London Declaration for Combating Antisemitism" which called upon:

> Parliamentarians [to] return to their legislature, Parliament or Assembly and establish inquiry scrutiny panels that are tasked with determining the existing nature and state of antisemitism in their countries and developing recommendations for government and civil society action.[1]

This call to action became the impetus for the establishment of the Canadian Parliamentary Coalition to Combat Antisemitism (CPCCA). Under the leadership of Citizenship and Immigration Minister Jason Kenney and International Steering Committee Chair, Professor Irwin Cotler, a delegation of eleven Canadian Members of Parliament attended the conference in London. Concerned

---

1 London Declaration on Combating Antisemitism, Lancaster House UK, 17 February 2009.

about the renewed emergence of new forms of antisemitism and backed by partnerships established with legislators from the international community, the CPCCA is tasked to carry out its mandate of inquiry and assist government to develop civil action to tackle the scourge of antisemitism in Canada.

The Canadian Parliamentary Coalition to Combat Antisemitism (CPCCA) was formed in March of 2009 and brought together twenty-two parliamentarians from all parties in the House of Commons. The CPCCA is not affiliated with the Government of Canada, or any non-governmental organization or advocacy group, but is a branch associated with the Inter-parliamentary Coalition to Combat Antisemitism (ICCA). The CPCCA is a multi-party coalition of concerned parliamentarians aiming to confront and combat the Canadian manifestations of the global resurgence of anti-Semitism. The CPCCA recognizes that antisemitism is, by its very nature, fundamentally opposed to the foundational values of Canada, including its multicultural identity, the Canadian Charter of Human Rights which guarantee o freedom from discrimination, as well as the values of the Universal Declaration of Human Rights.

From this stated mandate, the primary goals of the CPCCA and the subsequent inquiry has focused on identifying and defining the nature of antisemitism in Canada today; analyzing the extent of the problems based on sound evidence; and suggesting practical recommendations as to how the problem can be addressed. The Inquiry Panel was launched on June 2, 2009 with an open call for written submissions from the Canadian public.

Between June and November 2009, nearly two hundred written submissions were received. In assessing the submissions several criteria were established to determine which submissions to accept and to decide who to invite as part of the oral submissions and hearings. These included:

1) Where the written submission is antisemitic, anti-Zionist or more generally not respectful of human rights in which giving a platform to such a submission would contradict and undermine the purpose of the Committee, an oral submission should not be granted.

2) Where several written submissions are in essence similar, it should be sufficient to invite oral submissions from only one person or organization who made the submission as repetition should be avoided.

3) Written submissions need to be assessed for their seriousness and scholarship. Where written submis-

sions are insubstantial, state only the obvious, and add nothing to the knowledge of the Committee, it would seem pointless to invite the author(s) to make an oral submission.

4) The purpose of the Committee is to examine antisemitism, not the policy or practices of the State of Israel, whether in defence or land ownership or security or any other matter. Written submissions about the policy or practices of the State of Israel should be should not lead to an invitation to make oral submissions, because the written submissions deal with matters beyond the purview of the Committee.

5) Similarly, the purpose of the Committee is not to determine how one achieves peace in the Middle East. Any written submission, which in essence is directed to that subject, is also beyond the purview of the Committee and does not justify an oral submission.

6) In the same vein, the purpose of the Committee is not to take sides and favour one party or faction over another within Israel. Any written submission that in substance is an exercise of political partisanship for or against one of the political parties or factions in Israel would be considered improper as the basis for an invitation for an oral submission to the Committee.

From November 2009 to January 2010, the Inquiry Panel of the CPCCA held a series of ten domestic hearings into antisemitism in Canada. The hearings were held in the buildings of the Parliament of Canada and were open to the public. As part of this exercise, the Panel heard testimony and received full cooperation from ministers and government departments, local authorities and public bodies such as law enforcement agencies.

Despite the meticulous attention to detail, even before the completion of the Inquiry Panel and its subsequent report critics have attacked this process of selection and testimony. While not every group or individual who submitted materials was invited to provide oral evidence, we did hear from a broad cross section of opinions, including oral representations from a number of groups who expressed skepticism or reservations about our work. These groups and individuals expressed their views through submissions and in public media, even objecting to the very existence of this Inquiry. Even before a single witness had been called, a number of individuals accused the Inquiry of having been established with the ulterior motive of criminalizing criticism of Israel.[2] These attempts to discredit and silence pre-emptively an inquiry into the nature and extent of one of the most enduring and pernicious forms of hatred represents a misunderstanding of the nature of the problem and its modern complexity. At worst, these attacks are a worrying example of the wilful attempt of a small minority to use slight of hand techniques to justify and adhere to their own hateful agenda.

It is important to remember the mission of the CPCCA and the state of antisemitism in Canada. The Inquiry Panel recognized that racism, in any manifestation, is fundamentally opposed to the multicultural identity of Canada and to the Canadian values of human rights and human dignity. It also noted that while Canada is overall an extremely tolerant society, many minority groups in Canada have, to a great or lesser degree, been the targets of racist and discriminatory incidents or discourse. In every instance, such expressions of hatred are damaging to the communities that are targeted and to Canadian society more generally.

To recognize that there are multiple expressions of hatred in society is not to say that they are all the same in their source, scope or manifestation. In short, antisemitism is a distinguishable, sophisticated and virulent form of hate that necessitates being studied as it own phenomenon. Antisemitism is the oldest and most enduring form of hatred and has caused "catastrophic suffering, not only for Jews, but also for all those who are enveloped in that virus of antisemitism" as it has mutated over time.[3] Yet, as discussed in the United Kingdom's All-Party Report, the "high degree of integration and success" of the Jewish community means that Jewish people experience a model of prejudice and racism different from other communities. "Antisemitism is not always recognized for what [it] is, and Jews are not always recognized as victims of racism."[4]

Antisemitism is now a distinguishable form of hate in terms of its global dimensions. The problem is increasingly widespread, affecting societies and individuals around the world. Jews are currently the target of this global-

---

2 From the petition of Independent Jewish Voices concerning the CPCCA, "The CPCCA's goals is criminalize criticism of Israel and Zionism, not to hold impartial hearings," http://ijvcanada.org/sign-singex-petition-cpcca-hearings.

3 Testimony of the Honourable Irwin Cotler, November 2, 2009.

4 All-Party Report, UK, pg. 5.

ized antisemitism.[5] The United States Department of State's *Report on Global Antisemitism* has noted the disturbing rise of antisemitic intimidation and incidents is widespread throughout Europe, and cited "worrying expressions" of antisemitism outside of Europe and the Middle East, including New Zealand, Argentina and Canada.[6]

The Report noted that attacks on individual Jews and on Jewish property that occurred in the immediate post-Second World War period decreased over time and became primarily linked to vandalism and criminal activity. However, in recent years, these incidents have been more targeted in nature with perpetrators appearing to have the specific intent to attack Jews and Judaism. These attacks have deeply affected the sense of safety and well being of Jewish communities.[7] This globalized nature of antisemitism speaks to the interconnectedness of incidents occurring internationally and the occurrence of antisemitic incidents domestically. Spikes in antisemitic incidents are often linked to event in the Middle East.[8]

Antisemitism today is unique in the manner in which it manifests itself and morphs from localized and sporadic incidents to ideological, political, legalized and ultimately genocidal expressions of hatred. Traditional group libels—the attribution of negative characteristics to Jews—such as the blood libel, the economic libel and racism libel, continue to have traction in popular discourse and imagination. For example, Jews are currently being alleged to have been behind the September 11th terrorist attacks and Jewish doctors are blamed for deliberately infecting Palestinians and others with the AIDS virus.

The nature of contemporary antisemitism in Canadian society is complex, multifaceted, and emanates from multiple sources. Whereas "traditional" antisemitism is a form of hatred and discrimination aimed at Jews as a race, a new manifestation of antisemitism is increasingly taking hold internationally and in Canadian society. This new form of antisemitism has ironically, "marched ... under the protective cover of the United Nations, the protection of human rights, and under the struggle against racism itself."[9] That is, antisemitism is increasingly becoming focused on the role of Israel, as a Jewish State, in the conflict between Israelis and Palestinians and the greater Israeli-Arab conflict in the Middle East. Jews are collectively viewed as supporters of Israel

---

5 Testimony of Dr. Charles Small, November 2, 2009.
6 Released by the Bureau of Democracy, Human Rights, and Labor.
  Available online: *http://www.state.gov/g/drl/rls/40258.htm.*
7 Ibid.
8 Dr. Gregg Rickman, November 2, 2009.
9 Testimony of the Honourable Irwin Cotler, November 2, 2009.

and are seen by some people who refuse to distinguish between Israelis and Jews as legitimate targets in the fight to establish a Palestinian state or to eliminate the State of Israel.

In the most vile and clear expression of the new antisemitism, Jewish support for Israel and the notion of Israel as a criminal state is used to further traditional antisemitic themes. These manifestations use the discourse of politics, but in fact, constitute masked hatred. Traditional antisemitic libels are now being attached to the State of Israel and to Jews. Recent libels include an article in Sweden's popular newspaper, Afonbladet, alleging that Israelis abducted Palestinians in a conspiracy with American rabbis and killed them to steal their organs for transplant.[10] This refashioning of the traditional "blood libel" was also seen in a Canadian Islamic community newspaper in British Columbia, which posted on its website an article headlined "Ukrainian kids, new victims of Israeli organ theft."[11]

A similar new manifestation of traditional antisemitic behaviour can be seen on campuses where Jewish students are ridiculed and intimidated for any deemed support for the State of Israel, which is claimed by its enemies to have no right to exist. Individuals and governments who call for the destruction of the State of Israel and its inhabitants also exemplify this manifestation.

While traditional antisemitic acts, such as desecration of Jewish gravestones and firebombing of Jewish schools, are easy to identify, it is not always clear how to identify the point at which anti-Israel discourse becomes antisemitism. This has become an increasingly sophisticated and insidious form of discrimination meriting closer examination. As stated by the Honourable Denis MacShane:

> The old antisemitism, for me, is the classic millennium-old Jew hate that ends up in pogroms and ultimately the Holocaust, the obligatory expulsion of fleeing of Jews because they face physical violence or death. The "new" antisemitism seeks to belittle the status and identity of Jews within democratic communities, treat them as less that 100% full-class citizens, and oblige them to take up positions, particularly vis-à-vis Israel, they are uncomfortable with, which bring back into play the pernicious notion of the cabal or the secret

---

10 Tertimony of the Right Honourable Denis MacShane, November 2, 2009.

11 Available Online: *http://network.nationalpostcom/np/blogs/holy-post/archive/2010/01/08/muslim-paper-condemned-for-blood-libel.aspx*.

> lobby that gave rise to the "Protocols of the Elders of
> Zion", which now reappears in the idea of the Jewish
> lobby that controls capital and state policy.[12]

In the words of Toronto-based writer Navid Khavari, antisemitism "has desta-
bilizing and hurtfully harmful effects on all Canadians."[13] It is important to note
that while antisemitism by definition singles out Jews, its existence presup-
poses a willingness among at least some members of society to isolate and shun
or attack other groups. For this reason, even though opposing antisemitism is
important in its own right, the ongoing existence and international resurgence
of antisemitism is a sign that hatred of all types is far from extinct.

Hate breeds hate. While it may begin with the Jews, the group-based hatred
and stereotyping that we call antisemitism is unlikely to end with Jews. In the
words of Reverend Majed el-Shafie, an Egyptian Christian, and founder of One
Free World International:

> If we let this happen in Canada, and if we let antisem-
> itism rise in Canada, we will be next. The Bahais will
> be next, the Ahmadis will be next, the Christians will
> be next.[14]

Yet within this discussion, we all must be mindful of the concerns for the importance of free dialogue. For example, in her written testimony, Razia Jaffar,
President of the Canadian Council of Muslim Women, asserted that "silencing
such a dialogue is an injustice and an infringement on academic freedom, freedom of speech, association and belief."[15] Similarly, a Jewish organization, albeit
outside of the mainstream, expressed analogous unease about suppressing "legitimate concerns surrounding Israeli government policies that may seem to impinge
upon human right," suggesting that this would undermine the very democracy
that Israel, a multi-ethnic state, claims for itself so proudly.[16] As stated previously,
criticism of Israel is not, by definition, antisemitic. Israel is accountable, just like
any other state, for its act in accordance with its obligations under international
regimes dealing with human rights and international humanitarian law.

---

12 Testimony of the Honourable Denis MacShane, November 2, 2009.
13 Testimony of Navid Khavari, November 23, 2009
14 Testimony of Reverend Majed El Shafie, November 30,2009
15 Submission of Razia Jaffar, Present, Canadian Council of Muslim Women, August 2009.
16 Submission of David Abramowitz and Lyn Centre, Co-Presidents, United People's Order Canada.

The purpose of this book is to bring to public attention the dangers associated with new forms of antisemitism in both Canada and across the globe. The book is divided into three parts. The first part can best be described as an analysis of the nature of antisemitism including the multiple definitions and debates of the phenomenon. With this foundation in mind and borrowing from the CPCCA and ICCA Reports, the book delves into the incidents and state of antisemitism globally and in Canada and the creation and enforcement of the Ottawa Protocol.

The second part is entitled Engagements and serves as a collection of edited submission and testimony of expert witnesses and evidence related to the debates, discussions, and issues surrounding antisemitism. Compiled from a host of witnesses and professionals, the wide range of submissions covers a large cross-section of society on all sides of the issue, including academics, international activists, domestic police services, human rights organizations, legal scholars, educators and religious organizations. Also included are dissenting opinions and voices of concern related to the approaches advocated. Consistent with the principles of public discourse and free expression, it is also important to include contrary opinions in the hope of better understanding a phenomenon and to find the correct instruments to tackle such an issue.

The third and concluding section of this book highlights a call to action and the challenges in combating the rise of antisemitism in Canada. Through the exercise of the CPCCA Inquiry Panel and the advice offered by legislators and experts in the international community, recommendations are put forward as approaches to address antisemitism as systemic phenomena. Included in these are legal recommendations through hate speech and crime persecution, human rights legislation and training of police officers, educational outreach, research, inter-faith initiatives and to strengthen support through international and inter-governmental organizations such as the United Nations by promoting international peace, respect and tolerance.

Antisemitism Defined

In understanding the concept of antisemitism, it is important to differentiate it from terms similar and contrary to its definition. Antisemitism is a form of hatred, discrimination, and intolerance. Yet is also much more. Its uniqueness is what sets it apart for other forms of hatred, but ultimately blends into one another. In outlining the metamorphosis of the concept over nearly thousand years, it is important to reaffirm with conceptual clarity what antisemitism has come to mean.

In 2005, the European Union Monitoring Centre on Racism and Xenophobia (EUMC), the institutional body tasked with monitoring racism and antisemitism in EU Member States, produced a working definition of antisemitism:

> Antisemitism is a certain perception of Jews, which may be expressed as hatred towards Jews. Rhetorical and physical manifestations of antisemitism are directed towards Jewish and non-Jewish individuals and/or their property, toward Jewish community institutions and religious facilities. In addition, such manifestations could also target the State of Israel, conceived as a Jewish collectivity.[1]

As described in detail below, the concept of antisemitism frequently adapts to current political, economic, and social factors within domestic and international environments. A staple of this hateful rhetoric, antisemitism frequently charges Jews with conspiring to harm humanity and it is often used to blame

---

1 "A Working Definition of Antisemitism," adopted by the European Union Monitoring Centre on Racism and Xenophobia (EUMC), now the European Fundamental Rights Agency, 8 January 2005.

Jews for why things go wrong. It is expressed in speech, writing, visual forms, actions and employs sinister stereotypes, and negative character traits.

Contemporary examples of antisemitism in public life, the media, schools, the workplace and in the religious sphere could include:

- Calling for, aiding or justifying the killing or harming of Jews in the name of a radical ideology of an extremist view of religion.
- Making mendacious, dehumanizing, or stereotypical allegations about Jews as such or the power of Jews as a collective—such as, especially but not exclusively, the myth about a world Jewish conspiracy or of Jews controlling the media, economy, government or other societal institutions.
- Accusing Jews as a people of being responsible for real or imagined wrongdoings committed by a single Jewish person or group, or even for acts committed by non-Jews.
- Denying the fact, scope, mechanism (eg. gas chambers) or intentionality of the genocide of the Jewish people at the hands of National Socialist Germany and its supporters and accomplices during the Second World War and the Holocaust.
- Accusing the Jews as a people, or Israel as a state, of inventing or exaggerating the Holocaust.
- Accusing Jewish citizens of being more loyal to Israel, or to the alleged priorities of Jews worldwide, than to the interest of their own nations.

Examples of the ways in which antisemitism manifests itself with regard to the State of Israel taking into account the overall context could include:

- Denying the Jewish people their right to self-determination, e.g., by claiming that the existence of a State of Israel is a racist endeavor.
- Applying double standards by requiring of it a behavior not expected or demanded of any other democratic nation.
- Using the symbols and images associated with classic antisemitism (e.g., claims of Jews killing Jesus or blood libel) to characterize Israel or Israelis.
- Drawing comparisons of contemporary Israeli policy to that of the Nazi Germany.
- Holding Jews collectively responsible for actions of the State of Israel.

Criticism of Israel itself, however, similar to that leveled against any other country, cannot be regarded as antisemitic. Yet antisemitic acts are criminal when they are so defined by law, for example, denial of the Holocaust or distribution of antisemitic materials in some countries. Criminal acts are antisemitic when the targets of attacks, whether they are people or property—such as buildings, schools, places of worship and cemeteries—are selected because they are, or are perceived to be, Jewish or linked to Jews. These acts of violence represent the most basic and elementary characteristics of terrorism. In short, antisemitic discrimination is the denial of Jews of opportunities or services available to others and fundamentally violates human rights and human dignity.

Since 2005, the EUMC definition has been increasingly referenced and adopted by a variety of organizations and groups internationally, including by various courts, the Organization for Security and Cooperation in Europe and national inquiries of parliamentarians. The United Kingdom All-Party Parliamentary Inquiry into Antisemitism recommended that this definition be adopted and promoted by governments and by law enforcement agencies.[2] It has been referenced in the United States Commission on Civil Rights and in submissions to the United Nations Economic and Social Council Commission on Human Rights, Sub-Commission on the Promotion and Protection of Human rights. Currently, the European Forum on Antisemitism has translated the definition into thirty-two languages.[3] As such, this definition has formed the backdrop and standard definition of antisemitism as per the Canadian Parliamentary Coalition to Combat Antisemitism.

Traditional Antisemitism

Antisemitism is not a static concept but has changed through the years. As Mark Freiman, President of the Canadian Jewish Congress noted in his testimony to the CPCCA Inquiry Panel, "like other enduring infections, [antisemitism] survives by successfully mutating over time."[4]

Early Christian antisemitism was a form of religious intolerance that was based on the view that Jews had rejected Jesus and were complicit in his death. This perception "has been the most powerful justification for antisemitic persecution for two thousand years."[5] In the Middle Ages, Christians believed Jews to be children of the devil and allegations that Jews performed ritual murder led to "trials, burnings, torture, expulsion and massacres."[6] By the twelfth century, the blood libel—accusing Jews of slaughtering Christian children and consuming their blood for religious purposes—took hold.

---

2 Report of the All-Party Parliamentary Inquiry into Antisemitism, a subcommittee of the All-Party Parliamentary Group Against Antisemitism, London, UK, September 2005, p. 5.
3 Submissions of the American Jewish Committee, Kenneth S. Stern, p.3-4.
4 Testimony of Mark Freiman, December 7, 2009.
5 Kenneth L. Marcus, "Jurisprudence of the New Antisemitism", 44 Wake Forest L. Rev. 371, p.11
6 Ibid.

In the second half of the nineteenth century, there was a shift from religious antisemitism to a form of racial antisemitism. The evolution of antisemitism shifted from religious principles to those based upon nationalism and racial theory. This same era winessed the religious emancipation of many Jewish communities across Europe and the new mutated form of antisemitism viewed Jews as a distinct and genetically inferior race. This was the form of antisemitism, of course, that largely fuelled Nazi policy and Adolf Hitler's "final solution" which resulted in the murder of six million Jews in the Holocaust.

New Antisemitism

While the racial form of antisemitism that gave rise to Nazism is not completely extinct, the worrying record of such incidents demonstrates that the main and growing problem in Canada is what has been termed "New Antisemitism". New Antisemitism has come about as a form of political prejudice that finds expression in Islamism and also in certain ideologies and discourses[7] of the extreme left and right, which have been influenced by traditional antisemitic themes.

In line with these new developments, the EUMC definition recognized that Holocaust denial, holding Jews collectively responsible for Israeli policy, denying Jewish people their right to self-determination, the application of double standards that require Israel to behave in manners not expected or demanded of other democratic nations and using symbols and images associated with traditional antisemitism, are all forms of antisemitism.

The new antisemitism is "the form of this bigotry that cloaks itself in terms of a political discourse, directed towards Israel or Zionism the particular stereotypes and the defamations traditionally directed at the Jewish people."[8] As explained by Ruth Klein, National Director of the League for Human Rights of B'nai Brith Canada:

> In Canada, these dual themes of antisemitism and anti-Zionism run parallel and are used interchangeably, as has been mentioned before. We see this in the sharing of rhetoric and images between the extreme left and the extreme right. The extreme left will borrow Holocaust imagery and age-old Jewish stereotypes to attack Israel, while the neo-Nazis use the Middle East conflict as a justification for furthering

---

7 Testimony of Professor Alvin Rosenfeld, November 16, 2009.

8 Kenneth L. Marcus, "Jurisprudence of the New Antisemitism," 44 Wake Forest L. Review, 371, p. 4.

their anti-Jewish ideology. So whereas before the talk was of Jewish control of the media and Jewish control of the government and the financial world, the terminology now has changed. It's Israeli control. It's Zionist control.[9]

What is occurring is that traditional antisemitic themes are being applied to the State of Israel and its supporters.

Much of the anti-Zionist/antisemitic discourse today is a dehumanizing discourse. It is one that goes to the very character and essence of the Jews as a treacherous, devious people embarked upon domination of the Middle East, domination of the whole world, controlling the banks, the media, the United States—at least until the appearance of President Obama—controlling the White House, Congress, and the Pentagon. A global enemy. That is Nazi language. The description of the Jews/Zionist/Israel as the enemy of humanity is a dehumanizing discourse, and it is one that prepares the road. That's why I called it a "lethal obsession." It definitely prepares the road to genocide.[10]

To take one example, the depiction of Jews as those responsible for poisoning wells, which led to the allegations that they were responsible for the Black Death that swept Europe in the fourteenth century, has been revived in a number of new contemporary manifestations. Jews have been accused of creating and spreading the AIDS virus.[11] As recently as 2009, there was an international blood libel accusing Israelis of harvesting Palestinian organs. While it was widely condemned by society, it was published in a Canadian Islamic community paper, Al Ameen, which was reputedly reported by Israeli soldiers.[12] While this article has been subsequently condemned and removed from the organizational website, it nevertheless is a concern that such grotesque and antisemitic accusations are still being made today.

---

9 Testimony of Ruth Klein, November 30, 2009.
10 Submissions of the Canadian Jewish Congress, August 20, 2009, p. 2.
11 Submission of the Canadian Jewish Congress, August 20, 2009, p. 2.
12 Terry Glavin, "The Orgran-Harvesting Scare: A Mutant Offspring of Anti-Zionism & Classic Antisemitism," Chronicles & Dissent, January 5, 2010.

Contemporary Antisemitism

A significant source of antisemitism is found in both the radical left and extremist right of the political spectrum. As noted by the United Kingdom All-Party Inquiry, since Israel took control of the disputed territories of Judea and Samaria/West Bank, Gaza and the Golan Heights after a defensive war initiated by numerous Arab and Islamic nations, there has been a shift in sympathy away from Israel. Israel and Jews are increasingly viewed as part of the "establishment" and Arabs and Palestinians are seen as the oppressed.[13] Criticism of Israel was further fuelled by its counter-terrorism operations in response to the second Palestinian Intifada and by the American-led intervention in Iraq in 2003.

As explained by the Right Honourable Denis MacShane, United Kingdom parliamentarian and Chair of the United Kingdom All-Party Inquiry into Antisemitism, the left increasingly views the Palestinian struggle as the "most legitimate and noble struggle of the underdog."[14] This view, as he notes, is "perfectly legitimate" but it may also "trip over into anti-Semitism."[15]

This type of antisemitism is often seen on campuses across Canada,[16] where traditional antisemitic symbols and the targeting of Jewish students often occurs in the context of campus demonstrations and protests. In one example, in 2009, Jewish students at York University of Toronto, Ontario, were barricaded inside the Jewish Students' Association lounge by a mob of protesters. During Israeli Apartheid Week in 2009, a poster advertising the event depicted the Jewish State collectively in the role of child killer, with a gunship helicopter targeting a toddler holding a teddy bear. This, as noted by Ruth Klein of B'nai Brith Canada, "is the epitome of the modern-day blood libel."[17]

There are also examples of groups of Jewish students being targeted for negative treatment by their mere association with Israel. For example, OPIRG, a Student Federation in Ottawa that controls campus funding, was said to have refused to support an event put on by Hillel, a Jewish student organization. Hillel had planned to invite a Ugandan Jewish leader to discuss topics such as sustainable development initiatives and education among Christian, Muslims, and Jews in Uganda—a topic unrelated to Israel or Middle East politics. OPIRG, while acknowledging that this event was interesting, refused to help promote the even because of Hillel's purported support for Israel.[18]

---

13 Testimony of Dr. Fred Lowy, December 24, 2009, p.3.
14 Testimony of the Right Honourable Denis MacShane, November 2, 2009, p10.
15 Ibid.
16 Testimony of Dr. Fred Lowy, December 24, 2009, p.3.
17 Submissions of Ruth Klein, B'nai Brith Canada, August 2009, p. 3.
18 Testimony of Miriam Stein, November 16, 2009, p. 18.

As discussed by the United Kingdom All-Party Report, it is often difficult to define the boundaries between anti-Zionism and antisemitism. Many on the left are committed to fighting racism and would likely be resistant to the suggestion that they are engaging in antisemitic discourse. Indeed, most are likely unaware of the history of antisemitism and the impact that their use of traditional antisemitic iconography may have on Jews. Nonetheless, whether in purpose or effect, criticism of Israel that is unfounded, based on antisemitic tropes, or that uses antisemitic themes is discriminatory and harmful, and is cause for grave concern.

The twentieth century has seen the rise of a new ideology, commonly referred to as Islamism, which is responsible for a substantial component of contemporary antisemitism. While there is no clear and precise terminology to underline the fact that Islamism refers to a different phenomena than the religion of Islam, this is an important distinction. As the United Kingdom All-Party Parliamentary Inquiry noted, "there is much that the Jewish and Muslim communities can learn from one another in tackling racism."[19]

However, there is a "small" but "prevalent"[20] minority who subscribe to the ideology of Islam within Europe and North America. Islamism has been described by Professor Robert S. Wistrich, as "[undoubtedly]...the single, through not the only, major threat to the existence, physical and otherwise, of Jews today, but it is a much broader threat to Western society, to democratic norms and civic culture."[21] The doctrine of Islamist ideology has "at its core a form of genocidal anti-Semitism."[22]It is based on "zero tolerance" for the existence of any non-Muslim state in the Middle East. It views Jews in "conspiratorial terms" as enemies of Islam and has adopted the worst form of European antisemitism as part of its political programs.[23] This is evident in the antisemitic libels as propagated in the statements of Hezbollah and other jihadist organizations.[24] Along this same vein, what has been particularly troubling is to witness that the Czarist forgery, "Protocols of the Elders of Zion" has seen a resurgence of popularity in the Islamic world. As Dr. Charles Small pointed out, the Iranian revolutionary regime, Hamas, Hezbollah and other radical Islamist use the "Protocols of the Elders of Zion" to spread traditional forms of antisemitism while simultaneously dehumanizing the State of Israel in promoting new forms of antisemitic persecution and hatred.

---

19 All-Party Report, UK, pg. 26.
20 Testimony of Dr. Charles Small, November 2, 2009 p. 19.
21 Testimony of Professor Robert S. Wistrich, November 23, 2009, p. 18,
22 Testimony of Dr. Charles Small, November 2, 2009, p16
23 Testimony of Professor Robert S. Wistrich, November 23, 2009, p. 18
24 Ibid.

Antisemitism in Canada

Within Canada, the issues expressed globally are continually and increasingly finding a foothold. Yet the ability to understand the current scope and severity of the problem of antisemitism in Canada depends on two factors: 1) a shared understanding of what qualifies as antisemitism among those in a position to identify and report such activity; 2) an effective reporting system that allows the pooling and analysis of information from all relevant sources across Canada. Antisemitic incidents in Canada are currently identified and tracked in a number of different ways. From a legal perspective, prohibited antisemitic activity falls into two main categories: hate crimes and discrimination under human rights legislation.

a) Hate Crimes

The Criminal Code of Canada specifies four 'hate crimes' in sections 318 to 319 and 430. Under such legislation, hate crime is categorized as: advocating genocide; public incitement of hatred; the willful promotion of hatred; and, mischief to religious property. Under the Criminal Code, charges for hate crimes can only be brought forward with the permission of the Attorney-General.

In addition, section 718.2 of the Criminal Code states that when sentencing individuals found guilty of a criminal offence, courts may take into consideration evidence that a crime was motivated by bias, hate or prejudice, and are authorized to apply additional penalties based upon these motivations.[1]

With these extenuating circumstances in mind, in 2004, the Canadian Centre for Justice Statistics developed a national definition as to what, for the purposes of data collection, constitutes a "hate crime" as:

---

1 *Criminal Code, supra*, ss.318, 319, 320, and 718(2).

a criminal violation motivated by hate, based on race, national or ethnic origins, language, colour, sex, age, mental or physical disability, sexual orientation or any other similar factors.[2]

Under this definition, the quantitative collection of date related to hate crimes can offer a better picture to the plight of racist motivations of criminal offences.

Statistics Canada collects information on hate crimes via two surveys: the Uniform Crime Reporting (UCR) survey and the General Social Survey (GSS) on victimization. The UCR survey is conducted annually and gathers information from police forces on crimes that have been substantiated as motivated by hate. Developed in 1962 with the cooperation of the Canadian Association of Chiefs of Police the survey data reflects reported crimes that have been substantiated through police investigation from all separate federal, provincial and municipal police services in Canada. [3] The GSS, which began collecting hate crime data in 1999, is conducted every five years and gathers information from Canadians who self-reported being victims of hate crimes. The survey is designed to produce estimates of the extent to which person are the victims of offences, the risk factors associated with victimization, the rates of reporting to police and to evaluate the fear of crime and public perceptions of crime and the criminal justice system.[4]

Under the current regime of hate crime reporting, all police services are required to report hate crimes to the UCR. However, there is no requirement for tracking hate crimes based on the targeted minority groups.[5] While some police forces, like the Hamilton Police Services,[6] do track the number of incidents directed at the Jewish community, others do not.[7] As a result, it is impossible to do a comprehensive analysis of the level and nature of hate crimes across Canada. In addition, there is no current standardized definition of an antisemitic crime. The result is that for those jurisdictions that do break down hate crime by target group, it is still not possible to compare the level of

---

2 "Uniform Crime Reporting Incident-Based Survey" *Canadian Centre for Justice Statistics, Policing Services Program* (Statistics Canada, 2008), p.96.

3 *http://www.statcan.gc.ca/pub/85-002-x/2010002/sources-eng.htm#u2*

4 Ibid.

5 See Mia Dauvergne, "Police-reported hate crime in Canada, 2008", *http://www.statcan.gc.ca/pub/85-002-x/2010002/article/11233-eng.htm,* for an explanation on the surveys on hate crimes conducted by Statistics Canada.

6 Testimony of Deputy Chief Ken Leenderste, February 8, 2010, p 22.

7 For example, the Ontario Provincial Police does not keep track of crimes specifically against the Jewish community. Testimony of Commissioner Julian Fantino, December 8, 2009.

antisemitism across jurisdictions because the information is not collected in a standardized way.

b) Hate Incidents

Not all antisemitic incidents are clearly criminal. As explained by Monica Christian:

> Antisemitism is racism, and racism under any guise is deplorable. Antisemitic, racist and hateful comments are offensive to the vast majority of Canadians, but it must be said that this type of behaviour is not necessarily illegal.[8]

Similarly, Chief Bill Blair of the City of Toronto has noted that many of the types of activities referred to in the EUMC definition that are very offensive would, nevertheless, not be considered criminal in Canada.[9] Inspector John de Hass of the Vancouver Police noted that "we need a good analysis, not just of the crimes, but everything under it. The crimes are the tip of the iceberg".[10]

Under this framework, there is a serious underreporting of antisemitic incidents in Canada. Police records management systems do not record incidents where there is no violation of the law. Thus, if racial slurs are made but no crime is committed, no record is made.[11] Given that police are often the first point of contact for individuals who are victimized by such non-criminal yet clearly anti-Semitic incidents, it would be beneficial for police agencies to keep track of these incidents.

Within the Royal Canadian Mounted Police (RCMP), there is a clear policy of providing guidance and directing individuals to refer to their non-criminal complaints to the appropriate provincial or federal human rights commission.[12] Human rights codes at both provincial and federal levels have provisions that may address hate-motivated activity. These statutes prohibit a range of discriminatory practices, including those whose purpose is the incitement and spread of hatred. Individuals may bring complaints directly to these commissions which serve as an important repository of information about non-criminal antisemitic incidents in Canada in addition to the work done by several interested organiza-

8 Testimony of Detective Sergeant Monica Christian, December 8, 2009, p. 11.
9 Testimony of Chief Bill Blair, December 8, 2009, 17.
10 Testimony of Inspector John de Hass, February 8, 2010, p. 1.
11 Ibid.
12 Testimony of Assistant Commissioner Allen Nause, February 8, 2010, p. 1.

tions, such as the Friends of Simon Wiesenthal Centre and B'nai Brith Canada that track and report on antisemitic incidents in Canada.

History of Antisemitism in Canada
By Irving Abella

Irving Martin Abella, is an historian, academic and writer. He specializes in the history of the Jews in Canada and the Canadian labour movement. His books have included Coat of Many Colours: Two Centuries of Jewish Life in Canada (1990) and None is Too Many: Canada and the Jews of Europe 1933-1948 (1982). He is a professor at York University and is a former president of the Canadian Jewish Congress (1992 to 1995). In 1993, he was made a Member of the Order of Canada and a Fellow of the Royal Society of Canada. He is married to Rosalie Silberman Abella, who was appointed to the Supreme Court of Canada in August, 2004.

Pre-Confederation

In the period from approximately 1610- 1760, Jewish people were forbidden, by Royal edict, from entering New France. Following the victory of British troops on the Plains of Abraham in the 1760's, Jews began to settle in Canada. In 1832, French-Canadian politician Louis-Joseph Papineau sponsored a law granting to Jews full political rights in Canada and by the time of Confederation (1867) there were estimated to have been 1000 Jews living in Canada.

Post Confederation

Jews in Canada were the first in the British Empire to be emancipated, to be permitted to vote, allowed to accept government appointments and to be elected to legislatures. Under British rule, Jews were welcomed, integrated quickly, and built a vibrant community in Canada. There is no evidence that they confronted any antisemitism—at least until the latter years of the nineteenth century.

Beginning in the 1890s with the arrival of tens of thousands of Jewish refugees of the Russian pogroms, a blanket of antisemitism would settle over Canada that would not lift for the next fifty to sixty years. This was a particularly brutal time for Canadian Jewry—and for other minorities as well, particularly the Chinese. In the first fifty years of the twentieth century, Canada, like many other nations unfortunately experienced racism, xenophobia, and antisemitism. It was a period that witnessed the imposition of quotas, restrictions, and boycotts. Jewish people found themselves in a tenuous position in Canada and often experienced demeaning behavior and discrimination.

Unfortunately, in Quebec one prominent source of antisemitism emanated from the Church which feared that Jews were importing into their province 'subversive' ideologies which could potentially distract French Canadians away from Catholicism. Through their newspapers and sermons, many Church leaders often spread anti-Jewish sentiment throughout the province. In English-Canada anti-Jewish activity was led by intellectuals such as Goldwin Smith, the nation's most prominent scholar and editor who claimed that Jewish newcomers would destroy Canada and were 'dangerous' to whatever countries accepted them.

By the 1920s, Jews had in many ways became somewhat of a pariah in Canadian society. They were targets of abuse and were excluded from most professions, restricted in almost all universities, and legally prevented from living and vacationing in a wide variety of areas from coast to coast.

Few opportunities were available to Jewish people. Most firms would not hire Jews; they were barred from the civil service; department stores would not allow them to serve customers. Most hospitals were closed to Jewish doctors, and when a Jewish physician was inadvertently hired at a Montreal hospital, fellow interns went on strike until he was dismissed.

Universities, such as McGill and the University of Toronto openly restricted Jewish student enrolment and there were quotas on Jews in professional schools. In fact in the 1920s and 1930s there was not one Jewish professor in any Canadian university. There were no Jewish judges, and Jewish lawyers were excluded from all the large firms. As well, there were restrictive covenants on properties preventing them from being sold to Jews. Many clubs, hotels and beaches barred Jews and often displayed signs saying "Gentiles only."3

World War II

Clearly, the most disturbing discrimination against Jewish people took place during the ascendancy of the Nazi regime in Germany. Many Jews sought to escape from Germany and Europe. Unfortunately, antisemitism had permeated the upper ranks of the civil service in Canada and even Prime Minister Mackenzie King worried that Jewish immigration would "pollute" Canada's bloodstream. This was manifested in the statement that prevented further Jews from entering Canada.[13]

When in June of 1939, the passengers of the St. Louis, a ship full of approximately 1000 German Jews forced on board by the Nazis to look for a country that would accept them, pleaded with the Canadian government to allow them

---

13 Irving Abella and Harold Troper, *None Is Too Many: Canada and the Jews of Europe, 1933–1948* (Toronto: Lester & Orpen Dennys, 1986).

in, they were rebuffed and forced back to Europe where most would lose their lives in the Holocaust.

Post Holocaust

Since the Second World War and the Holocaust antisemitism in Canada has been on the decline and Jewish immigration to Canada has increased; this is primarily a result of relaxed government policies on immigration. In 1948 alone, over 10,000 Jewish holocaust survivors immigrated to Canada and by 1961, Canada was home to over 255,000 Jews.

New ideas and leaders replaced the old order; attitudes, old habits and traditions .were slowly transformed. The creation of the state of Israel changed stereotypes about the Jew and overt antisemitism was reduced, though as is evident from these hearings, it did not disappear.

According to a report produced by the Library of Parliament, "in the 1980s and 1990s, antisemitism was manifested mainly through historical revisionism and Holocaust denial."[14] The coalition heard from various witnesses that Holocaust denial is still prevalent today, stemming primarily from Iranian President Mahmoud Ahmadinejad.

Present

According to Alan Golshlager, President of the Ontario region of the Human Rights league of B'nai Brith Canada, "We are seeing the emergence of a new form of anti-Semitism." He explains that "The censure leveled at Israel and all of its actions, and the total lack of recognition for its accomplishments (and there are many) have become a breeding ground for the anti-Semitism that engulfs every Jew on the planet."4 A report from the library of Parliament also noted that "contemporary anti-Semitism seems to be on the rise, and related to the Israel-Palestine conflict."5 It must be noted, that the panel heard plenty of testimony which disputes the equation of anti-Israelism to anti-semitism. [15]

Current Nature of Antisemitism in Canada

As has been noted elsewhere, antisemitic incidents are on the rise globally. There has been "a serious rise of antisemitism in Europe almost without parallel or precedent since the Second World War."[16] Resolution 1563 of the

---

14 Thompson, Daniel, *A History of Anti-Semitism in Canada and Worldwide from 1880 to the Present* (Ottawa: Library of Parliament, 2009).

15 Alain Goldschläger, *Antisemitism In Canada: Variations of Space and Time* (Toronto: League for Human Rights, B'nai Brith Canada, 2009).

16 Submission of the Honourable Irwin Cotler

Parliamentary Assembly of the Council of Europe noted that "far from having been eliminated, antisemitism is today on the rise in Europe. It appears in a variety of forms and is becoming relatively commonplace."[17] Indeed, 2009 saw the highest incidence of attack on Jewish person, institutions and property ever recorded in countries like the United Kingdom and France.[18]

The Community Security Trust (CST), a British charity that records and analyses antisemitic incidents in the United Kingdom, recorded 924 antisemitic incidents in 2009. This represented the highest annual total since it began recording antisemitic incidents in 1984, and is 55% higher than the previous record in 2006. The CST found that the main reason for this record spike was the "unprecedented number" of antisemitic incidents recorded in January and February of 2009, during and after the war between Israel and Hamas in Gaza. The number of incidents recorded did not return to relatively normal levels until April, some three months after the war ended.[19]

Unfortunately, the global upward pattern in antisemitic incidents is reflected in the Canadian experience. According to the Honourable Jason Kenney, Minister of Multiculturalism, Citizenship, and Immigration, while the situation in Canada is not as grave as in some other Western societies, antisemitism is still a "significant and growing problem in Canada."[20] Jews in Canada are disproportionately targeted. According to data compiled by Statistics Canada on hate-motivated crimes, in 2006, 2007, and 2008, hate crimes against Jews formed the second-most frequently reported category of hate crime, second only to hate crimes against African-Canadians.[21] In each of the three years, antisemitic incidents accounted for 15-16% of all reported hate crimes. From 2007 to 2008, the number of antisemitic incidents increased by 42%, up from 116 in 2007 to 165 in 2008. It is important to note that there has been a generalized issue of under-reporting of hate incidents.

Overall, there were 265 religiously motivated hate crimes in 2008, up by ninety-two incidents over 2007, equating to 53%. Twenty-four per cent of reported hate crimes that year were motivated by religion and of these, six-

---

17 "Resolution 1563: Combating Antisemitism in Europe," Parliamentary Assembly of the Council of Europe (2007).

18 "Study: Anti-Semitism in Europe hit new high in 2009", June 1, 2011, http://www.haaretz.com/jewish-world/news/study-anti-semitism-in-europe-hit-new-high-in-2009-1.284032

19 Community Security Trust, "Antisemitic Incidents Report 2009": http://www.thecst.org.uk/docs/CST-incidents-report-09-for-web.pdf, p.4

20 Testimony of the Honourable Jason Kenny, February 8, 2010, p. 18

21 See also testimony of Inspector John de Hass, of the Diversity & Aboriginal Policing Section of the Vancouver Police Department, who noted that in Vancouver, the Jewish population suffers the second-highest number of bias, hate or prejudice incidents of any identifiable group (February 8, 2010, pg. 20)

ty-two percent were targeted against the Jewish community.[22] There are indications that in some locations, the proportion of hate crimes that target the Jewish community is increasing. In Calgary, for example, while the actual number of hate incidents has steadily dropped over the past five years, the number of antisemitic incidents has steadily risen. The results have been that the proportion of such incidents that are targeted against the Jewish community has risen from about 1.9% in 2005, to 8.8% in 2008. The indications based on this evidence suggest that further increases in the statistics are to be expected.

As Ruth Klein of B'nai Brith stated, police experts and sociologist agree that only about ten percent of victims ever come forward to report their victimization.[23] As discussed above there is a lack of consistency among agencies and within police forces as to how antisemitic incidents are recorded. However, while looking at the absolute number of incidents reported by various agencies may therefore not be reflective of the actual number of incidents occurring, the trends noted by individual organizations are nonetheless instructive. The League of Human Rights of B'nai Brith Canada's 2009 Audit of Antisemitic Incidents demonstrates the continuing escalation of antisemitism in Canada. There was an 11.4% increase documented in 2009 over the 2008 figures. The 2010 Audit detailed 1,306 antisemitic incidents, representing a 3.3% increase over the 2009 data.[24] This continues a general upward trend. There has been nearly five-fold increase in the number of antisemitic incidents recorded over the past decade.[25] The incidence of antisemitic incidents in 2010 was the highest on record in the twenty-eight-year history of the League's Audit.[26]

Related and equally concerning is the view among professionals that the level of hostility toward the Jewish community is increasing. According to Doron Horowitz, current director of community security of UJA Federation of Greater Toronto, there has been an increase in local antisemitic incidents—including in Calgary, Barrie, Ottawa, and Hamilton.[27] In this view, not only has there been an increase in antisemitic act, but "there is an increase in intention. There is an increase in hostility."[28] Yet this data on antisemitic incidents reveal only half of the picture. The incidents recorded generally include attack on Jewish person, property and institutions—in other words, traditional manifestations of antisemitism. However, they do not capture incidents of antisemitic

---

22 Testimony of Kristina Namiesniowki, December 8, 2009, p1.

23 Testimony of Ruth Klein, November 30, 2009, p. 16

24 Available online: *http://www.jewishtribune.ca/tribune/PDF/audit2010/ENAudit2010.pdf*

25 Available online: *http://www.bnaibrith.ca/files/audit2009/MAINAUDITENG.pdf*

26 Available online: *http://www.jewishtribune.ca/tribune/PDF/audit2010/ENAudit2010.pdf*

27 Testimony of Doron Horowitz, December 8, 2009, p. 9.

28 Ibid

discourse. Further as pointed out by the Honourable Irwin Cotler, this data does not make obvious the fact that the rise in traditional antisemitism is inextricably related to the rise in new antisemitism, that contemporary antisemitism is "insidiously buoyed by a climate receptive to attacks on Jews because of the attacks on the Jewish state."[29]

Contemporary Forms of Antisemitic Incidents

As the statistics present, the majority of hate crimes against Jews were mischief-related.[30] Former Ontario Provincial Police Commissioner, Julian Fantino has noted that in Ontario, the most common type of incident of antisemitism takes the form of mischief to property including religious properties and other Jewish entities. However, more serious offences of advocating or promoting genocide and the wilful promotion of hatred occurring across Canada including incidents of fire bombings between 2000 and 2007. In most acts of antisemitic mischief were perpetrated by youths.[31]

B'nai Brith Canada recorded 1,135 antisemitic incidents in 2008, 70.7% of which were categorized as, "harassment" incidents, 28% as vandalism, and 1.2% of which were described as violent incidents.[32] This has been collaborated by a Statistic Canada report released in June 2011 on police reported hate crimes, the number of crimes targeting the Jewish community in Canada spiked by 71% between the period of 2008 and 2009, accounting for the most significant rise in hate crimes motivated by religion.[33] As Detective Sergeant Monica Christian, of the Hate Crimes Unit of the Ottawa Police Service, points out, there has been a "changing face to the conventional acts of anti-Semitism." While swastikas are still being painted on walls and cemeteries are being desecrated, "the hate itself has now grown and festered and manifests itself in different ways." In particular, the Internet has emerged as a key "modern-day venue for the

---

29 Submission of the Honourable Irwin Cotler

30 Deputy Chief Ken Leenderste of the Hamilton Police Service testified that the majority of hate crimes directed against the Jewish community in Hamilton were in the form of mischief to property, usually in the form of graffiti (Testimony of Deputy Chief Ken Leenderste, February 8, 2010, p. 22); Both Hamilton and York Region police reported that the majority of their hate/bias crimes were mischief offences. In Calgary in 2009, 46% of hate/bias crimes involved assault, 33% involved mischief and 14% involved threats. 73% of reported hate/bias crimes involving religion (e.g. antisemitism) were mischief-related (Written Submissions of Murray Stooke, p. 1.); In Toronto, though the Jewish Community makes up only 4% of the population, 30% of all hate/bias crimes reported to the Toronto Police Service are targeted against the Jewish community. The most commonly reported of the hate/bias crimes is the crime of mischief, representing 75% of the total reported hate crimes (Testimony of Chief William Blair, December 8, 2009, p. 13).

31 Testimony of former Commissioner Julian Fantino, December 8, 2009, p. 12.

32 Submissions of B'nai Brith Canada, p. 9.

33 Available online: *http://www.statcan.gc.ca/pub/85-002-x/2011001/article/11469-eng.pdf*

spreading of hate rhetoric." Social media sites such as Facebook and Twitter are becoming more problematic in promoting the rise of antisemitism.[34]

Notwithstanding the general decline of White Supremacist movements in this country, incidences, such as the rise of the "Aryan Guard", a White Supremacist group from Calgary created in 2007, have become systematic of a more general rise of antisemitism and racism across Canada. The Calgary Jewish Community Council pointed out that the Aryan Guard's "recruitment efforts ... appear to be successful as the number of participants in the White Pride rallies is growing. However, each Aryan Guard rally or parade is met with an even larger number of counter-demonstrators." [35] While a decisive majority of Canadians recognize that antisemitic violence and hate crimes are an affront to Canadian values, antisemitic hate groups continue to operate within Canada.

The issues of rising antisemitism across Canada, however, are not limited to Calgary, but are being experienced across Canada. This has been evident in Quebec. Quebec is the province with the second highest number of antisemitic incidents in Canada, following Ontario. Of the 1,135 cases reported to Statistics Canada in 2008, 245 took place in Quebec.[36] What is particularly worrying is that a significant number of the most serious recent acts of antisemitism have taken place in Quebec. As in other jurisdictions, antisemitic incidents in Quebec tend to be tied to the situation in the Middle East. There was evidence that institutions, such as the union movement in Quebec, who traditionally speak out on issues of social justice, have at times remained silent in the face of injustices, including the firebombing of Jewish institutions, and this may further cultural divides.[37]

In an attempt to make sure that intolerance within the province is kept in check Quebec leaders have made special efforts to ensure that "the Quebec values of tolerance, respect, non-violence and the ability to embrace the richness of good intercultural relations come first."[38] In 2007, the Lieutenant Governor of Quebec appointed a two-person commission - the Bouchard-Taylor Commission - to investigate the issue of reasonable accommodation in Quebec. The mandate was to study the socio-cultural integration model in Quebec and review interculturalism, immigration and secularism and the theme of Quebec identity.[39] Yet the recent debates in Quebec on reasonable accommodation,

34 Testimony of Detective Sergeant Monica Christian, December 8, 2009, p. 10.

35 Submissions of Calgary Jewish Community Council.

36 Testimony of Moise Moghrabi, December 1, 2009, p. 13.

37 Testimony of Fo Niemi, December 1, 2009, p. 5.

38 Testimony of Adam Atlas, December 7, 2009, p. 3.

39 Reasonable accommodation is the concept of requiring systems or institutions to change in order to adjust and meet the needs of individuals with certain characteristics (for example, disabilities, sex,

including the debate concerning the place of religion in public spaces, have had the result of fanning the flames of antisemitism in Quebec. Fo Niemi, executive director of the Center for Research-Action on Race Relations (CRARR), has stated that these debates often have served as a platform for public expressions of racism, including towards the Jewish community.[40]

Moise Moghrabi, Quebec Regional Chair of the League for Human Rights of B'nai Brith Canada, explains "… wholesale rejection of religion is a mainstay in their lives by Quebeckers, and for that reason, requests for accommodation by the Jewish community and requests for accommodation on the basis of religious justifications may be seen as going against Quebeckers' desire to escape from the bonds of religion."[41] With this in mind, the fight against antisemitism must take place "effectively and equally in French and in English. It needs to take into account the special dynamics of the French-speaking collectivity in Canada …"[42]

In addition, what has become particularly worrying is the rise in the rash and brazen acts of violence and intimidation against members of the Canadian Jewish community. Some examples of recent incidents of antisemitism in Canada include:

- In January 2011, four synagogues, a Jewish school and a daycare had their windows smashed in targeted vandalism attacks in Montreal.[43]
- In January 2010, a freelance reporter received an email telling her to stop working for the kikes if she wants to be taken seriously.[44]
- In March 2010, a synagogue was desecrated, religious objects ruined, and the bima[45] defaced with swastikas.[46]
- In May 2010, a playground in Victoria, BC was vandalized with antisemitic graffiti reading "No Jews", "Warsaw Ghetto" and a swastika.[47]
- On December 25, 2009, Al Ameen, an Islamic community newspaper in British Columbia, printed a story entitled Ukrainian kids,

---

race), in order to allow for their full participation in those institutions. The March 2008 report is entitled the "Consultation Commission on Accommodation Practices Related to Cultural Differences," and is often referred to as the Bouchard-Taylor Commission—the names of its two Commissioners.

40 Testimony of Fo Niemi, December 1, 2009, p. 5.
41 Testimony of Moise Moghrabi, December 1, 2009, p. 14.
42 Testimony of Fo Niemi, December 1, 2009, p. 6.
43 The Toronto Star, "Jews fear 'orchestrated campaign' of hate after attacks in Montreal," (accessed January 30, 2011), http://www.thestar.com/news/canadaarticle/923034--jews-fear-orchestrated-campaign-of-hate-after-attacks-in-montreal.
44 Available online: http://jewishtribune.ca/tribune/PDF/audit2010/ENAudit2010.pdf.
45 A bima is the religious term for the podium in synagogues where the Torah/Bible is read from.
46 Available online: http://jewishtribune.ca/tribune/PDF/audit2010/ENAudit2010.pdf.
47 Ibid

new victims of Israeli "organ theft"[48] alleging that Ukrainian orphans had been spirited into Israel for purposes of harvesting their organs for transplants.

- In 2009, at York University in Toronto, Jewish students were barricaded inside the Jewish Students' Association lounge by a mob of protesters.[49]
- In September 2009, a Jewish university professor in Halifax was sent a letter with antisemitic slurs addressed to "Tribe of Judah" at his home address.[50]
- In August 2009, a Thornhill, Ontario synagogue's interior was defaced with antisemitic slurs.
- In May 2009, in Montreal, a flyer depicting Jews as genocidal murderers was distributed throughout the Outremont area.[51]
- In April 2009, a Toronto playground was defaced with the words "Jew free zone", "Jews not welcome", along with Nazi symbols.[52]
- In March 2009, a blog containing antisemitic content threatened a university's Jewish Studies Centre in Ottawa: "We need to identify the Zionist Kikes and their handmaiden. Time to draw up list, time is soon."[53]
- In January 2009, at an anti-Israel rally in Toronto, protesters' chants included "Jews are our dogs", and "Jewish child, you're gonna f***in' die. Hamas is coming for you."[54]
- In December of 2008, a Calgary man was punched in the face when he responded "so what if I am" to a group of individuals who asked if he was Jewish (he was not).[55]
- The words "Six million more" was written on the wall of a synagogue in Calgary.[56]
- At the University of Guelph, graffiti was found in the University Centre with the message "Kill all Jews" and "Allah destroy all Israel."[57]
- In November 2008, swastikas and the phrase "dirty jew" [sic] was scrawled on the vehicle of a Jewish student at Queen's University.[58]

---

48 Testimony of Inspector John de Haas, February 9, 2010, p. 21.
49 Submissions of Hillel of Greater Toronto & Testimony of Daniel Ferman, November 16, 2009, p. 17.
50 98 League for Human Rights of B'nai Brith Canada, 2009 Audit of Antisemitic Incidents, pp 13-15.
51 Ibid
52 Ibid
53 Ibid
54 Ibid
55 Submissions of Kelly Mergen, Calgary Police Service, Diversity Resources Unit.
56 League for Human Rights of B'nai Brith Canada, 2009 Audit of Antisemitic Incidents, pp 13-15.
57 Submissions of Guelph Jewish Student Life.
58 Submissions of Queens' University Hillel.

One particularly serious category of criminal incident deserves special attention. Jewish communities in Canada had on nine occasions, over the past
decade, been the target of bombings:
- 2007: firebombing of the YM-YWHA Ben Weider Jewish Community
  Centre in Côte-des-Neiges. [59]
- 2006: firebombing of the Skver-Toldos Orthodox Jewish Boys School in
  Outremont.[60]
- 2004: firebombing of the United Talmud Torah elementary school in
  Montreal.110 [61]
- 2002: firebombing of Quebec City's Beth Israel Synagogue.[62]
- 2002: firebombing of Agudas Israel Synagogue in Saskatoon.[63]
- 2002: firebombing of a Montreal theatre playing a Jewish film.[64]
- 2000: three Molotov cocktails thrown into Edmonton synagogues (twice
  at Beth Shalom synagogue, and once at Beth Israel synagogue). [65]

These incidents represent the extreme nature of antisemitism as not just a form
of racial slander but as forms of violence that violate the most basic human rights
and lead to the creation of terror against the Jewish people.

Such forms of violence and hate have found ample breeding ground with the
Internet and social networking sites. These are now being used to spread hatred.
As Dr. Manfred Gerstenfeld, Director of the Post-Holocaust & Antisemitism
Program, Jerusalem Center for Public Affairs, has written anti-Semitism,
"… has adapted itself to the internet. Spreading antisemitism there is increasingly effective," leading to the potential for the development of a culture in
which such displays of hate and intolerance become "socially acceptable". This
has come about with the effect of Web 2.0—websites that allow for interactive,
user-centered design and contribution to content—and increase the possibil-
ities of the spread of hate. Web 2.0 promotes the "idea of multiple narratives
rather than the quest for a single truth. Where it makes a choice between these
narratives, promoting some and hiding others, this is done by pure democracy.

59 CBC News, "Montreal man sent to prison for attacks on Jewish school, centre," (accessed
   January 30, 2011), http://www.cbc.ca/canada/montreal/story/2009/02/12/mtl-firebombing-bulphred-0212.html.
60 Ibid.
61 CTV News, "Arrests made in Jewish school's firebombing," (accessed January 30, 2011), http://www.ctv.
   ca/CTVNews/Canada/20040515/firebombing_arrests_040514/.
62 2002 Audit of Antisemitic Incidents, (League for Human Rights of B'nai Brith Canada, 2003), accessed on
   March 2, 2010, http://www.bnaibrith.ca/publications/audit2002/audit2002-02.html.
63 Ibid.
64 Ibid.
65 CTV News, "Defacing of Edmonton Synagogue Condemned," (accessed on March 2, 2010), http://www.
   ctv.ca/CTVNews/Canada/20051227/edmonton_synagogue_051227/.

The community gets the truth it already believes."[66] Within these environments, the implicit and explicit social pressures inherent in these fora may
result in conformity of opinions and normalization of hateful ideas.

It is clear that the Internet is leading to the spread of conspiracy theories and
other antisemitic content. For example, according to US-based Southern Poverty
Law Centre, there are 12,000 white supremacist propaganda videos and Holocaust-
denial pseudo-documentaries openly available on video-sharing websites such as
YouTube.[67] The presence of such disturbing websites such as "Kaboom," an example of a "suicide-bombing game," and "Ziofacism.net," a Montreal blog featuring
stereotypes of Jews, claims that Jews were involved in the 9/11 terrorist attacks
and blame Israel's intelligence agency for a supposed terrorist attack on Montreal's
metro system have found a voice with many antisemitic groups.[68] The explosion of
Holocaust denial on Facebook is a particularly concerning development about the
effect that exposure to such websites may have on youth.

This proliferation of antisemitic websites makes it very difficult to accurately
or comprehensively monitor antisemitic content on the web. In addition, the
existence of sites in other languages poses further difficulties in effective monitoring. The ability to locate such sites is further complicated by the existence of
"disinformation or stealth sites" that have neutral names, but represent fronts for
hate. For example, the website "martinlutherking.org" is actually a front for a
white supremacist group used to spread misinformation about Dr. King.[69]

All of these factors, as well as the speed with which new content and
technologies are developing, pose important challenges to addressing these
issues through legal means. As discussed by Dr. Gerstenfeld: "This whole
field has developed far too fast for governments to act effectively against it."[70]
The Honourable Andrew Swan, Minister of Justice and Attorney General of
Manitoba, echoed this sentiment:

> Hateful statements are very difficult for any individ-
> ual police force, any individual province, or any one
> country, for that matter, to monitor and control. The
> Internet, as we know, is a great place for the cowardly
> to hide and to spread their hate. We will do what we

66 Andre Oboler, "Online Antisemitism 2.0: "Social Antisemitism" on the "Social Web"" No. 67,
   1 April 2008/ 25 Adar Sheni 5768. Available online: *http://www.jcpa.org/JCPA/Templates/ShowPage.
   asp?DRIT=3&DBID=1&LNGID=1&TMID=111&FID=624&PID=0&IID=2235&TTL=Online_Antisemitism_2.0._.*

67 Testimony of Matthew Johnson, December 1, 2009, p. 3.

68 Testimony of Avi Benlolo, November 30, 2009, p. 15.

69 Testimony of Matthew Johnson, December 1, 2009, p. 3.

70 Testimony of Dr. Manfred Gerstenfeld, November 16, 2009, p. 6.

can to try to shut down these sites and bring people to justice, but it is a challenge. I don't pretend to be an expert on technology. I know that there are frustrations with where the servers are located, with where the systems are that may be beyond the jurisdiction of law enforcement in Canada.[71]

Many international hate sources are now located on servers in the United States where that country's First Amendment often protects their content.

Internationally, the Council of Europe's Convention on Cybercrime is an international treaty that has attempted to address Internet crimes by harmonizing national laws and improving investigative techniques and increasing cooperation among nations, in assisting with the extradition and prosecution of cyber-hate. The Convention was signed by Canada in 2001, but has not yet been ratified. Currently there is great difficulty for police services in obtaining lawful access to internet communications. In late 2010, the current Government of Canada introduced three bills that would assist police and intelligence officers to intercept and survey online communications and to access personal information from internet service providers (ISPs) about their subscribers.

The "Additional Protocol to the Convention on Cybercrime" concerning the criminalisation of acts of a racist and xenophobic nature committed through computer systems, was signed by Canada in 2005, but has not yet been ratified. The Additional Protocol requires signatory states to adopt legislation and the necessary measures to criminalize the distribution and making available to the public racist or xenophobic material through computer systems, intentionally and without right. It requires member states to pass legislation that would cover racist insults and threats.

Antisemitism on Campus

Reflective of the open hostility, intimidation and violence against Jewish group in Canada, perhaps no contemporary form of antisemitism in Canada is as rampant as the climate of antisemitism on university campuses. In recent years, evidence has mounted in which this phenomenon is becoming a serious and growing concern on some Canadian campuses. While this phenomenon takes many forms, including traditional expressions of antisemitism, it is increasingly manifesting itself in terms of anti-Israel discourse. This new antisemitic

71 Testimony of the Honourable Andrew Swan, February 8, 2010, p. 4.

discourse has expressed several characteristics including: the denial of the Jewish people the right to self-determination; the use of symbols and images associated with traditional antisemitism; comparisons of contemporary Israeli policy with that of Nazi Germany; and the collective blame of Jewish people for the actions of the State of Israel. In accordance with the EUMC Working Definition of Antisemitism, such discourse crosses the line from legitimate criticism of Israel into antisemitism.

Such discourse is creating, in some cases, an inhospitable climate for Jewish students on campus. As described by Dr. Karen Eltis, Professor of Law at the University of Ottawa:

> The global phenomenon of antisemitism that draws on traditional motifs but extends from the individual to the collective Jew, Israel, is spilling over into Canadian campuses and creating a hostile environment of intimidation, fear, and demonization, in which violence, both psychological and even physical, is increasingly extended legitimacy.[72]

Jewish students, particularly those who are forthrightly supportive of Israel, have faced harassment from other students, hostility from professors, smears on their ancestral homeland and libelous attacks on their personal integrity for supporting that homeland. As summarized by Raphael Szajnfarber, former president of Hillel Ottawa:

> Many Jewish students [have been] made to feel unwelcome on Carleton University's campus by the anti-Israel activists. Indeed, the anti-Israel activists were so vicious in their tactics and so unrelenting in their verbal abuse, that nearly every day, I received calls from crying students, or students who no longer wanted to go to class because they felt intimidated by their colleagues, and even some of their professors.[73]

Similarly, Shelley Faintuch, the Community Relations Director of the Jewish Federation of Winnipeg testified that:

---

72 Testimony of Dr. Karen Eltis, December 7, 2009, p. 5. 41
73 Submissions of Raphael Szajnfarber.

> Our students have been feeling rather beleaguered.
> A number of groups are bringing in speakers who
> are characterizing Israel as an apartheid state and
> who are making our students feel unsafe and unwel-
> come. ... Despite the fact that we don't have an Israeli
> Apartheid Week, our students have told us that the
> environment is becoming more and more malignant
> for them.[74]

Such incidents have led to a climate of intolerance and fear on some Canadian university campuses.

In addition, such experiences are not only limited to students, but to educators as well. As Dr. Noemi Gal-Or, a Jewish professor of Israeli origin in the Department of Political Science, at Kwantlen Polytechnic University in Surrey, British Columbia, has noted antisemitic incidents have become increasingly overt over time.[75] Such a climate in British Columbia is reflected throughout Canada and is part of a global phenomenon. As Dr. Gal-Or has noted:

> [there is an] "atmosphere" when attending conferences
> in Europe and elsewhere. However, developments
> abroad have increasingly been spilling over into
> Canada, and becoming more pronounced on our coun-
> try's post-secondary education campuses. While for
> long exhibited in form of sub-text in many academic
> circumstances, it has recently turned explicit.[76]

Against this tide of hate, many faculty members sympathize with Jewish students but feel uncomfortable speaking out because they fear repercussions in their own academic circles.[77]

That antisemitism is a growing problem on Canadian campuses is, unfortunately, reflective of a problem that is occurring on campuses around the world. For example, the UK Report concluded that "Jewish students feel dispropor-tionately threatened in British universities as a result of antisemitic activities

---

74 Testimony of Shelley Faintuch, November 30, 2009, p. 19.
75 Submissions of Noemi Gal-Or. For example, in early 2009, after a series of incidents where a
   Canadian-Palestinian student made provocative antisemitic and anti-Israeli comments, Dr. Gal-Or
   entered her classroom on February 16, 2009, to find "You exist, therefore I am offended," in
   conjunction with a test referring to a revolution in Palestine, and a map of Israel and a Palestinian flag.
76 Testimony of Noemi Gal-Or, November 23, 2009, p. 2.
77 Testimony of Immediate Past President, Hillel at Queen's University, November 16, 2009, p. 23.

which vary from campus to campus."[78] Similarly, the U.S. Commission on Civil Rights found that "Many college campuses throughout the United States continue to experience incidents of antisemitism, a serious problem warranting further attention."[79]

In addition, in February 2006, a Conference on Academic Antisemitism was held in Amsterdam. The Conference brought together an international group of participants from civil rights organizations, academic and student organizations to discuss how antisemitism is being manifested on campuses around the world. Participants in the conference came up with recommendations to the Organization for Security and Cooperation in Europe (OSCE) on ways to combat antisemitism at universities across North America and Europe.[80] The recommendations state, in part:

> Antisemitism has no place in higher education. However, in recent years universities on both sides of the Atlantic have had to grapple with this problem. We've witnessed reports of speakers in academic settings employing classic antisemitic stereotypes, demonising Jews, and demonising Israel. We have also seen the growth of petitions to boycott and exclude Israeli professors, students, and universities from academic exchange programs. Divestment campaigns and the rhetoric surrounding them are also problematic ... We fear that this age-old disease may poison a new generation.[81]

As Professor Patrick Monahan, Vice-President Academic and Provost, York University, testifies, "conflicts around the Middle East and the debate over the conflict in the Middle East have become the most challenging issues in terms of free expression on university campuses."[82] As recent events illustrate, there is a challenge facing university administrators in terms of achieving the difficult and important balance between the need to provide a safe, harassment-free learning environment for all, and the need to promote and protect the value of freedom of expression. This problem was the focus of a conference held at York

---

78 All-Party Report, UK, p. 42.

79 U.S. Commission on Civil Rights, *Briefing Report on Campus Antisemitism*, July 2006. Available online: http://www.usccr.gov/pubs/081506campusantibrief07.pdf.

80 Testimony of Sheldon Levy, November 24, 2009, p. 6.

81 Available online: http://www.osce.org/cio/25705.

82 Testimony of Patrick Monahan, November 24, 2009, p. 13.

University in 2009 entitled "Israel/Palestine: Mapping Models of Statehood and Paths to Peace." The conference was intended to "to explore which state models offer promising paths to resolving the Israeli-Palestinian conflict, respecting the rights to self-determination of both Israelis/Jews and Palestinians."[83]

However, it was reported to us that notwithstanding the ostensible purpose of the conference as described, the reality was that at this event "anyone who challenged the Palestinian perspective was intimidated or labelled a racist ... At times, those presenting a different view were subject to abuse and ridicule."[84] The event "instead of offering a fair and balanced debate ... used the veil of academic freedom to legitimize calls for the elimination of the Jewish state and promoted the view that Zionism has an inherent tendency towards war crimes."[85]

Universities are the intellectual centre of Canadian society and the free exchange of ideas in an open climate of tolerance is the cornerstone of academic life. This rise of incidents is particularly concerning because of the implications that in this exchange Jewish students and faculty may feel the need to self-censor or to hide their Jewish identity in the context of an increasingly unwelcoming climate. Given the fundamental role that universities play in shaping the mindset and opinions of coming generations, it is vital for universities to maintain an environment where freedom of speech can pre-vail. The removal of free debate from university life, with no effective counter-point to bigoted views, may have particularly long-term, damaging consequences.

The presence of barriers similar to those that impede efforts at objectively measuring and understanding the level of antisemitism in Canadian society in general, have arisen with respect to efforts to understand the level of antisem-itism on Canadian campuses. Students who feel that they are the victims of antisemitic incidents have a number of places they may go to report them, including campus protection services, Jewish student organization, and admin-istration or youth counselling service on campus.[86]

Yet many do not report these incidents at all. There is no university-wide understanding of what constitutes antisemitism. As noted by Ruth Klein of B'nai Brith Canada, it is difficult for universities to keep statistics on antisemitic incidents when they do not have definitions in their policies.[87] Mirroring the

---

83 Available online: *http://www.yorku.ca/ipconf/index.html.*

84 Quote of Na'ama Carmi who presented at the conference, in submissions of Hillel of Greater Toronto.

85 Submissions of Avi Benlolo, President and C.E.O. of Friends of the Simon Wiesenthal Center for Holocaust Studies.

86 Testimony of Francine Page, November 24, 2009, p. 14.

87 Testimony of Ruth Klein, November 30, 2009, p. 20. See also testimony of Kenneth Stern, American Jewish Committee, November 23, 2009, p. 20, who states that it is "it incumbent upon universities to do a survey of their students, faculty, and others to see how these issues are panning out, and not just in terms of antisemitism but bigotry in general."

problems within the police services, there is no university-wide systems in place to collect and share information on incidents that occur on campus.

While there are no reliable statistics in terms of the absolute number of antisemitic incidents on campuses across Canada, there are reliable indications that such incidents are on the rise. The League for Human Rights of B'nai Brith Canada's 2009 Audit of Antisemitic Incidents reported that cases of antisemitism on Canadian university campuses had risen by 80.2% from 2008 to 2009. The report notes that this statistic is "even more alarming given that the number of incidents has increased almost four-fold since 2006".[88] The report noted the relationship on campuses, as in Canadian society more generally, of the level of antisemitic incidents to events in the Middle East. Specifically, the level of incidents intensified significantly during the war in Gaza in January 2009.[89] The 2010 Audit reported eighty-six antisemitic incidents on university campuses, down from the 2009 figure, but still a significant increase from the thirty-six reported incidents in 2006.[90]

The following represents a sample of some of the incidents that have occurred in connection with Canadian academic life in recent years:

In March 2010, a York University student was charged by police with running a virulently antisemitic website (filthyjewishterrorists.com). He blamed his troubles with the law on "Jewish Kikes".[91]

- In February 2010, during Israeli Apartheid Week, a threatening message was sent via Facebook to a Jewish student at the University of Western Ontario.[92]
- In September 2009, in Guelph, Ontario, antisemitic graffiti was scrawled on the door of a university campus residence where Jewish students lived.[93]
- In February 2009, it was reported that at York University, Jewish students who were involved with a petition to impeach student government were "barricaded" in the Jewish student lounge by a group of protesters. Police were called and the students had to be escorted out of the lounge to safety. On the way out, York University Student Daniel Ferman, who was involved in the incident, testified that he was called a "fucking Jew" and was told to "Die, Jew".[94]

---

88 Available online: *http://www.bnaibrith.ca/files/audit2009/MAINAUDITENG.pdf.*
89 Available online: *http://www.bnaibrith.ca/files/audit2009/MAINAUDITENG.pdf.*
90 Available online: *http://ljewishtribune.ca/tribune/PDF/audit2010/ENAudit2010.pdf.*
91 Available online: *http://ljewishtribune.ca/tribune/PDF/audit2010/ENAudit2010.pdf.*
92 Available online: *http://ljewishtribune.ca/tribune/PDF/audit2010/ENAudit2010.pdf.*
93 Available online: *http://www.bnaibrith.ca/files/audit2009/MAINAUDITENG.pdf.*
94 Testimony of Daniel Ferman, November 16, 2009, p. 17. 48

- In January 2009, the Ontario branch of the Canadian Union of Public Employees brought forward a proposal to ban Israeli academics from teaching at Ontario Universities. In response to an appeal from the Palestinian Federation of Unions of University Professors and Employees, Sid Ryan, President of CUPE Ontario stated "we are ready to say Israeli academics should not be on our campuses unless they explicitly condemn the university bombing and the assault on Gaza in general."[95] This statement was removed shortly after it appeared and was replaced with a statement calling instead for a boycott "aimed at academic institutions and the institutional connections that exist between universities here and those in Israel".[96]

- In January 2009, university and college professors and employees in Quebec called for a boycott of Israeli academic institutions. Professors from Concordia University, McGill, Université de Quebec À Montreal, Université de Montreal, and numerous other postsecondary institutions in Quebec signed this petition.[97]

- In January 2009, Jewish students in Vancouver B.C. were chased and assaulted on campus. MAINAUDITENG.pdf. [98]

- In January 2009, *The Manitoban*, the student newspaper at the University of Manitoba, published an article that asked, "Do you see the parallel between Palestinians in open prisons attacked with phosphorous bombs and Jews slaughtered in Nazi Germany?"

- At Queen's University, Hillel was forced to remove its "response wall" which was meant to be a space for people to share their feelings after walking through a Holocaust education display, due to the overwhelming number of antisemitic remarks, including remarks denying the Holocaust.[99]

- On Holocaust Remembrance Day in 2009, the York University Free Press published cartoons featuring Israelis dressed as Nazis shooting Palestinians into a mass grave labelled "Gaza". Another cartoon shows a dead Palestinian in a concentration camp wearing a prisoner's uniform and a keffiyeh.[100]

---

95 "Ontario union calls for ban on Israeli professors" National Post, Monday, January 5, 2009, *http://www.nationalpost.com/news/story.html?id=1144758.*

96 "CUPE pulls Ryan proposal from union web site," National Post, January 14, 2009, *http://network.nationalpost.com/np/blogs/fullcomment/archive/2009/01/14/steve-janke-cupe-pulls-ryan-proposal-from-union-web-site.aspx.*

97 Available online: *http://www.mcgilldaily.com/2009/02/academics_petition_for_israel_boycott/* and *http://www.tadamon.ca/post/2827.*

98 Available online: *http://www.bnaibrith.ca/files/audit2009/MAINAUDITENG.pdf.* 49

99 Submissions of Queen's University Hillel.

100 Submissions of Hillel of Greater Toronto.

- In 2008, the group at Queen's University called Solidarity for Palestinian Human Rights reportedly had several cartoons posted on its Facebook page demonizing Israel. Two of the cartoons explicitly equated Jews with Nazis, while a third image showed Jews preparing to drink the blood of Palestinains—evoking the traditional antisemitic blood libel.[101]
- In November 2008, a Jewish student's vehicle was defaced with several swastikas and the phrase "dirty Jew" written across the windows.[102]
- In April 2008, Natan Sharansky, a refusenik with the civil rights movement in Russia and Cabinet minister in Israel came to speak at York University and was shouted down and prevented from speaking.[103]
- In April 2008, public facilities on the University of Western Ontario campus were defaced with antisemitic graffiti.
- In March 2008, after an Israeli incursion into Gaza, the SPHR at Queen's University placed a large banner in the student centre commemorating "Victims of the Gaza Shoah." Shoah is the Hebrew word for the Holocaust.[104]
- On March 10, 2008, immediately following a terrorist attack on an Israeli Yeshiva on March 10, 2008, the Excalibur at York University published an article that stated: "It's no wonder why Yeshivat Merkaz Harav school was attacked." The article subsequently went on to justify the attack because the school had a curriculum that combined Talmudic studies with military service. Complaints from Hillel to the paper apparently did not prompt an apology for the offensive nature of the article.[105]
- In February 2008, "Death to Jews" was reportedly shouted repeatedly at an anti-Israel rally held on the McMaster University campus.[106]
- In 2007, Jewish students reported to Queen's University Hillel that their sociology professor had accused Canadian Jewish Organizations (such as the Canadian Jewish Congress) of a conspiracy to manipulate Canadian foreign policy. The professor later apologized.[107]
- In March 2004, the Queen's University Palestinian Human Rights association distributed literature portraying Jews with big noses and carrying large sacks of money. Controversy over the issue made it into the Queen's

101 Submissions of Queen's University Hillel.
102 Ibid.
103 Testimony of Zac Kaye, November 16, 2009, p. 16. 50.
104 Submissions of Queen's University Hillel.
105 Ibid.
106 "No charges after year-long investigation of Mac rally" on the website of Macleans On Campus, accessed on June 1, 2011,
   http://oncampus.macleans.ca/education/2009/01/31/no-charges-after-year-long-investigation-of-mac-rally/.
107 Submissions of Queens University Hillel.

Journal, where the President of the club denied the antisemitic nature of the cartoon on the basis that "Palestinians are Semites too."[108]

- The visiting Israeli consul-general was prevented by protesters from speaking at Simon Fraser University in British Columbia in 2004.[109]
- In March 2003, a student group, Solidarity for Palestinian Human Rights (SPHR), at York University reportedly included on its display table a yellow Star of David inscribed with slogans referring to ethnic cleansing.[110]
- In September 2002, violent protesters prevented former Israeli Prime Minister Benjamin Netanyahu from speaking at Concordia University in Montreal.[111]
- Ehud Barak, also a former Israeli prime minister, was subsequently prevented from speaking at Concordia based on the university's assessment that threats of further violence by anti-Israeli protesters would materialize.[112]

This is by no means a comprehensive list of recent incidents and does not even include all incidents that occurred across Canadian university campuses. Nevertheless, in addition to demonstrating the variety and severity of incidents on Canadian campuses, these incidents highlight a number of specific, and deeply troubling issues.

Academic boycotts, such as those proposed by CUPE and a coalition of academics in Quebec, are a serious concern. The UK Inquiry received similar evidence regarding academic boycotts. The UK Report noted that though the motivations of boycotters may not be themselves antisemitic:

> ...the effect of their actions would be to cause difficulties for Jewish academics and students. The

108 Ibid.

109 Prof. Alain Goldschläger, "The Canadian Campus Scene," from Manfred Gerstenfeld (ed.) Academics against Israel and the Jews, September 2008, available online: http://www.jcpa.org/JCPA/Templates/ShowPage.asp?DRIT=3&DBID=1&LNGID=1&TMID=111&FID=624&PID=0&IID=2614&TTL=The_Canadian_Campus_Scene.

110 Prof. Alain Goldschläger, "The Canadian Campus Scene," from Manfred Gerstenfeld (ed.) Academics against Israel and the Jews, September 2008, available online: http://www.jcpa.org/JCPA/Templates/ShowPage.asp?DRIT=3&DBID=1&LNGID=1&TMID=111&FID=624&PID=0&IID=2614&TTL=The_Canadian_Campus_Scene.

111 Prof. Alain Goldschläger, "The Canadian Campus Scene," from Manfred Gerstenfeld (ed.) Academics against Israel and the Jews, September 2008, available online: http://www.jcpa.org/JCPA/Templates/ShowPage.asp?DRIT=3&DBID=1&LNGID=1&TMID=111&FID=624&PID=0&IID=2614&TTL=The_Canadian_Campus_Scene.

112 Prof. Alain Goldschläger, "The Canadian Campus Scene," from Manfred Gerstenfeld (ed.) Academics against Israel and the Jews, September 2008, available online: http://www.jcpa.org/JCPA/Templates/ShowPage.asp?DRIT=3&DBID=1&LNGID=1&TMID=111&FID=624&PID=0&IID=2614&TTL=The_Canadian_Campus_Scene.

majority of those who have institutional affiliations
to Israeli universities are Jewish, and thus the consequences of a boycott would be to exclude Jews from
academic life.[113]

The UK Inquiry found that the "singling out" of Israel was alarming. Boycotts
had not been suggested against other countries and discourse surrounding the
boycott debate often moved beyond reasonable criticism into antisemitic demonization of Israel, using Nazi analogies and the suggestion of Israel as "a fascist
state."[114] Such calls to boycott contact with academics working in Israel represent an assault on academic freedom and intellectual exchange.

It is clear that the visits of pro-Israeli speakers to Canadian campuses often serve
as a flashpoint for conflict and, in some cases, harassment. Some Jewish students feel that their school administrations do not treat these visits consistently
by failing to protect the ability of pro-Israeli lecturers to speak and providing greater access and protection of pro-Palestinian speakers, some of whom
spread antisemitic viewpoints. Universities, as institutions for open debate and
free expression, have failed to adopt clear and consistent guidelines aimed at
protecting the security of speakers on campus. This has become evident that
campus media been used as a vehicle to promote antisemitic views.[115]

Most alarming has been the role that Canada universities have played role in
the campus phenomenon known as Israeli Apartheid Week (IAW).[116] This event
was first launched at the University of Toronto in 2005 and now occurs on many
university campuses across Canada and around the world.[117] These weeks are
uniformly well-organized, aggressive campaigns designed to make the Jewish
state and its supporter pariahs. According to Alvin Rosenfeld, "in the past we
would say that's just kids, that's just political theatre ... but that was the old
days ... this is very well organized ... a national organization ... funds and organizes Israeli Apartheid Week."[118]

---

113 All-Party Report, UK, p. 41.

114 All-Party Report, UK, p. 40.

115 "HonestReporting Canada (HRC) denounces YU Free Press' Publication of 'Anti-Semitic' Cartoons"
on the website of HRC, accessed June 1, 2011,
http://www.honestreporting.ca/news_article_name/987654yorku.aspx.

116 Dr. Manfred Gerstenfeld, "How to Fight the Campus Battle against Old and New Anti-Semites: Motifs,
Strategies, and Methods," December 1, 2009. Available online: http://www.jcpa.org/JCPA/Templates/ShowPage.
asp?DRIT=3&DBID=1&LNGID=1&TMID=111&FID=624&PID=0&IID=2235&TTL=Online_Antisemitism_2.0._.

117 "Past Israeli Apartheid Weeks" on the website of Apartheid Week, accessed April 2, 2010,
http://apartheidweek.org/en/pastapartheidweeks.

118 Testimony of Alvin Rosenfeld, November 16, 2009, p. 12.

Groups come together to demonize Israel as a Jewish homeland and use campuses as their staging ground because the audiences are captive. The use of the term apartheid is, to use the language of the EUMC Working Definition of Antisemitism, a "[denial of] the Jewish people their right to self-determination ... by claiming that the existence of a State of Israel is a racist endeavour." The activities of IAW are often associated with drawing comparisons of contemporary Israeli policy to that of the Nazis, and holding Jews collectively responsible for actions of the state of Israel. For examples, posters put up in early 2009 to promote IAW featured an Israeli helicopter bombing a helpless Palestinian child clutching a teddy bear, inside a concentration camp.[119] This display is symptomatic of the IAW and it's the use of "symbols and images associated with classic antisemitism."

During IAW, Jewish students are often afraid to be visibly Jewish on campus because they are wary of being harassed. Hillel of Greater Toronto submitted that:

> At the University of Toronto, 'Israeli Apartheid Week'
> is the primary source of problems for Jewish students.
> The organizers and supporters of 'IAW' single out
> Israel from all other nations on earth, set a negative
> tone on campus, hold one-sided events with little aca-
> demic merit, exclude Hillel students and staff from
> events, and typically flout school protocol regarding
> use of space on campus.[120]

IAW's proponents have tended to hijack any open and honest dialogue regarding the Middle East and have fostered on various campuses a hostile and sometimes unsafe environment identifiable Jews and advocates for Israel. Such experiences are antithetical to academic debate and devoid of the integrity and nuance that should govern the Canadian university system.

The supporters of Israeli Apartheid Week, and similar events, have rigorously claimed that any critique of their messages or tactics is an attempt to stifle free speech. Abigail Bakan, Head of the Department of Gender Studies and Professor of Political Science at Queen's University states that "there are indications of a chilly climate associated with free expression on university campuses in regard to defense of Palestinian human rights and critiques of Israel's policies

---

119 Submissions of Hillel of Greater Toronto.
120 Submissions of Hillel of Greater Toronto.

and practices."[121] This argument should be rejected. Freedom of speech requires balance and the opportunity for both sides to be heard, a concession which IAW proponents seem less willing to make than their opposition.

One cannot deny the complexity surrounding the issues in the Middle East, and the desire of many Canadians, especially on campus, to debate and propose solutions to those issues. Yet the best resolutions and recommendations for complex problems can only be developed through serious and rigorous debate, free of intimidation and threats. The concept of Israeli Apartheid Week, like the comparison of Israel to an apartheid state in general, is aimed at delegitimizing the State of Israel, and demonizing those who support it. Due to its sheer size and nature, we are concerned about the intimidating effect this experience has on Jewish students.

Actions such as the Legislative Assembly of Ontario passing of a motion condemning Israeli Apartheid Week on campus and the intimidation that it creates are welcomed actions. Because of the commitment to free speech, and to the maintenance of open discourse on university campuses, despite the vulgarity of Israeli Apartheid Week, it would be inappropriate for university administrators to refuse to allow the event to take place.

However, protection of the safety of Jewish and pro-Israeli students must be guaranteed while in pursuit of free debate. The abuse of the podium by faculty who feel at liberty to transfer their anti-Israel opinions to their students and to punish those whose views they do not share cannot be tolerated. As Professor Gil Troy argued: "I support academic freedom; I oppose educational malpractice ... Unfortunately, that often happens when professors turn their lecterns into political soapboxes ... and their students feel harassed for disagreeing."[122] The Immediate Past President of Hillel at Queen's University testified that at Queen's University:

> SPHR [Solidarity for Palestinian Human Rights], which runs Israeli Apartheid Week, allied with several professors and set up what were called checkpoints outside of several classrooms that would simulate going through a West Bank checkpoint ... a number of students, Jewish and non-Jewish ... felt that they had no possibility of opting out of these checkpoints because they were mandatory parts

---

121 Submissions of Abigail Bakan.
122 Testimony of Dr. Gil Troy, December 7, 2009.

of their class. Some were specifically put on days
when there were assignments due, so the students
had to go to these classes. They felt they were being
harassed, and they felt there was an abuse of podium
going on.[123]

Incidents of antisemitic activity on campus, unfortunately, have not been
isolated to the organization of IAW but have increasingly been advocated by
Student Unions and other campus groups.

As Dr. Fred Lowy, President Emeritus of Concordia University, explained
from 1999 to 2002, a group of "anarchist activist students ... effectively took
over the student government of the University." This group allied itself to a
group of "activist Muslim students and agreed to promote their causes, which
included targeting Jewish students and Jewish causes." This escalated to what
ended in a well-publicized riot that caused the cancellation of a speech by Israeli
Prime Minister Benjamin Netanyahu in 2002. After that event the group was
defeated in student government.

The Ontario Public Interest Research Group (OPIRG) has often been
perceived to be discriminatory against Jewish students. For example, OPIRG-
Ottawa refused to give support, in name or financially, to any events sponsored
by Hillel Ottawa, because of their "relationship to apartheid-Israel and Zionist
ideology."[124] Miriam Stein, in quoting a letter OPIRG-Ottawa sent to Hillel
Ottawa to indicate their concern:

> In Hillel Ottawa's mandate, it specifies that Hillel ...
> promotes the support of the Jewish state: The State of
> Israel. OPIRG-Ottawa views Hillel's steadfast support
> of Israel to be a position that alienates Palestinians and
> undermines respect for their personhood, mobility
> rights and basic human rights. Accordingly, OPIRG-
> Ottawa cannot formally endorse Hillel Ottawa or
> events sponsored by it. OPIRG-Ottawa bases its deci-
> sion on Hillel's political support of Zionism, while
> it is open to working with Jewish organizations and
> other organizations that respect basic human rights
> for Palestinians.

---

123 Testimony of Immediate Past President, Hillel at Queens University, November 16, 2009.
124 Testimony of Miriam Stein, November 16, 2009, p. 18.

Particularly troubling are actions in which university students' mandatory fees are given to OPIRG to support its activities. At the University of Ottawa, students are able to opt out of paying this fee, and receive a refund, but only by requesting the refund from OPIRG representatives directly - a process that is often burdensome and intimidating to Jewish students. As Hillel of Greater Toronto notes, the Students Against Israeli Apartheid, which sponsors and organizes Israeli Apartheid Week in Toronto, is a working group of OPIRG, despite OPIRG's mandate requiring it to be non-partisan.[125]

Faced with these difficulties university administrator have faced numerous challenges in addressing these issues and incidents. There are often differences in how they perceive the problem of antisemitism on their campuses, as well as in their vision of how administrations should respond to it. While most would stress that Canadian universities are safe,[126] they do recognize that campuses have had significant problems with antisemitism in recent years. Some administrators were more willing than others to recognize that a problem exists on their campuses. For example, Ryerson University President Sheldon Levy articulated steps that his institution's administration had taken to create a more inclusive campus. He noted that "for 99% or some very large number of people, these are not issues. We have to never let them becomes issues by not accepting the one percent, because the one percent will grow if one tolerates intolerance."[127]

Yet in some cases, there appeared to be a disconnection between students who had first-hand experience of incidents of antisemitism on campus and administrators that deny there is any problem. For example, one representative claimed that the extent of Israeli Apartheid Week was a small out-of-the way information table and two poorly attended events.[128] This ran contrary to the evidence by students at this same school that IAW is the primary source of problems for Jewish students, and that it sets a "negative tone on campus." [129]

Jewish students on most Canadian campuses are safe and do not experience generalized antisemitism in their daily lives on campus. However, administrators have a responsibility to act even if only 1% of their population is affected. By failing to recognize that there is a problem on their campuses, some university administrators are failing in their duties to protect all students. This is especially problematic because, on the one hand, administrators were eager to claim an absence of antisemitism on their campuses, but on the other hand,

---

125 Submissions of Hillel of Greater Toronto.
126 Testimony of Fred Lowy, November 25, 2009, p. 3.
127 Testimony of Sheldon Levy, November 24, 2009, p. 6.
128 Testimony of Robert Steiner.
129 Submissions of Hillel of Greater Toronto.

they exhibited little knowledge about the events which tend to spark the most antisemitism. In reference to posters for IAW that portrayed Israel as a child killer, university administrators had no idea what kind of material was being distributed on campus.[130]

While administrators are steadfast on the value of freedom of expression on university campuses, and recognize their job to "teach our students how to participate in deep and intimate conflicts with mutual respect", it seems that some administrators are ignoring the problems on their campuses, an, thereby they tolerate an environment where intimidation is employed as a tool to silence opposing opinions. On a limited number of university campuses, antisemitism is a serious problem of which, taking the most charitable view, some university administrators are unaware. At the other extreme, some administrators are, in fact, aware of the extent to which antisemitism exists on their campuses, but are unwilling to admit this fact or to take the steps needed to eliminate it.

130 Testimony of Ruth Klein, November 30, 2009, p. 19.

Part II: Inquiry Testimonials

Rabbi Andrew Baker

Rabbi Andrew Baker is Director of International Jewish Affairs for the American Jewish Committee. He has been a prominent figure in addressing Holocaust-era issues in Europe and in international efforts to combat anti-Semitism. In January 2009, he was appointed the Personal Representative of the OSCE Chair-in Office on Combating Anti-Semitism and has been reappointed in each successive year. The Organization for Security and Cooperation in Europe, an intergovernmental body of 56 nations headquartered in Vienna, has become a central arena for addressing the problems of a resurgent anti-Semitism.

He has played an active role in confronting the legacy of the Holocaust. He is a Vice President of the Conference on Jewish Material Claims against Germany, the Jewish umbrella organization that has worked on restitution issues for half a century. In 2003, he was awarded the Officer's Cross of the Order of Merit (First Class) by the President of Germany for his work in German-Jewish relations. He was a member of Government Commissions in both the Czech Republic and Slovakia that were established to address the claims of Holocaust Victims.

Rabbi Baker was a founding member of the National Historical Commission of Lithuania and involved in restitution negotiations there. He currently serves as co-chairman of the Lithuanian Good Will Foundation, established in 2012 to administer communal compensation payments. In 2006, the President of Lithuania presented him with the Officer's Cross of Merit for his work. For similar work he was awarded the Order of the Three Stars by the President of Latvia in 2007. He helped the Romanian Government establish a national commission to examine its Holocaust history and served as one of its founding members. For this work he was awarded the National Order of Merit (Commander) by the President of Romania in 2009.

Rabbi Baker directed AJC efforts in the development and construction of the Belzec Memorial and Museum, a joint project of the AJC and the Polish Government on the site of the former Nazi death camp in Southeastern Poland. In May 2006 he was appointed by the Prime Minister of Poland to a six year term on the International Auschwitz Council, the official governmental body that oversees the work of the Auschwitz State Museum.

A long-time resident of Washington, DC, Rabbi Baker has served as President of the Washington Board of Rabbis, President of the Interfaith Conference of Washington and Commissioner on the District of Columbia Human Rights Commission.

A native of Worcester, Massachusetts, Rabbi Baker received a B.A. from Wesleyan University and a Masters Degree and Rabbinic Ordination from Hebrew Union College-Jewish Institute of Religion in New York City. He is the father of four children.

Oral Testimony of Rabbi Andrew Baker, Personal Representative, OSCE Chairman-in-Office on Combating Anti-Semitism and Director, International Jewish Affairs, American Jewish Committee, delivered to the Canadian Parliamentary Coalition to Combat Antisemitism via teleconference on 23 November 2009.

I join my colleagues in expressing appreciation that you've organized these hearings. The mere act sends a message not only here in Canada but also to other countries. By no means would one imagine Canada to be a place where this problem is the most serious. And by doing this, you recognize the value and the importance of having a focused and a serious and comprehensive examination, and I hope other countries will as well.

You have my written submission. I know time is brief, so I want to make a few key points. And I speak more now out of my experience this year as the personal representative of the OSCE chair on combating antisemitism, which has allowed me to look at and take up the issue in various countries of the 56 members of the OSCE. What we see, certainly what we've heard, at least as I've listened today, is that the central element of antisemitism, or the problem of antisemitism, in many countries is to be found in public discourse—in the media, on the Internet, in newspapers, at public events, demonstrations, and the like. It's important to recognize that this itself can, not always but can, become a physical security threat for Jews and members of the Jewish community. So speech does matter!

Now how to address it, how to deal with the problem, is a challenge all countries face. In some cases, efforts have been made to deal with it through legislation by limiting hate speech, by criminalizing hate speech. This is something I know you wrestle with to a degree here in Canada, as well.

From what I've observed, my sense is that legislation often does not work. It may exist but it is not uniformly or frequently imposed. In some cases where court examinations have been brought, the length of time between bringing a case and reaching some settlement can often be months or even years. Penalties, when penalties are applied, may be so limited as to really not be a deterrent. And I think in some countries, the mere fact that you have a legal process has allowed political leaders to be quiet, whether by choice or whether by law, to be able to say this is now a matter for the prosecutor, a matter for the courts, and they won't speak. I think we need to do more to determine the best ways of dealing with this hate speech. But most of us recognize a critical element is for political leaders, civil leaders, to speak clearly, loudly, and swiftly to make such expressions taboo, as best they can.

In many countries, antisemitism is recognized but it is not monitored. Data are not recorded. Even in countries that do make special efforts to record hate crimes, many don't disaggregate the data so you can see what examples we have of antisemitism. Again, in various places it is left to law enforcement to record incidents. So if you have an issue, if you have a question of antisemitism in public discourse, many countries don't criminalize it, so it won't be recorded by police. In some countries that do criminalize it, the attitudes are such that victims or observers have little confidence that anything will come of it, so they're also not reporting to the general public or to authorities.

This being the case, I think we've seen an unfortunate circle in various European countries in the early part of this decade. Incidents were taking place. They weren't noted. They weren't recorded. Authorities looked at what they had and simply saw this as not being a problem. I think until it became such an extreme battle among Jewish communities who experienced and recognized one reality, with political authorities who came late to recognize it as well, we had a serious disconnection. So the importance of understanding and monitoring these incidents cannot be underestimated.

If governments are not prepared to do it, NGOs, Jewish communities, other elements of civil society should step forward. There are ways of monitoring and recording data in an organized, standardized way so that they can be easily accessible to government authorities and certainly to those who are trying to monitor and understand what's taking place.

One reference to this working definition of antisemitism was generated, initially, by the European Monitoring Centre, which is now officially part of the European Union Fundamental Rights Agency. It may not be the best definition, though I think it is a very good definition of antisemitism, but it has the added value of being developed by an agency of the EU, of what is now a union of 27 countries. It has been put to use in various training materials developed by the ODIHR in the OSCE, again, an umbrella of 56 countries, and I think that imprimatur makes it especially valuable, so that one cannot point a finger and say, "Well, this is your subjective view", or "This comes from a former minister of the State of Israel or a professor of Jewish studies", but rather this is something that has become a formal document of a European Union agency.

I would like to take this opportunity, even though I realize your primary focus is looking at this problem here in Canada, to urge you as members of Parliament to see how you might be engaged as well in combating this problem internationally. I think the OSCE is one venue where Canada, as a full member, can sit around the table and take up this issue, where you as parliamentarians can join in the OSCE parliamentary assembly meetings where this subject is also raised. There is every expectation that next year, in 2010, the incoming chair of the OSCE, the Government of Kazakhstan, will mount a high-level conference that will focus on the problem of anti- Semitism as well as other forms of intolerance, and there's a clear role for Canada to play.

I would also add that through your own foreign ministry, through your own ambassadors and embassies around the world, you can see that your government makes note of what takes place, and perhaps can bring to these countries, in your own contribution to their civil societies, the positive elements of the experience you have here in Canada. While I realize much of the focus of the discussion has been to bring forward the problems that exist in Canada, I think we all recognize there are a lot of good practices going on in this country as well that could usefully be shared with others.

Rabbi Andrew Baker*
Personal Representative of the OSCE Chair-in-Office on Combating Anti-Semitism

Anti-Semitism in Public Discourse
An essential element of the problem in many countries is the presence of antisem- itism in public discourse. It is offensive and pernicious in its own right, but it can also contribute to a climate which poses a security threat to Jews and Jewish institutions. The capacity to counter this antisemitism is frequently lacking.

Many European countries have laws which restrict or punish hate speech. They are intended to address incitement to racial or religious hatred which may appear in public speeches, in books, newspapers and other media, and on the Internet. This includes fomenting anti-Semitism and, in some cases, Holocaust denial. Rarely is the problem the legislation itself, but rather it is the infrequent and often unsuccessful record of employing it.

By way of example and drawing from some of my OSCE country visits and other personal experience:
  • In Spain there have been only two successful cases of prosecuting Holocaust denial in the last twenty years, and both of them took over seven years to adjudicate. In a country where the Jewish population is less than one one-hundredth of one percent the society is likely to know

---

* The testimony of Rabbi Baker is comprised of both an oral submission presented to the Canadian Parliamentary Inquiry into Antisemitism on 23 November 2009, and written submission presented to the Panel outlining the presence of antisemitism throughout the public discourse within OSCE member states. Full unabridged transcripts of Rabbi Baker's testimony can be found at http://www.cpcca.ca/inquiry.htm.

Jews only from their depictions in the press and media. As it is generally accepted that the Spanish media frequently depicts Israel in a negative light, some officials have suggested that this contributes to the population's low opinion of Jews.

- In Lithuania in 2004, the General Prosecutor opened a case against the publisher, Vitas Tomkus, after his newspaper ran a series of articles entitled "Who Rules the World?" loosely based on the *Protocols of the Elders of Zion* and illustrated with Nazi-like cartoons. Political leaders, although privately disgusted with the articles, remained publicly silent as the months-long investigation proceeded. A year later, when the case came to trial Mr. Tomkus was found guilty. But he was not required to appear in court and the $1,000 fine had little deterrent value to this multi-millionaire publisher. Such articles still appear regularly in his newspapers.

- During this last year the Jewish Community of Greece appealed to a 1979 hate speech law in its case against the author Kostas Plevris, who wrote that the Holocaust is a "profit making myth" invented by the Jews. Although initially found guilty, the decision was reversed on appeal. It seems that many judges are conflicted about a law that restricts freedom of speech, and the High Court will soon take up the larger question if its usefulness. Perhaps as a way to tacitly express its own dissatisfaction with the court results, the Greek Foreign Ministry held a public ceremony in Athens this summer where it honored Greek Holocaust survivors.

- Last week I sat in the Jewish Community offices in Bucharest while the President of the Jewish Federation described the personal attacks on him in the newspaper of the right-wing Greater Romania Party. Nearly two years have passed since he filed suit, but so far the public prosecutor has not responded. (Ironically, on my first visit to Romania in 1993, I sat in the same room and heard the late Rabbi Moses Rosen describe similar personal attacks on him from the very same newspaper.) I met later with the Justice Minister/Foreign Minister Catalin Predoiu during this visit, who readily acknowledged the lack of clarity in the law and its limited effectiveness. To his credit the Minister used the occasion of my visit to issue a statement stressing the moral obligation of public officials to speak out against acts of anti-Semitism.

- We also witnessed a similar example of this problem in Sweden earlier this year, when the newspaper *Aftonbladet* published a report from Gaza claiming that Israeli soldiers were harvesting organs from Palestinians they had killed. This updated version of the medieval blood libel charge was openly denounced by political leaders in the United States and in some European capitals. However, the Swedish Foreign Ministry maintained that its press freedom laws did not permit its own public officials to criticize the article, and it rebuked its Ambassador to Israel for doing so. It did indicate that an official ombudsman had the authority to investigate and bring charges if was determined that racial incitement laws were violated. It was quickly decided that they were not.

- The Internet is often cited as an unchecked source for all manner of hate speech including anti-Semitism. Even those countries with some experience at reining in extremist material in traditional media admit to difficulties when it comes to this source. But it is not only impressionable young people—the most frequently cited target—who are affected by it. Three years ago the Government of Latvia and its Jewish Community reached an agreement on legislation that would resolve all outstanding property restitution claims. But by the time the bill reached Parliament, opposition to the legislation—much of it spread via the Internet and anti-Semitic in nature—so unnerved its Members that it failed to pass. During my visit to Riga Latvian authorities conceded that whenever the subject of Jewish property restitution is raised in public they anticipate a spike in anti-Semitism.

We can certainly reach some general conclusions from these examples. Put simply, many hate speech laws have the unintended consequence of letting political leaders off the hook. In the United States, Canada and other countries with strong free speech protections, manifestations of racism, anti-Semitism, and other extremist views in public discourse are generally addressed (and can only be addressed) by strong and swift rebukes from political and civic leaders. In this way such hateful speech is marginalized and isolated. But in countries with legislative remedies some political leaders will refer to the legal process as a reason or excuse not to speak out. As we see in practice those legal decisions are generally months or years away. In the meantime, there is no clear message being delivered that such hateful speech is unacceptable. Consider too that even some decent, mainstream political leaders, fearing the success of extremist movements, see calculated benefits in maintaining an ambiguous stance.

The OSCE Representative on Freedom of the Media, speaking at a Roundtable on the problem of anti-Semitism that we convened on March 17, 2009 in Vienna, also cited special difficulties in countries with a Communist or authoritarian past. Because all speech was once monitored and controlled, he argued, prosecutors and judges are often reluctant today to pursue cases or impose penalties on those who violate hate speech laws despite having legislation to do so. Some of them have difficulty understanding that it is possible to limit some forms of speech while still vigorously protecting the principle itself.

In nearly all places anti-Semitic speech is understood to be included within the larger categories of inciting racial, ethnic or religious hatred. But virtually no penal code includes a specific or detailed description of anti-Semitism, which means it is not always recognized by prosecutors or judges or (as witnessed in Sweden) by official ombudsmen.

Where they do exist, Holocaust denial laws are not uniform. In some places denial alone is illegal; while other countries require proof that the denial of the Holocaust is part of an intentional effort inflict pain on survivors or members of the Jewish community. As a result prosecution under such a law can also vary widely.

Monitoring Anti-Semitism

Accurate and recognized monitoring of antisemitic incidents is frequently lacking or incomplete. The newly released ODIHR Hate Crime Report reveals that many governments are still lax in monitoring and recording hate crime data or in aggregating the data they do have so as to better understand who are the perpetrators and the victims. But the problem is especially acute when the goal is to combat anti-Semitism. (A summary of the findings with regard to anti-Semitic incidents is appended to this report.)

In countries where hate speech is not restricted, government authorities are unlikely to record such incidents. The poor record in many countries which do have such laws frequently deters citizens from even filing suit. Physical attacks on persons or the vandalizing of synagogues and cemeteries may be monitored (although with all the same gaps and limitations of hate crimes more generally), but they still ignore the anti-Semitism that appears in the press, on television, at public demonstrations, on the Internet and in anonymous hate mail. When these anti-Semitic incidents are not recorded or are underreported it conveys the misimpression to political leaders and policy makers that the problem itself is not so important.

Governments must be encouraged to do a better job of monitoring and recording anti-Semitism, and we should continue to do everything to urge them to live up to their commitments. But in the interim we can do more to assist local Jewish leadership in various countries or regions to develop their own monitoring centers and to do so in a standardized and internationally recognized way so that public authorities can accept their results.

A Working Definition of Anti-Semitism

In 2004, when the European Monitoring Center (EUMC) conducted its first study of anti-Semitism in the then 17-member European Union, it recognized the need for an operative and common definition of the phenomenon. At the time more than half of its national monitors had no definition at all, and of those that did no two were alike. In light of this the EUMC, now the EU Fundamental Rights Agency, developed a working definition, which has been adopted by the ODIHR, by the US State Department Special Envoy for Combating Anti-Semitism, and by Parliamentary Committees in Germany and the UK, among others. This definition (a copy of which is appended to this testimony) provides an overall framework for understanding what it is and offers a series of examples designed to aid police, monitors and NGOs in their work. It also describes where animosity toward the State of Israel also becomes a form of anti-Semitism.

In some countries the working definition is part of police training programs, as it is in ODIHR's Law Enforcement Officers Program (LEOP) manual, which trains police to respond to hate crimes. In nearly all meetings during my country visits I shared the definition with government officials, who welcomed it. Those of us who are focused on the problem may not fully realize that a lack of understanding on the part of these officials is not uncommon. While physical attacks on identifiable Jewish targets may be easily recognized as anti-Semitic in nature, certain public discourse or the vilification of the Jewish State may not be so readily identified. Therefore, increasing the circulation of this working definition is a useful tool that we can promote.

I hope the Members and Staff of the Canadian Parliamentary Coalition to Combat Antisemitism find this report helpful in its work. If I can be of further assistance—whether in elaborating further on these points or providing additional information—I will be pleased to do so.

Yehuda Bauer

Yehuda Bauer (Scholar-in-Residence) is Professor Emeritus of History and Holocaust Studies at the Harman Institute of Contemporary Jewry, Hebrew University of Jerusalem and academic adviser to the Yad Vashem Foundation. Bauer is fluent in the Czech, Slovak and German languages, Hebrew, Yiddish, English, French and Polish. He has been a visiting professor at Brandeis University, Yale University, Richard Stockton College, and Clark University. Professor Bauer was the founding Chair of the Vidal Sassoon International Center for the Study of Antisemitism, the founding editor of the Journal for Holocaust and Genocide Studies, and served on the editorial board of the Encyclopedia of the Holocaust, published by Yad Vashem in 1990. Bauer has received the Israel Prize, the highest civilian award in Israel. In 2001, he was elected a Member of the Israeli Academy of Science. In 2009, he was awarded the Royal Norwegian Order of Merit for his meritorious services to humanity. Professor Bauer is author to over a dozen books, his latest book "The Death of the Shtetl", is currently in print (Yale University Press).

Professor Bauer currently serves as academic adviser to Yad Vashem and is the Honourary Chair of the International Holocaust Remembrance Alliance (IHRA).

Professor Yehuda Bauer[*]

Professor Emeritus, Hebrew University of Jerusalem, Academic Advisor, Yad Vashem Institute as an Individual

Oral Testimony of Professor Yehuda Bauer, Professor Emeritus, Hebrew University of Jerusalem, Academic Advisor, Yad Vashem Institute, as an individual, delivered to the Canadian Parliamentary Coalition to Combat Antisemitism via teleconference on 16 November 2009.

I would like to thank you and your committee for having me present some issues and possibly some answers to the problems that you are addressing.

My concern is a global one and an historical one. I think the first issue that one has to consider is what antisemitism actually is. Of course, "antisemitism" is the wrong term for what we are dealing with. There is no "Semitism" that you can be "anti". Therefore, antisemitism is really a nonsensical word. It was coined by a German journalist and anti-Jewish agitator by the name of Wilhelm Marr in 1879 in order to differentiate the new nationalist and racist Jew hatred from the traditional religious one that preceded it.

We use that term for a variety of problems that arise in modern society. We use it for discrimination against Jews and for anything between a moderate dislike of Jews to murderous hatred. But I think we have to realize that when we use that term, we use something that does not really describe what we mean. What we actually mean is Jew hatred—in other words, the idea that Jews are some kind of disturbing factor in modern society.

This, of course, has historical roots of tremendous importance, which we won't go into now. Modern antisemitism, post-World War II, was obviously influenced by the Holocaust. Any contemporary anti-Jewish propaganda relates one way or another to that event.

I think antisemitism has become a global issue, not just a Canadian, American, British, European, or Muslim countries issue. It has become a problem that all of humanity has to deal with. Let me put it very clearly: antisemitism was a major, if not *the* major, factor in the development of Nazi ideology, which directly led to World War II, which caused the deaths, in Europe alone, of 35 million people. Close to 6 million of these were the Jews who were murdered by the Nazis; 29 million were non-Jews.

---

[*] The testimony of Professor Bauer is comprised of an oral submission presented to the Canadian Parliamentary Inquiry into Antisemitism on 16 November 2009, a subsequent written supplication in response to Panel members' questions and written submission presented to the Panel outlining historical and contemporary antisemitism. Full unabridged transcripts of Professor Bauer's testimony can be found at http://www.cpcca.ca/inquiry.htm.

In other words, 29 million non-Jewish people were killed largely because of Jew hatred. I emphasize that: non-Jews were killed because of hatred of Jews. If there's any good reason for non-Jewish people to fight antisemitism, I think that historical experience should lead them to do that.

My second point is that we always thought antisemitism was a result of economic problems, of economic downturns. The post-World War II incidents of antisemitism—in my paper, I analyze four such waves of anti-Semitism—show very clearly that this was not the case. In some cases, antisemitism was caused by economic downturns. In others, it was certainly not caused by economic downturns but by cultural problems, political problems, and of course by the ongoing Israeli-Palestinian confrontation in the Middle East, which was not the cause of antisemitism but was a trigger for antisemitism.

In other words, my contention is that if there should be some kind of compromise or solution one way or another of the Israeli-Palestinian confrontation, there certainly will be a weakening of antisemitic propaganda, but it will not disappear. Proof of that can be seen in the development of radical Islamic anti-Jewish propaganda before the establishment of the state of Israel. Even if some kind of arrangement should be reached in the Middle East region, there is no chance, I think, of antisemitism disappearing.

Antisemitism can be fought over time, basically by two strategies. One is the recognition of the right of every group to have its own culture and independence—cultural, political, and so on. That would include the Jews along with many other groups. The other one is to undercut the basis for antisemitism.

The basis for antisemitism is the fact that the Jews are neither better nor worse than anyone else is, but their culture is certainly different, and it is that difference on which the enemies of the Jews focus. Once one recognizes that, one can then develop strategies to fight it. One can encourage the idea that every group, including the Jews, has its own right to separate development and to recognition as a group.

Of course, this can only happen in democratic societies. In the present situation, we have to say that we are dealing with two kinds of worlds. We are dealing with the world of, roughly speaking, so called western democracies. "Western", of course, includes Australia and Japan, so the term is not really geographical but cultural. We also deal with the non-democratic world, where the impact of fighting anti-Semitism is necessarily extremely limited. I think we have to recognize that the possibility of fighting antisemitism in Pakistan or other places like that is limited by our limitations of influencing these societies from the outside.

Pakistan is an excellent example, because there is not a single Jew there. There was one there and they killed him. That was the American Jewish journalist Daniel Pearl.

So we are dealing with two separate issues with one underlying base. That underlying base is the traditional and cultural hatred of the Jewish people because they are different. Israel has become another case of a development from the Middle Ages; in the Middle Ages, it was the individual Jew who was hated, persecuted, and so on, but now it is the collective Jew.

The collective Jew is the state of Israel as a Jewish state. The hatred of Israel is really a direct configuration of the Middle Ages and the early modern periods. I think that when one realizes this, one can then move forward in order to deal with it.

My recommendations to your committee would be on a number of points.

- First, I think your example and the example of Britain should be followed. There is an initiative in Britain for an international parliamentary union of parliamentary representatives fighting antisemitism; in other words, a global parliamentary movement that will include more and more parliaments in the democratic or even half-democratic world in order to face this issue.

- The second point is education. You can't deal with academic antisemitism, for instance, without realizing that the students who are following antisemitic propaganda are the sons and daughters of parents who, one way or another, may influence them in one way or the opposite way—in other words, for or against antisemitic propaganda. So the issue is about educating not only the children but also the adults. It means introducing programs into schools that will be not only with the children but with their backgrounds, with their peer societies and parent societies.

Those are two of my main recommendations. Of course, any kind of political alliance between Canada and other countries to fight antisemitism will be extremely welcome.

Thank you very much.

Supplementary Statement provided by Professor Yehuda Bauer to the Canadian Parliamentary Coalition to Combat Antisemitism, Ottawa, Canada on November 21, 2009.

Ladies and Gentlemen,

I was not very satisfied with my responses during our teleconference the other day, especially as I was not asked to comment on the questions I received prior to it. I hope you will agree to read the following comments on those queries.

Question 1. *"Do you see any similarities in attitudes towards Jews today and in the 1930s?"*

Yes, there are some parallels. The ideological base of Nazi antisemitism was a purely illusionary series of accusations that had nothing to do with reality: a world Jewish conspiracy (an accusation one can read in the writings of the Church Fathers, Origen, Cyprien, John Chrysostomos, and others), the blood libel, the charge that Jews control the world's media, the charge that Jews corrupt "Aryan' civilization, etc. Jihadist accusations, as put forward by Sunni radicals such as Yussuf Qaraddawi, or Imams in the main Mecca mosques, or ideologues such as Abdullah Azzam, and their pupils, echo these thoughts. The differences between that and today's situation are rooted in the different cultures: a European tradition of anti-Jewishness on the one hand, and an Islamist view that sees the Western world of infidels as the overall enemy, with the Jews serving as its spearhead. That world they actively seek to destroy.

In the Middle Ages, the Jew as an individual was seen as the servant of Satan and viewed as a pariah. Today, Israel, as the collective Jew, serves this role. The individual Jew today is viewed as a member of a worldwide conspiracy, i.e., Jews are viewed as a disciplined collective, each member of which represents all. This was the view of extreme antisemites in the 1930s as well. However: in the 1930s, there were quite a number of governments who supported antisemitism; apart from Germany, these were, for instance, Poland, Romania, Hungary, and others, in various degrees. Today, no Western government supports anti-Jewish agitation and, as is well known to panel members, the OSCE is formally committed to fighting antisemitism.

Question 2: *"You make the case that the threat against the Jews today is another genocide and therefore we cannot 'repeat past mistakes'. What were these mistakes and how do we avoid repeating them?"*

I did not say that anti-Jewish threats are genocide, but that incitement that may lead to genocide is punishable under the UN Convention on the Prevention and

Punishment of the Crime of Genocide (December 9, 1948). Thus, Iranian threats against Israel can be translated into reality only by destroying Israel as a Jewish state, and that clearly implies a campaign of mass murder directed against an identifiable ethnic/national group (as foreseen in the Convention). The Iranian President should therefore be liable to prosecution under the Convention, to which his country is a signatory. In the past, statements such as that of the Nazis (e.g., Hitler's speech to the Reichstag of January 30, 1939), which clearly indicated a desire to annihilate the Jews, were brushed off as rantings of a violent antisemite. We should adopt the view that if people with some power and influence constantly repeat a certain ideological world-view, they will do their best to realize their plans if they get the chance. Talk leads to action; not always, but very often. Radical anti-Jewishness is a position that has been verbally expressed in the past, and very often attempts were then made to translate it into practice, whether these attempts were successful or not. This does not apply to antisemitism only, but is true of ideological convictions generally. Radical anti-Jewishness, whether of an extermi-natory kind or less than that, is being expressed today in both the West and parts of the Moslem world (but not in China, India, Indonesia, Tunisia, in most African countries, etc.), and should be taken at its face value.

Question 3: "Is there an explanation for the fact that the present wave of antisemitism, while generally a phenomenon restricted to the middle classes, is widespread in the media, in universities, and in "well-manicured circles"?"
The first groups to join the National-Socialist Party in Germany as groups or unions were the students, the university teachers, and the Teachers' Union. In the Churches, antisemitism was taught and spread by the elites, before it was adopted and popularized by the lower clergy. In the US, there were restrictions on Jews studying at Harvard until the 1950s, while the economy was open to them, and they were free to vote and be elected. In Britain, during the war, there was a spontaneous outburst of pro-Jewish sentiment in 1942/3, demand-ing action to rescue European Jews and offering homes for Jewish refugees, while Clementine, Churchill's wife, declared that she will not have a Jew cross the threshold of her home. The media are somewhere between the general pop-ulation, and the elites, depending on their quality, and they will reflect both, on different occasions, and in different outlets. Waves of antisemitism after 1945 were never led by blue or white-collared workers' organizations, but by lower or upper middle-class groups incited by ideologues coming from the upper strata of society. Neo-Nazis in the West today are clearly semi-primitive groups, but their ideologies are contrived by intellectuals who use clever orchestration to

do their bit. Antisemitism, and this is crucial for understanding the phenomenon, comes from the fact that while Jews and their culture or civilization are
neither better nor worse than any other, they certainly are different. Had the
Jews stayed in their hilly country and continued to live by what may be called
acrobatic agriculture, ploughing the hard soil of their hills to plant whatever
they could, as they originally did, they would have been just another oddity in
the cultural pluralism of our world, with their peculiar monotheism and their
set of social ideas and ideals. But they spread outwards, for reasons that I could
but will not explain here, and carried their culture on their backs, so to speak,
walling themselves off from their host populations in order to preserve it. They
formed a well-known, but strange, minority everywhere.

That meant they were easy scapegoats whenever a society sought to transfer guilt for any problem that arose onto someone else. In Christian Europe,
and partly in the New World afterwards, there was the central issue of a
Christianity that sought to persuade society of the truth of its concepts, and it
had to differentiate itself from the father religion/civilization in order to do so.
The same applied later to Islam. Antisemitism became a basic postulate of the
successor religions/cultures. All this made it a central, almost self-understood
premise of high culture and its bearers, before it became the ideology of the
masses—which of course it did become. Modern national societies, based in
the Christian-Moslem world, tend to continue this. Antisemitism is, therefore,
not (only) a prejudice, but a cultural phenomenon. Hence, its prevalence in
"well-manicured" circles.

**Question 4: "You make the connection between Soviet Communism, National
Socialism, and Islamism—do you believe that current trends in radical
Islamism have the realistic capability to transform into the same sadistic
and genocidal creations of the last century?"**
Firstly, let us leave out the "sadistic". Sadism is not peculiar to Nazism,
Communism, Islamism, or any other genocidal movement. It has been part,
unfortunately, of human behavior, since time immemorial (a recent find in
Talheim, in Germany, of a Neolithic mass grave showed that a large number
of humans were murdered there by other humans, and that babies' skulls were
smashed and their bodies speared; you didn't have to wait until Hitler).

Current trends in radical Islam have the realistic power to persuade very large
numbers of people to adopt its teachings. They are having quite some success
in contemporary Pakistan, for instance, and the ideas are spreading in places
like Egypt, Sudan, Saudi Arabia and elsewhere. Radical Islam teaches the love of

Death, as against the love of Life of all the other ideologies/religions, including moderate Islam (in Indonesia, Bangladesh, in North America, and elsewhere). Recent statements by Moslem liberals tell us about the effectiveness of radical teachings in mainstream Moslem societies (a recent example: Mansour Al-Hadj, a Saudi liberal, on his education, in www.aafaqmagazine.com, October 24, 2009). The problem is not just that radical Islam, still a minority, spreads as such, but that its ideas are increasingly being accepted by the mainstream. This is seen for example by the twisting and turning of the most important Islamist theologian, Mohammed Sayyid el-Tantawi, the Sheikh al-Azhar in Cairo, who had to withdraw his opposition to suicide bombing after being pressured by his students and colleagues at al-Azhar. There are, as you know, 1.3 billion Moslems in the world, and they are potential followers. The answer to the problem is to support the considerable number of non-radical and anti-radical, devout, Moslems, who (rightly) see Islam as another world religion that can be interpreted, and has been interpreted, as a religion of peace (example; the millions of Sufis, a pietistic branch of Sunni Islam). The outside world cannot solve the problem. This has to be done by the millions of Moslems who love life, though they may not fear death.

Question 5: "What impact does the large Muslim population in Europe have on attitudes towards Jews and Israel?"

There are an estimated 23 million Moslems in Europe today. The demographic catastrophe that has befallen Europe will cause a sharp reduction of the native populations (in Russia, Poland, Germany, Spain, Italy, etc.); ageing will necessitate immigration from the outside, and hence a necessary cultural reorientation. There is a well-known opposition to further immigration, especially from Moslem areas, but it seems to me that the possibility to reduce or stop this immigration is not very likely to succeed, especially as the pressure from (Moslem) African and other areas to enter Europe shows no sign of abating. These Moslem immigrants come from very varied backgrounds.

A Kurd, will in most cases, not enter a Turkish mosque, and a North African Moslem will not be comfortable in a Black African mosque, either. To treat the Moslem population as though they were cut from the same cloth is a basic mistake. Radical Islam is a minority view, but it is growing, because of the lack of integration of large groups of Moslem into local culture(s). There are some successes, though: many Turkish immigrants into Germany are slowly being integrated. Some positive signs can be seen in Switzerland. The problem has not arisen, yet, in Eastern Europe, but there can be little doubt that the development of local economies will bring larger number of

Moslems there, too. In Central and Western Europe it arises mainly with second-generation immigrants, who often are the first to be dismissed from work, and who feel the intense dislike towards strangers of the locals which results in discrimination. The hatred of many young Moslems is directed mainly against the host country, its symbols, and culture. Radical Islamic propaganda and violence are the work of usually newly immigrated imams and other ideologues, but they fall on fertile ground because of the factors mentioned above. The result is withdrawal into traditional Islam, which is interpreted, in a radical fashion (not unlike parallel fundamentalist Christian and Jewish indoctrination).

Anti-Jewish texts from the Kor'an and the Hadith form the textual basis for opposition to Jews. The Israeli-Palestinian confrontation provides a powerful trigger. Radical Moslems in Europe—and elsewhere - do not actually know much about the Mideast issues, but simplistic slogans suffice as incitement to hatred that sometimes translates into action: 'Jews kill Moslems' serves all such purposes. To fight Jews, and their collective expression, i.e. Israel, then becomes a jihadist project, though the real target are the French, Dutch, British, and other, societies. Christianity ('crusaders' religion') and Judaism are seen as allies fighting the true faith. In the eyes of radicals, Israel becomes the spearhead of the anti-Moslem conspiracy.

What can be done against this? At OSCE meetings in Berlin and Cordoba, I suggested that Islamophobia and antisemitism are linked and should be addressed simultaneously, because hatred of Moslems by locals is a major factor in producing antisemitism. Furthering integration of Moslems into European society and advancing a carefully-graded multiculturalism (which includes acceptance of local languages and European cultural symbols by the Moslem minority) is, I believe, the only way to move forward. And it can only be done with the support of non-radical Moslems. This may apply to the growing Moslem population of Canada as well.

Question 6: "How influential is the expression of radical Islam throughout media outlets in the Muslim world? Moreover, is there any way to curb this rising trend?"
The main Islamist outlets are websites on the net. These sites change constantly, so as not be to be subject to interference by anti-Islamist factors. They can be found at any time through the Washington-based www.memri.com (Memri = Middle East Media Research Institute). Memri makes available not only Islamist sources, in English, German, and Hebrew, but also plans to expand to Polish

and Swedish; it also makes available anti-Islamist, liberal, and democratic voices from the ME. Its sources are in Arabic, Turkish, Farsi, and Urdu, so the coverage is very wide. There is no way to estimate how many people in the Moslem world access radical websites, which also include video material. Not everyone who reads them is a follower of radical Islam, and not all followers of Islamism read these websites. The problem is that ideas from Islamist sources penetrate into mainstream media outlets such as El-Jazeera, or the main printed papers in Egypt, Turkey, and Pakistan.

The Shi'a form of Islamism differs in many important respects from the Sunni version, though the desire for world control, the absolute truth of Islam, and the willingness to use force are common to both. Shi'a Islamism is willing to countenance a controlled form of parliamentary democracy, as in Iran— controlled by the supreme authority of clerics; the Sunni variety is opposed to any participatory politics, on principle: Allah has given humans all the laws they need, in the Kor'an, the Hadith, and the Shariyah, and all that they have to do is to nominate devout clerics to interpret them correctly. Therefore, when men (women don't count anyway) presume to make laws, they are guilty of blasphemy. The struggle between radical Sunna and radical Shi'a is real and bitter, takes place over internet and print, and should be utilized by non-radical Moslems and Western opponents of radical Islam. That is one of the main avenues of struggling against antisemitism.

Question 7: *"How would you propose governments in the West best deal with the growing phenomenon of radical Islam?"*
First, by reaching out to non-radical Moslems in their own countries and beyond, in a non-patronizing way, offering cultural equality, but without yielding on Western-type democracy and Western culture and its values. Western universities should be supported when they educate non-Moslems and Moslems in both Islamic culture on these principles, provided support by Islamic states of the relevant departments is discouraged (Saudi, Turkish, Iranian, and sometimes Libyan money is made available at these institutions in order to further anti-democratic, antisemitic and radical anti-Israeli propaganda; of course, freedom of access to anyone must be protected, but governmental encouragement can and should be selective).

Second, by encouraging non-radical Moslems to engage in theological argument against the radicals, and protect them from radical attacks (such attacks often come not from Moslems, but from misled non-Moslem supporters of radical Islamic demands, especially at universities). Third, by supporting economic and social advances in Moslem countries which are not linked to Western economic interests. Fourth, by engaging in a form of dialogue with Moslem countries that makes it clear both that the West appreciates and respects Islam and its culture, and at the same time strongly insists on its own. Fifth, introduce in any contacts and friendly alliances with Moslem governments provisions that will insist that radical Islam has to be fought tooth and nail.

Final, marginal, comment: at the hearing, Dr. Gerstenfeld insisted on attacking Norway and Sweden for alleged governmental support of antisemitic tendencies there. It should be stated clearly that even if he was right—which he emphatically is not—antisemitism and violent anti-Israeli hatred, masquerading as anti-Zionism, in Scandinavia (which of course exists there as everywhere else) is totally marginal to antisemitism in Europe and the Americas generally. In fact, however, the Norwegian war-time resistance movement, supported by the overwhelming majority of the population, rescued half of Norwegian Jews—the others were indeed delivered to the Germans by collaborators of the Quisling movement (collaborators with the Nazis existed in all countries under German rule, even in Denmark). Norway was the first, and so far the only, country whose (Labor) government paid full and complete restitution to the Jews of Norway for what Nazi Germany and its Norwegian collaborators did to the Jews.

At the moment of writing, Norway is the Chair of the International Task Force for Holocaust Education, Remembrance, and Research, and Ambassador Tom Vraalsen, the Chair, had the ITF pass a program which centers on the fight against anti-Semitism. Yes, a Norwegian minister attended a violent anti-Israeli meeting and did not walk out when revolting slogans were uttered. That does not make the government into an antisemitic ogre. Sweden, also under a Labor government, organized the first ever inter-governmental conference on Holocaust education, in 2000 (attended by Canadian governmental representatives), which passed the so-called Stockholm Declaration that, inter alia, also made anti-Semitism an issue to be addressed (as I wrote that declaration, I can testify to the determination of the Swedes to deal with this issue, among others). Dr Gerstenfeld has a problem with liberals and left-wingers, which is fine, but that should not deter us from looking at things as they are in reality. Not every right-winger is a friend of Jews and Israel, and not every liberal is an enemy.

Written Submission Prepared by Professor Yehuda Bauer for the Canadian Parliamentary Panel on Antisemitism

Antisemitism, Historical and Contemporary

Why did Nazi Germany start World War II? There is a broad consensus among
historians that the war broke out because the Nazi leadership wanted to gain
control over Europe, and it believed that in order to do that it needed the supply
of food and raw materials that could only be gained for Germany if it conquered
the Ukraine and the Caucasus, after eliminating Poland and removing the threat
of a two-front war by defeating Britain and France. There was little pragmatic
logic behind this, because it is clear that they could have got all that by ordinary
trade with the USSR—Stalin was eager to avoid war, and was willing to supply
Germany with everything it needed. The real reason was ideological: Hitler and
his followers believed that in order to control Europe, and beyond that, the danger of Bolshevism had to be removed. In the only memorandum he ever wrote
himself, in August, 1936, directed to Göring and not intended for publication,
Hitler laid out the economic conditions for a war within four years. That was
essential, he wrote, because otherwise Bolshevism would conquer Germany
and annihilate the German people (sic!). Bolshevism, he said, had as its aim the
replacement of all the leading strata of human society with International Jewry.
Bolshevism was, as he had said elsewhere, a Jewish project, and it was allied to
the Jewish plutocracy that ruled America and the West, as he later said in his
famous speech to the Reichstag on January 30, 1939. Clearly, then, World War
II was motivated by an ideology at whose core was the belief in a world Jewish
conspiracy. In other words, the war, with its 35 million dead in Europe alone,
was in no small degree the product of an antisemitic ideology. To put it bluntly:
29 million non-Jews died, in part, because of antisemitism. That would appear
to be a good enough reason to fight it today, seventy years after.

Since 1945, there have been four waves of antisemitism. The approximate
dates are 1958-1960, 1968-1972, 1987-1992, and 2000 to the present. Analysis
has shown that the motivations were different in each case, and in the third,
the one starting in 1987, and the fourth, economic motivation was/is largely
absent. That means that our traditional explanations that modern antisemitism
always has something to do with economic downturns are inaccurate. Political,
economic, or theological crises can all be causes of a phenomenon that cannot
be explained monocausally. Why is there antisemitism? Basically, because the
Jews produced a civilization that differed in some central aspects from the civilizations around them. Monotheism may have been invented by the Egyptians
during the times of Akh-en-aton, the Sabbath may originate in Babylon (the
name shabbat-sabbatu is Babylonian), others may have tried to limit or abolish
slavery, Hebrew social legislation may have precedents elsewhere, but only the

Jews combined all these elements in a religious-ethnic-social civilization that developed over a long period of time. On that basis there developed a way of life, with changing, but clearly defined customs that solidified into laws sacralized by religious belief. Jews were/are certainly no better or worse than others, but they are/were different in the way they conducted their lives. Had they stayed in their hilly land, they would have been another peculiar oddity; but they spread. Everywhere the Jews went they carried their distinctive civilization with them, which marked them off against their environment. Crises of whatever source could cause this basically defenseless, well-known yet strange, minority, to be seen as the reason for the crisis, and therefore they were often subject to discrimination or attack, although, contrary to accepted wisdom, in most places at most times this did not happen and they were not persecuted. However, Jew-hatred is the oldest group hatred that exists, preceding racism; thus, Blacks who acknowledged Roman gods and were free men, could become Roman citizens. Jews refused to acknowledge other gods, they would not share in the food of their neighbors, and on the whole they kept themselves separate. This solidified in the theological dispute with Christianity and Islam. Economic stresses came later, and contrary to Marxist interpretations, they were the result of the theological tensions, not the other way round.

This Christian theological basis for antisemitism is today slowly eroding. Vatican II in 1965 was a first step, acknowledging the baselessness of the deicide accusation. Christian Churches are slowly developing the idea that there may be several ways to serve God, and that theirs may not be the only one. Theological antisemitism is not dead, but it is weakening, and in the struggle against contemporary antisemitism the Christian Churches are often allies, not opponents.

However, many hundreds of years of an antisemitic culture have had their result in the formation of an underlying latency of antisemitism that waits to explode when aroused by some outside crisis. In the post-1945 era this has been complicated by two major events of a political and cultural nature: the impact of the Holocaust and the establishment of Israel. The Holocaust created an unease about the Jews, especially of course in Europe, where people have to live with close to six million ghosts, created by a deadly mutation of European culture. As the famous saying goes—the Europeans cannot forgive the Jews for Auschwitz. Periods of self-accusation and beating of breasts alternate with periods in which everything is done to turn the Jews into perpetrators, nowadays even Nazis, in order to liberate the heirs of European culture from the burden of genocide. The establishment of Israel caused a widespread feeling of relief on the one hand: we don't have to bother about the Jews anymore, they have made good, they will create a new Christianity for us, or a new socialism—a humanistic, idealistic society that will bring salvation to a sick world. The kibbutz, the Weitzmann Institute of Science, the Hebrew University, and Itzhak Perlmann took the place of the Christian Savior, or provided an alternative to Stalin's Communism. On the other hand, antisemites turned the victims into perpetrators, David into Goliath, and when occasion arose, everything was and is done to identify Israel with evil. In both cases, Israel is singled out, a collective deity or an evil force. Jews as a collective entity are never equal to others. That is antisemitism.

The Israeli-Palestinian confrontation provides ample material for an antisemitism that sees itself as anti-Zionist, and not anti-Jewish. Indeed, one can be, in theory at least, anti-Zionist without being antisemitic, but only if one says that all national movements are evil, and all national states should be abolished. But if one says that the Fijians have a right to independence, and so do the Malays or the Bolivians, but the Jews have no such right, or that that right should be revoked, then one is anti-Jewish, i.e. antisemitic. The UN and its Commissions and Committees often single out Israel as a pariah nation, and the status of the collective Jew, i.e. Israel, becomes akin to the status of the individual Jew in the Middle Ages.

Israel is locked in a bitter struggle with Palestinian nationalism, which is no less legitimate than the Jewish one is. Israeli policies on the West Bank and the Gaza strip may be mainly reactive to terrorism which has been branded as crime, but they cause serious violations of human rights, and result in terrible suffering of the local population. Compromises that were suggested, failed, and seem currently impossible of achievement as both sides are ruled by elites that oppose any compromise that would be acceptable to the other side. However, antisemitic latency in the West latches on to that tragic dispute in order to brand the Jews as mass murderers and Nazis, in order to solve the social psychological problem caused by the Holocaust. Facts do not matter there—the total number of Palestinian victims of the second Intifada, since September 2000, until today, is slightly over 6500 (and about 1000 Israelis, including Israeli Arabs, almost all of them civilians, were killed by Palestinians in the same period), which is about one half of the daily number of Jews shipped to Auschwitz from Hungary in the spring of 1944. Any kind of simplistic comparison becomes totally ridiculous—e.g. to the Kashmiri or Sri Lankan or Sudanese situations, never mind World War II. The reason for the vile attacks on Jews in the West is not based on facts, but on a basic cultural trend that latches itself onto real events which it distorts: *antisemitism is not a prejudice but a basic cultural phenomenon.* A realistic approach would sharply criticize Israel in the context of its justified defense against terrorist suicidal homicide, and seek a compromise between two national movements fighting over a very small piece of real estate. But we are not talking about a realistic approach; we are talking about antisemitism.

It appears that the present, fourth wave of antisemitism, in the West, is a basically upper middle class, intellectual phenomenon. It is widespread in the media, in universities, and in well-manicured circles. Typical is the statement of the French ambassador to Britain at a cocktail party, later reported in the British Press, referring to Israel, with diplomatic finesse, as that "shitty little country." What is important here is not the statement itself, but the fact that that gentleman felt perfectly at ease making it in an environment he was sure would understand and appreciate it. Students at Western universities identify with the Palestinian struggle without really knowing the facts of the situation. I am also pro-Palestinian, as I believe that Palestinians deserve independence and equality, but I also believe that the armed struggle of Hamas and Islamic Jihad consists largely of acts of barbarity and inhumanity that in turn provoke inexcusable Israeli behavior. It is easy to cross the line from criticism of a government policy to antisemitism. The US, even after Obama's election, and Israel, are the world's evil forces, and in any case the US is governed by Jewish interests - another well-worn antisemitic myth. In addition, many Europeans have not forgiven the Americans for having liberated them, first from Hitler, and then from Stalin.

One should not generalize: many Europeans (and most Americans), especially of the working and middle classes, but also among the elites, are opposed to these antisemitic trends. It is my view that this wave will pass in time, and of course if a compromise in the Mideast conflict were found, the situation would ease, but unless one deals with the root causes, it will reappear again later. The conflict did not cause today's antisemtitism, but it partly triggered it, and certainly enhanced it. Yet on the whole, it is not Western antisemitism that causes me to worry, but something else: Islamic radicalism.

On May 7, 2002, a program was broadcast on the Egyptian TV station IQRAA, financed by Saudi money. The program was directed at Moslem women. A charming TV personality, Ms. Doua Amer, asked little Basmallah, a 3 ½ year old girl—'Do you know who the Jews are?' 'Yes'. 'Do you like them?' 'No.' 'Why?' ' Because they are monkeys and swine ... and also because they tried to poison the wife of our prophet.'

A whole world is being influenced by such teachings. There are today some 1.3 billion Moslems in the world. Radical Islam is the ideology of only a minority of Moslems, but it is spreading. It is that ideology that fuels international terrorism. The usual response to it, in the US but also in some other places, including

Israel, is that it should be fought by armed force. Is that the correct answer? No, because you cannot fight an ideology by force only.

Islam and radical Islam are not the same thing. Literal interpretation of Islam may lead to radicalism, but that can be said of Christianity and Judaism and other religions as well. Islam is as capable of developing a more liberal, non-literal, milder religious approach that will recognize the validity, or at least partial validity, of other belief systems, as others are. Thus, for instance, there is the very large Sufi movement, a pietistic, peace-loving Islamic direction; there are moderate Moslems in the West, and some very courageous liberals in the Moslem world itself.

What does the Sunni version of radical Islam believe in? The central element is the conviction that Western civilization has passed its peak, and that the future lies with (radical) Islam. The final aim is the conquest not just of the Middle East or Asia, but ultimately, by conversion or force, of the world. The second element is the desire to abolish politics as such. God-Allah has told the world, through his prophet, the Hadith traditions and the Shari'a, how men (women don't count) should govern themselves, and what laws they should follow. Any human intervention, through parliamentary democracy or any type of autocracy is blasphemy, because it means that men decide what they should do, whereas God has already decreed what should be done. The world should be run by men trained in Islamic law, and national and territorial boundaries should be simply a matter of convenience. Hence also comes the third point: radical Islam aspires to the abolition of national states, first and foremost Arab national states. Thus, Hamas and Islamic Jihad in Palestine do not demand a Palestinian national state, but an Islamic state of Palestine, which would be almost as anti-Christian as anti-Jewish: Christians, and those Jews who will survive the genocide that is planned for Israeli Jews, will be subject peoples in Islamic Palestine, with no political rights whatsoever. Lastly, Islamism is a utopian ideology. It promises a wonderful, peaceful world, ruled by God Himself, and thus aspires to the end of history as we know it—there can be no history after the establishment of the rule of God. I have said it many times, with an apology to Lord Acton: all utopias kill, and radical, universalistic and apocalyptic utopias kill radically and massively.

Modern radical Islam was founded by Hassan el-Banna in Egypt in 1928 (the Moslem Brotherhood), and developed as a result of its social policies into a major force in Egyptian society. Many Moslem governments were and are incapable of providing basic necessities to a population that is growing by leaps and bounds. The resulting destitution and despair was answered in Egypt by the

Brotherhood establishing village clinics, building sewage systems and schools, the famous madrassas. They got the money by reinstituting a major principle of religious social policy, the tithe. Even the poorest were asked to give a few pennies each week for the upkeep of these institutions, and of course richer members of the Brotherhood had to chip in with substantial sums. The same principle is followed today by Hamas and Islamic Jihad in Gaza. In return, children and adults are being taught to accept the literal interpretation of Islam and the anti-American and anti-Jewish phobias developed by the radicals.

What are the sources of radical Islam? Moslem civilization, which was the main world culture in the early Middle Ages, did not develop parallel to the West because it did not develop individualism and a middle class that would struggle for supremacy against the forces of conservatism and feudalism. Islamic religious ideology preached opposition to change. In the Moslem countries, autocratic regimes could therefore rely on a reactionary clergy that had a mass basis in the population, and fought successfully against Moslem intellectuals and entrepreneurs that sought to change Moslem society. Today, radicals in Moslem society have to contend not only with the West, but with the industrialized Far Eastern countries as well, which is why the struggle has become global. Radical Islam is fighting not just against the West, but against civilization as such, and when you read what they have to say about Hindus, for instance, you realize that here you have a megalomaniac intention of elimination of all pagan beliefs, such as those of the Hindus and the Buddhists.

I would go further than that. We have seen three major ideologies emerging during the twentieth century, and in many ways continuing into the present: Soviet Communism, National Socialism, and Islamism. There are of course vast differences between them, but there are also some parallels. All three aspired to world supremacy. Belief in radically exclusivist religious or quasi-religious ideologies led/lead to the establishment of dictatorial regimes that would suppress all other belief systems. Their utopias were/are designed to establish a classless society in which historical dialectics will no longer be operative, and an end of time will come. In a utopia you don't need laws, or parliaments that make laws. In all three cases, nationalism was or is to be opposed, in favor of a universalist totalitarianism.

All three ideologies saw or see the Jews as a main enemy. We all know about National Socialism. Stalin's state saw the Jews as the spearhead of Western imperialism, and apparently wanted to deport all the Soviet Jews to Siberia, where most of them would have perished. Radical Islam says, basically, the same thing: the Jews are the spearhead of Western civilization, and they are traditionally the enemies of Islam.

Anti-Jewish ideology has been a part of the development of radical Islam since the late twenties of the last century. The chief ideologue of the movement was Sayid Qutb, an Egyptian official who spent some years in New York and became convinced that the West is decadent and dying. In 1950 and the following years he wrote a number of brochures that are, to this day, the guiding texts of radical Islam. One of them was devoted to the Jews—two years after the establishment of Israel. Traditional Kor'anic elements became intermingled with the legacy of European, and chiefly Nazi, antisemitism. In the Kor'an, Jews are called apes and swine. They are also branded (wrongly) as the most determined opponents of Islam. However, there is more than that—in line with European antisemitism, Jews are seen as the actual rulers of the West, especially of the US, through the media supposedly controlled by them, and through political influence. Thus, Islamistic antisemitism sees the fight against the Jews as a central piece in its program, paralleled only by their desire to eliminate the present corrupt Sunni Moslem governments, and replace them with Islamic states. The language used by the media in some (by no means all) Moslem countries is clearly and unmistakably genocidal. Radical Islam wants to annihilate the Jews, contrary to the medieval Islamic principle of seeing them as the People of the Book, who were granted an inferior, but guaranteed status in Islam. Nazi ideology which led to the Holocaust is repeated here, albeit dressed up differently.

How far is this antisemitic ideology influenced by the Israeli-Palestinian conflict? Sayid Qutb, writing two years after the establishment of Israel, saw the occupation of a piece of land 'liberated' for Islam by its original conquest in the seventh century, and its successful defense against the Crusaders later on, as a blasphemy, especially as the despised Jews did it. In 1967 came another, terrible, defeat that could only be reversed by the total annihilation of the offending people; the Jews had rebelled not only against the stable order of things as established in Islamic tradition, but theirs was a rebellion against God himself.

A compromise reached with the Palestinians would undoubtedly reduce the rhetoric and with it the danger, but it would not eliminate it. However, a compromise is prevented, at the moment, by the ruling elites on both sides. The maximum each side would be willing to offer falls far short of the minimum demanded by the other.

Radical Islam is of Egyptian inspiration. Sayid Qutb was executed by the Nasserist regime in 1966, because Qutb's anti-nationalist ideology was viewed as a great danger by the Nasserist regime. Qutb was followed by other Egyptian

Brotherhood members—Sheikh Yussuf Karad'awi, who preaches in Qatar, Mohamed Salih al 'Awa in Egypt, and Osama Bin Laden's ideologue and deputy, Dr. Ayman al-Zawahiri, an Egyptian pediatrician. Sheikh Ahmed Yassin, the founder of Hamas, had been a member of the Brotherhood. The outstanding non-Egyptian figures were Abul 'Alah el-Maududi, a Pakistani who died in 1979, and Abdullah Azzam, a Palestinian.

There is no way of estimating the strength of the radicals in the Moslem world. What we know is that in countries such as Pakistan, Egypt and Syria there is a growth of radical sentiment which finds its expression in official media outlets, sermons that are broadcast by radio and TV, and a great deal of literature. There are also opposing trends of a more liberal, or moderate, or open kind, but they appear to be a distinct minority. And there is a violent, often murderous, enmity between the Sunni and the Shi'a versions of Islamic radicalism.

This, then, is the major danger that confronts us, as defenders of a universalist civilization guided by the belief that groups of people are entitled to develop their specificity in the context of some kind of democratic world order. We are faced with a genocidal threat to the Jewish people, and then quite explicitly to others: Christians, secularists, Hindus, Buddhists, animists, Confucians, and anyone who does not accept Islam. One of the characteristics that differentiate radical Islam from Nazism and Communism is the lack of a centralized structure and, Bin Laden apart, the absence of a uniting charismatic figure that would combine ideological leadership with political authority. Radical Islamic movements are many and varied, though the differences between them are minuscule. They aid and support each other, quarrelling over local leadership and tactics, but are united in purpose. It is much more difficult to combat a movement like that than it was to face a centralized hostile bureaucracy.

There is a threatening background to all that. Sayid Qutb was not totally mistaken—the West indeed is faced with problems of decadence and regression. The populations of Europe are declining. The 23 million Moslems in Europe today are not, most of them, radicals—yet. But they do not integrate culturally. The number of Jews in the world is static, below the 13 million mark, and is destined to decline markedly in the next half century. Radical Islam does have a chance, and world civilization must defend itself against that threat. To repeat—the threat is genocidal, and we have been in that scenario before. We must not repeat past mistakes.

Rabbi Reuven Bulka

Rabbi Dr. Reuven P. Bulka has been Rabbi of Congregation Machzikei Hadas since 1967. He hosts Sunday Night with Rabbi Bulka on 580 CFRA and is a regular contributor to Ask the Religion Experts in the *Ottawa Citizen*. He received Rabbinic ordination from Rabbi Jacob Joseph Rabbinical Seminary in 1966 and a Ph.D. in Logotherapy from the University of Ottawa in 1971. He also received an Honourary Doctorate from Carleton University in 2006. He chairs the Trillium Gift of Life Network, responsible for organ and tissue donation and transplantation in Ontario, and is a member of the board of Canadian Blood Services.

He is the founder and chair of Ottawa Kindness Week and chairs the Hospice Ottawa West campaign. Rabbi Bulka has written over 35 books and more than 100 articles, and has made 345 blood/platelet donations. On June 28, 2013, he was appointed a member of the Order of Canada. He is married to Leah (Kalish-Rosenbloom) and they are blessed with many children and grandchildren.

Thank you very much, Mr. Chairman, and distinguished members of the committee. Thank you for the invitation to share some thoughts with you this morning. I'd like to begin by making a comment not on antisemitism, but on pro-semitism.

I think it's fair to say that even though we're debating some pernicious evils that our lurking in our great country, it is also important to realize that there are many, many champions who basically love Jewish people. I've experienced it in my many years here in Canada. I think it is probably logical to say that if it were not the case, then a committee such as this couldn't actually happen. The people who are on the committee are all people who have, in their lifetime, exhibited this, and I think that we are fortunate in Canada that we have, I think, the overwhelming majority of people who love Jewish people. When we speak about antisemitism, the context of it is not that this is the majority of what Canada is all about. It's a problem within Canada, but it doesn't speak about what Canada is.

I'd like to share with you a little bit of our own personal history as a synagogue.

I came to Canada in 1967. The simple math is I've been here over 40 years, and the synagogue that I am the rabbi of was a very open synagogue. We locked the doors at night, but during the day, the doors were open. Anybody could come in. Anybody could leave. All that changed in 1991. It was around the Gulf War. It was a watershed. We started getting threatening calls. I myself, my life was threatened, and we had to start doing what many other synagogues across Canada had to do, which was basically to lock our doors, to put a system in where you had to identify yourself before you entered, and to have security in place that is costing us, who can ill afford it, thousands of dollars a year just to protect our membership.

This is not the Canada that I came to in 1967, and it's sad that this is the case, but unfortunately, it is the case. I'd like to think—and I think that you'll probably all agree, and I've heard it from my colleagues before me—antisemitism is not specifically a Jewish problem. It's, for all of us, a Canadian problem, because we pride ourselves on being a great country which is welcoming and open and embracing, and antisemitism threatens, because of the fact that it is underlined by hate, that it's consuming fury will know no boundaries.

Jews have always been the first line of offence when it comes to antisemitism but never the last line, and while this may be the case again here, the spillover into the Canada that we want to maintain is one that we cannot take any chances on in terms of allowing anti-Semitism of any form to fester in any way or shape, in any place, in any nook and cranny, or across the country.

A little while ago, when I found out that I was going to be appearing before you, I sent an email out to my congregation, and I asked them whether they had experienced antisemitism in their lifetime and their impressions about it. I got some interesting responses, from the usual stuff of names that they were called, sometimes by kids who unfortunately were just repeating what they heard in their homes, to threats against their lives; one who wrote to me that they had to move, in Ottawa, from one neighbourhood to another because of the constant threats that were being levelled against them.

The campuses have been a place where many Jewish kids feel uncomfortable, and let's not delude ourselves into thinking that this starts at the campuses. I got some emails from people who deal a lot with what's going on in the high schools.

They report to me many incidents in many of the high schools here in Ottawa of antisemitic comments and actions, which is basically unacceptable, as you all know.

One that particularly hit was from someone who has a store on the ByWard Market, which is a stone throw from here. He actually sent me a picture of a swastika that was painted on his store. He has a visibly Jewish store. This happened on Yom Kippur, the holiest day of the Jewish year. This is not the Canada that we want to see.

Perhaps the graphic in my mind that sticks out the most is when by chance I was downtown a number of years ago and there was a demonstration that had just come off Parliament Hill. Some of the placards said those ugly words, "kill the Jews". That was on Parliament Hill. We have a major problem in that context.

The thing that I want to share with you is on the simple question of, what do we do with this? How do we counter antisemitism?

To me, the very simple answer is teach, teach, teach. In my capacity as chair of the Trilium Gift of Life Network we're trying to have a new generation of children who think positively in terms of organ donation. We have started a program which hopefully will be taught in every single high school in Ontario. It's called One Life, Many Gifts. The importance of this will be imprinted on children as they're going forward into maturity.

The concern I had about what was happening with antisemitism, the ill will that is engendered, and the general feeling of the absence of love, shall I say, motivated me a little while ago to start something in Ottawa called Kindness Week. I think this is the way we need to go to fight antisemitism amongst others. You know you can fight antisemitism to a certain extent, but more importantly it's the question of how to promote pro-semitism and hopefully envelope the country in the Canadian embracing spirit so that antisemitism doesn't have a chance and would be embarrassed to rear its head.

Kindness Week in Ottawa came this year through legislation in Queen's Park in all of Ontario. My hope is that it will eventually become a dedicated week in Canada. We don't profess that other than that week people shouldn't be kind, but we do suggest that the way around the dark forces of hate is to create a climate of accommodation, a climate of embracing, a climate of kindness.

We are in a battle and this is one in which we cannot relent for a moment. It's very easy to hate. It's much more difficult to love. It's much more difficult to create the climate and the institutions of love and respect than it is to throw a rock.

We need to create foot soldiers. Those foot soldiers are the children of the next generation. We owe it them. We owe it to the legacy of our founding fathers and mothers that children, as they go through any school system, elementary, high school, by the time they get to university they have been so inoculated against hate that when they see it they will reject it.

Thank you very much.

Avi Benlolo

Avi Benlolo is a prominent Canadian human rights activist dedicated to promoting tolerance, justice and human rights. His academic focus included in-depth research on the Holocaust, antisemitism and racism. Through his work on genocide studies he documented survivor testimony from multiple genocide events around the world. In 2012, the Government of Canada appointed him to the Task Force for International Cooperation on Holocaust Education. The Lieutenant Governor General of Ontario recently awarded Mr. Benlolo with the Queens Diamond Jubilee Medal for service to Canada and his community. Mr. Benlolo is the Founder and guiding force behind the annual Spirit of Hope Benefit, Freedom Day, the Tour for Humanity mobile Tolerance Training Center, "Compassion to Action" Holocaust education missions, the Toronto based Tolerance Training Education Center and many other unique and innovative Friends of Simon Wiesenthal Center (FSWC) programs and events. As President and CEO of FSWC he has published opinion pieces in the Toronto Star, Huffington Post, National Post, Montreal Gazette, Calgary Herald, Canadian Jewish News and other publications. He regularly gives interviews on radio and television and participates in academic panels on the Holocaust and genocide.

1. Introduction

When it comes to human rights, Canada is the most progressive, tolerant, and respectful country on earth.   Unfortunately, antisemitism has emerged as a major problem in Canada over the last decade. It has manifested itself in many ways ranging from the traditional (vandalism and graffiti) to the extreme (fire bombings of schools, community centres and synagogues) and now to the subversive - an antisemitism which permeates institutions and threatens to change the very fabric of this nation.

A 2009 Angus Reid poll says that 47% of Canadians do not hold favourable views of Judaism, and 14% believe Judaism teaches violence.   These statistics may signal that many Canadians could harbor or adopt antisemitic attitudes, unless proactive measures are undertaken.

What concerns the Friends of Simon Wiesenthal Center today is the creeping institutionalization of antisemitism in Canada by prominent unions, universities, churches and businesses, and some human rights organizations. Much of today's antisemitism manifests in anti-Israel agitation around boycotts, divestment and sanctions. It deploys an unfair double standard against the Jewish state, singling out of Israel alone for one-sided, harsh criticism and calls for punitive actions. Some of the criticism approaches open incitement that contributes to hatred of Israel, Judaism, and the Jewish people in the mainstream of society.

2. Universities

Antisemitism, fueled by the demonization of Israel, has been a growing problem on Canadian campuses in many ways such as the violent protestors who blocked Israeli PM Benjamin Netanyahu from speaking at Concordia University in September 2002. Since then, a climate of hate and intolerance has spread to university campuses across Canada. The normalization of virulently anti-Israel invective at demonstrations, attacks against "Zionists", biased lectures and conferences have spawned an atmosphere in which Jewish students, faculty, and staff feel targeted and vulnerable.

2a. University of Toronto

The University of Toronto is the birthplace of "Israeli Apartheid Week," an event which, since its inception in 2005, has spread to over 40 university campuses across the globe. The week-long series of lectures and demonstrations conveys and inculcates the idea that Israel is responsible for "ethnic cleansing" and the "colonization of all Arab lands." Avi Benlolo, president and CEO of

Friends of Simon Wiesenthal Centre (FSWC) states, "Students have come to us and have reported that they feel intimidated, threatened, and uncomfortable attending university at this time of wrongful behavior and unrest." By enabling Israeli Apartheid Week to occur, the University of Toronto (and now other Canadian universities) is complicit in perpetuating and spreading accusations and propaganda designed to vilify Israel and the entire Jewish community.

2b. York University

In June 2009, York University hosted a highly controversial conference titled, "Israel/Palestine: Mapping Models of Statehood and Paths to Peace," which received national media attention. While the event was promoted as a dialogue on peaceful solutions in the Middle East, the conference speakers presented the One-state solution as the only viable option. Moreover, many of the speakers are heavily involved in anti-Israel campaigns. Instead of offering a fair and balanced debate, the conference used the veil of academic freedom to legitimize calls for the elimination of Israel as a Jewish state.

York University has also been the setting for a series of threats against Jewish students, and direct attacks on individuals and groups. On February 4th 2009, a York student who is actively involved in pro-Israeli campus organizations received a phone call that violently threatened him and his family. Police investigated for hate crimes. During that same week, another Jewish student reported that she was assaulted by an Anti-Israeli protestor. At a press conference on February 11th 2009, Jewish students were berated with antisemitic and anti-Israeli slogans. Fearing for their safety, these students took refuge in the office of a student group on campus. Anti-Israel demonstrators surrounded the room, and police had to be called in to escort the Jewish students to safety.

Moreover, the guise of academic freedom is used as protection for and cover-up of the hateful mislabeling of Israel as a "Nazi" and "apartheid" state. In such an environment, Jewish students are reporting incidents of threats and intimidation. Unless proactive counter measures are taken, antisemitism on Canadian campuses will continue to fester.

3. Businesses

The use of antisemitic and anti-Israel rhetoric by and against Canadian businesses has become a far too frequent occurrence. Three recent examples serve to illustrate how anti-Semitism has permeated the Canadian business community.

3a. Mountain Equipment Co-op

In April 2009, a group of Mountain Equipment Co-op members proposed a resolution at its annual meeting that sought a boycott of Israeli products and the termination of transactions with its three Israeli suppliers. This collection of members, which was mostly comprised of schoolteachers, mislabeled Israel as an apartheid state.

While Israel is a free democracy, MEC does have a wide range of suppliers from countries with questionable human rights records. However, there was no similar call for a boycott of MEC's 23 suppliers from China, a country with a repressive government that has been responsible for a plethora of human rights abuses. MEC justified its business relationships with Chinese companies by claiming that such interactions can encourage human rights. However, a resolution to boycott Israel would have directly contradicted this assertion. Although the members ultimately voted down the resolution at the annual general meeting, the fact that the issue came under discussion signifies antisemitism in action.

3b. Le Select Bistro

In June 2009, an exhibit of the Dead Sea Scrolls was set to open at the Royal Ontario Museum. In anticipation of the opening, the owner of Le Select Bistro, a restaurant in downtown Toronto, posted comments on the restaurant's website urging its customers to boycott the ROM's exhibit. The restaurateur claimed that the exhibit features "artefacts seized by Israel in its 1967 surprise war which ... led to the seizure and the ongoing military occupation of many lands." The message went on to read that "[b]y showcasing these artefacts, the ROM is violating Canada's responsibilities under the UNESCO Conventions and Protocols."

The restaurateur's vilification of the State of Israel is unfair in its use of one-sided facts and distortion of history to condemn one country. The call for a boycott of the Dead Sea Scrolls, which were written in Hebrew by Jewish ancestors and purchased legally by the modern State of Israel, illustrates a direct attempt to undermine and expunge Jewish culture. These critics are intentionally misrepresenting facts by claiming that the ancient manuscripts are stolen artefacts that were obtained by an aggressive war and occupation. These claims are untrue, and belie the tradition and vivacity of Jewish culture.

3c. Targeting Indigo Books & Music Inc.

In 2007, Indigo Books & Music Inc. was the subject of boycotts and protests. The demonstrators maligned Indigo CEO Heather Reisman's involvement with

the Heseg Foundation, a charitable organization that provides University schol-
arships for former Israeli soldiers. In one instance, an anti-Semitic caricature
of Ms. Reisman was distributed by the Coalition Against Israeli Apartheid. The
same coalition disrupted Indigo lectures on several occasions.

The recurring use of anti-Israel rhetoric by and against Canadian businesses
represents the normalization of hate in the Canadian corporate domain. Sanctions,
boycotts, and divestments that exclusively target Israel and ignore well-documented human-rights abusers, are signs of antisemitic behavior and prejudicial
attitudes that compromise the integrity of the Canadian business sector.

4. Unions

Some prominent Canadian Trade Unions have been transformed into instruments for advancing anti-Israel and antisemitic agendas unrelated to the unions'
primary agendas. Such actions may be the result of naiveté or underlying prejudices held by individuals. The recurring charges against Israel by unions are
exemplified here.

4a. CUPE Ontario

CUPE Ontario has been fomenting anti-Israel agitation for many years—having
passed boycott, sanctions and divestment resolutions and produced "educational
material" like "The Wall Must Fall"—referring to Israel's security barrier.
Most recently, in February 2009, the Ontario division of the Canadian Union
of Public Employees (CUPE) responded to the Gaza War by passing a motion
that strengthened calls for boycotts, divestment, and sanctions against Israel,
including a full academic boycott. This resolution is consistent with CUPE
Ontario's systematic blaming of only one side in a complex conflict.

4b. CUPW

In April 2008, the Canadian Union of Postal Workers (CUPW) supported a resolution calling for boycott, divestment and sanctions against Israel. The CUPW
resolution mislabeled Israel as an "apartheid state" and "demand[ed] that the
Israeli-West Bank barrier be immediately torn down." These resolutions exclusively blame one side in the conflict, and demean Israel as an Apartheid state.

4c. Positive Example set by the Carpenters' Union

In September of 2008, the Canada Council of Carpenters adopted a resolution that supports the pursuit of peace and democracy in the Middle East. The
Carpenters' Union explicitly expressed its support for "Israel as a democratic

nation state built on foundations of equality, equity, justice and freedom" and rebuked other trade unions for "attempting to undermine the legitimacy of Israel's democracy." The measures taken by the Carpenters' Union prove that Canadian trade unions do have the potential to be vehicles for balanced and fair voices for international understanding.

5. Rights Groups

In recent years, the agendas of some Rights groups have embraced boycott, divestment and sanction campaigns against Israel. Here is one example of how one rights group became an apparatus for the spread of anti-Semitic rhetoric.

5a. Toronto Pride Week

Over the past few years, Toronto's Pride Week has become a venue for anti-Israel demonstrations. The organization "Queers Against Israeli Apartheid" (QuAIA) has been allowed to march in the parade with banners reading "End Israeli Apartheid" and signs equating Zionism with Nazism. Although Pride Toronto states on its website that it adopts and upholds the City of Toronto's policy statement prohibiting discrimination and harassment and protects the right to be free of hate activity, the inclusion of QuAIA in the parade directly contravene this policy.

Toronto lawyer and gay rights advocate Martin Gladstone emphasizes that anti-Israel advocacy has no relevance to the event, stating, "It's supposed to be a celebration of diversity, inclusion and tolerance. But it's a microcosm of the antisemitism that's happening globally."

In April 2008, Jewish community leaders met with the Pride committee to address our concerns. However, the committee ignored the complaints. This hateful display recurred in June 2009.

6. Community Violence and Radicalism

History shows that antisemitic rhetoric and attitudes can lead to radicalism and violence. In Canadian communities, antisemitism has been inflamed by lectures from extremist speakers, erupting in numerous violent displays.

6a. Radical Speakers

On April 5, 2009, the Palestine House organization hosted Ekrima Sabri, Imam of the Al-Aqsa Mosque in Jerusalem; and Atallah Hannah, the Greek Orthodox Bishop of Sebastia, as featured guest speakers in Mississauga, Ontario. Both have well-documented histories of making antisemitic remarks that incite hate and violence against Jews and others.

In February 2005, Sabri, quoting from a debunked antisemitic screed, said that "anyone who studies The Protocols of the Elders of Zion and specifically the Talmud will discover that one of the goals of these Protocols is to cause confusion in the world and to undermine security throughout the world."

In July 2008, Hannah explained that he "do[es] not believe in so-called 'peace with Israel' because peace cannot be made with Satan."

Despite the openly hateful and dangerous messages of these men they, and others like them, are regularly invited to speak in Canada.

6b. Street Violence

During the 2009 Gaza War, Canadian citizens exercised their democratic right by taking to the streets to rally and demonstrate in support of both sides of the conflict. However, at protests in Toronto and Montreal, many anti-Israel protestors shouted slogans advocating the killing of Jews and the obliteration of Israel. They held signs equating Israel with Nazi Germany and burned Israeli flags.

Such hatemongering has no place in Canadian society and poses a threat to the safety of Canadian citizens. The dissemination of vitriol and misinformation only serves to encourage hateful ideologies and violence.

7. Internet Hate

- Antisemitism frequently appears online. In August 2008, the hateful and antisemitic content of www.realjewnews.com appeared on the site's Canadian ISP provider. Although the website was shut down, it reappeared on a foreign ISP provider and continues to promote hate through blatant misinformation.
- A University of Toronto student was investigated by the RCMP and OPP for comments he posted on various sites and chat rooms. Salman Hossain called for the murder of Jews and Canadian soldiers, including one instance in which he explicitly expressed a desire to "shoot a few Jews down." As of July 15, 2009, Hossain had yet to be prosecuted for hate crimes.
- In March 2009, in the wake of the Gaza War, a middle school in Richmond Hill, Ontario, reported online hate messaging wherein a Jewish student was ridiculed and targeted for her political and religious affiliations.

To contain and marginalize antisemitism in Canada and elsewhere, individuals who spread hate in this fashion must be brought to justice. To that end, in 2009, FSWC released Digital Terrorism and Hate 2.0, an annual interactive CD-ROM report on online extremist operations.

8. Conclusion

As antisemitism proliferates across various sectors of society, including universities, businesses, unions, rights groups, Churches, NGOs, community and speaker venues, and online, it threatens the very core of Canadian Life. Not only does antisemitism vilify Israel, it incites hatred, and encourages Canadians to be less accepting and tolerant of others.

The mainstreaming and institutionalization of antisemitism threatens the security and well-being of Canadian Jews and the preservation of Canadian values. There is a need for increased awareness that this hatred is gaining ground, and for the adoption of direct and strong action to ensure that such prejudices and injustices are openly opposed on moral and, when appropriate, legal grounds. Antisemitic rhetoric and behaviour can never be allowed to compromise our community's safety or our individual constitutional rights.

In addition to countering the hate directly, The Friends of Simon Wiesenthal Centre welcomes every opportunity to assist with any initiative that would encourage positive dialogue, create meaningful experiences, develop tolerance, and engage in respectful outreach that contributes to responsible and constructive approaches toward living and working together.

Honourable Irwin Cotler

Irwin Cotler has been a Canadian Member of Parliament since 1999 and is former Minister of Justice and Attorney General of Canada. Currently he is the Liberal Special Council on Human Rights and International Justice. Mr. Cotler is also a member of the House of Commons Foreign Affairs Subcommittee on International Human Rights, and Chair of the All-Party Save Darfur Parliamentary Coalition.

Prior to his election, Mr. Cotler was a Professor of Law at McGill University, Director of its Human Rights Programme and Chair of InterAmicus, the International Human Rights Advocacy Centre. His dedication to humanitarian causes has earned him the Order of Canada, among many other awards, including nine honourary doctorates.

An international human rights lawyer, Professor Cotler served as Counsel to former prisoners of conscience including Andrei Sakharov & Nathan Sharansky in the Soviet Union, Nelson Mandela in South Africa Nelson Mandela, and more recently as International Legal Council to Shoaib Choudhury, a Muslim Bangladesh journalist.

A noted peace activist, Professor Cotler has been engaged—both as scholar and participant observer—in the search for peace in the Middle East. A leader in the struggle against impunity and the development of international humanitarian law, Professor Cotler served as Counsel to the Deschênes Commission of Inquiry in the matter of bringing Nazi war criminals to justice; filed amicus briefs before the International Criminal Tribunals for former Yugoslavia and Rwanda; and was leading advocate for the establishment of an International Criminal Court.

Mr. Cotler is currently Chair of the Inter-Parliamentary Coalition for Combating Antisemitism (ICCA), which brings together Parliamentarians from around the world to lead the fight against resurgent global antisemitism. Its principal purpose is to share knowledge, experience, best practice, and recommendations, encouraging their dissemination in an attempt to deal more effectively with contemporary antisemitism. He is one of six International Steering Committee members of ICCA who helped organize the London Conference on Combating Antisemitism in February 2009.

Honourable Irwin Cotler*

Member of Parliament for Mount Royal, Professor Emeritus McGill University and Chair of the Inter-Parliamentary Coalition for Combating Antisemitism

Written Submission Prepared by Honourable Irwin Cotler for the Canadian Parliamentary Coalition to Combat Antisemitism.

Global Anti-Semitism: Assault on Human Rights

Introduction: Anti-Semitism Old and New—Definition and Distinction

What we are witnessing today—and which has been developing incrementally, sometimes imperceptibly, and even indulgently, for some thirty-five years now—is a new sophisticated, globalizing, virulent and even lethal Anti-Semitism, reminiscent of the atmospherics of the 30s, and without parallel or precedent since the end of the Second World War.

The new anti-Jewishness overlaps with classical antisemitism but is distinguishable from it. It found early juridical, and even institutional, expression in the United Nations "Zionism is Racism" resolution but has gone dramatically beyond it. This new antisemitism almost needs a new vocabulary to define it; however, it can best be identified using a rights-based juridical perspective.

In a word, classical or traditional antisemitism is the discrimination against, denial of, or assault upon, the rights of Jews to live as equal members of whatever host society they inhabit. The new antisemitism involves the discrimination against the right of the Jewish people to live as an equal member of the family of nations—the denial of, and assault upon, the Jewish people's right even to live—with Israel as the collective Jew among the nations. Observing the complex intersections between the old and the new antisemitism, and the impact of the new on the old, Per Ahlmark, former leader of the Swedish Liberal Party and Deputy Prime Minister of Sweden, pithily concluded:

> Compared to most previous anti-Jewish outbreaks,
> this [new antisemitism] is often less directed against
> individual Jews. It attacks primarily the collective

---

* Testimony of Hon. Cotler consist of a written submission presented to the Canadian Parliamentary Inquiry into Antisemitism, outlining the global characteristic of contemporary antisemitism and the political and cultural undertones of renewed discrimination against Jews.

Jews, the State of Israel. And then such attacks start
a chain reaction of assaults on individual Jews and
Jewish institutions ... In the past, the most dangerous antisemites were those who wanted to make the
world Judenrein, 'free of Jews'. Today, the most
dangerous anti-Semites might be those who want
to make the world Judenstaatrein, 'free of a Jewish
state'[1]

Regrettably, indices of measurement for the new antisemitism have yet
to be developed. Indeed, this may account for the disparity between the vis-
ceral feelings of Jews and the reports of social scientists still following the old
antisemitism paradigm. According to the traditional indicators—such as discrimination against Jews in housing, education, or employment, or access for
Jews to major positions in the political, economic, scientific and academic are-
nas—it would appear, falsely, that antisemitism is in decline.

What follows is the missing conceptual and analytical framework—a set of
eight indices—to identify, pour content into, monitor, unmask and combat this
global threat whereby the new antisemitism builds upon—and incites to—traditional hatred. We need this paradigm shift in our thinking.

Two important caveats underpin this analysis. First, none of the indicators
is intended to suggest that Israel is somehow above the law, or that Israel is not
to be held accountable for any violations of law. On the contrary, Israel, like
any other state, is accountable for any violations of international law or human
rights. The Jewish people are not entitled to any privileged protection or preference because of the particularity of Jewish suffering.

Second, I am not referring to critiques—even serious critiques—of Israeli
policy or Zionist ideology, however distasteful or offensive some of these critiques might sometimes be. But the converse is also true: antisemitic critiques
cannot mask themselves under the exculpatory disclaimer that "if I criticize
Israel, they will say I am antisemitic". In the words of New York Times commen-
tator Thomas Friedman: "Criticizing Israel is not antisemitic, and saying so is
vile. But singling out Israel for opprobrium and international sanctions, out
of all proportion to any other party in the Middle East is antisemitic, and not
saying so is dishonest".[2]

---

1 Per Ahlmark, "Combating Old—New Anti-Semitism", Yad Vashem, April 11, 2002.
2 Thomas L. Friedman, "Campus Hypocrisy", New York Times, October 16, 2002.

The State of Global Antisemitism Today: Indices of Identification

1. State-Sanctioned Genocidal Antisemitism

The first indicator—and the most lethal type of anti-Jewishness—is what I would call genocidal antisemitism. This is not a term that I use lightly or easily; rather, I am using it in its juridical sense as set forth in the *Convention on the Prevention and Punishment of the crime of Genocide*. In particular, I am referring to the Convention's prohibition against the "direct and public incitement to genocide."[3] If antisemitism is the most enduring of hatreds and genocide is the most horrific of crimes, then the convergence of this genocidal intent embedded in antisemitic ideology is the most toxic of combinations.

There are three manifestations of this genocidal antisemitism. The first is the state-sanctioned—indeed, state-orchestrated - genocidal antisemitism of Ahmadinejad's Iran. This intent is further dramatized by the parading in the streets of Teheran of a Shihab-3 missile draped in the emblem "Wipe Israel off the Map", while demonizing both the State of Israel as a "cancerous tumour to be excised" and the Jewish people as "evil incarnate".

A second manifestation of this genocidal antisemitism is in the covenants and charters, platforms and policies of such terrorist movements and militias as Hamas, Islamic Jihad, Hezbollah and Al-Qaeda, which not only call for the destruction of Israel and the killing of Jews wherever they may be, but also for the perpetration of acts of terror in furtherance of that objective. For instance, Hamas leader Mahmoud al-Zahar proclaims that, "before Israel dies, it must be humiliated and degraded," while Hezbollah leader Hassan Nasrallah has said that "If all the Jews were gathered in Israel it would be easier to kill them all at the same time".[4]

In a lesser known, but no less defamatory and incendiary expression, Nasrallah has said that "if we searched the entire world for a person more cowardly, despicable, weak and feeble in psyche, mind, ideology and religion, we would not find anyone like the Jew. Notice, I do not say the Israeli." Shiite scholar Amal Saad-Ghorayeb, author of the book *Hezbollah: Politics and Religion*, argues that such statements "provide moral and ideological justification for dehumanizing the Jews." In this view, she added "the Israeli Jew becomes a legitimate target for extermination and it also legitimizes attacks on non-Israeli Jews."[5]

The third manifestation of this genocidal antisemitism are the religious *fatwas* or execution writs, where these genocidal calls in mosques and media are

---

3 The Genocide Convention, in Article 3, expressly prohibits the "direct and public incitement to genocide".

4 Quoted in Amal Saad-Ghorayeb, *Hezbollah: Politics and Religion*, Pluto Press, 2001.

5 Jeffrey Goldberg, "In the Party of God: Are Terrorists in Lebanon Preparing for a Larger War?" *The New Yorker*, October 14 and 21, 2002.

held out as religious obligations, and where Jews and Judiasm are characterized as the perfidious enemy of Islam. Israel emerges here not only as the collective Jew among the nations, but as the Salman Rushdie among the nations.

In a word, Israel is the only state in the world today—and the Jews the only people in the world today—that are the object of a standing set of threats by governmental, religious and terrorist bodies seeking their destruction. And what is most disturbing is the seeming indifference—even the sometimes indulgence—in the face of such genocidal antisemitism.

2. Political Antisemitism: Denial of Fundamental Rights

If genocidal antisemitism is a public call for - or incitement to - the destruction of Israel, political antisemitism is the denial of Israel's right to exist to begin with, or the denial of the Jewish people's right to self-determination, if not their very denial as a people. There are four manifestations of this phenomenon.

The first is the denial of the Jewish people's right to self-determination— the only right consecrated in both the *International Covenant on Civil and Political Rights* and the *International Covenant on Economic, Social and Cultural Rights*. Jews are being singled-out and discriminated against when they alone are denied this right. As Martin Luther King, Jr. put it: "this is the denial to the Jews of the same right, the right to self-determination that we accord to African nations and all other peoples of the globe. In short, it is antisemitism."[6]

The second feature of political antisemitism involves denying the legitimacy, if not the existence, of the State of Israel itself. Just as classical antisemitism was anchored in the denial of the very legitimacy of the Jewish religion, the new anti-Jewishness is anchored in the denial of the very legitimacy of the Jews as a people, as embodied by the Jewish State, Israel. In each instance, then, the essence of antisemitism is the same—an assault upon whatever is the core of Jewish self-definition at any given moment in time—be it the Jewish religion, or Israel as the civil religion or juridical expression of the Jewish people.

A third manifestation of political antisemitism is the denial of any historical connection between the Jewish people and the State of Israel, a form of Middle East revisionism or "memory cleansing" that seeks to extinguish or erase the Jewish people's relationship to Israel, while "Palestinizing" or "Islamicizing" the Arab and Muslim exclusivist claim. If "Holocaust Revisionism" is an assault on Jewish memory and historical experience, "Middle East Revisionism" con-

---

6 Martin Luther King, Jr., quoted in Seymour Martin Lipset, "The Socialism of Fools: The Left, the Jews and Israel", *Encounter*, December 1969, page 24. See also: John Lewis, "I Have a Dream for Peace in the Middle East: Martin Luther King, Jr.'s Special Bond with Israel", *San Francisco Chronicle*, January 21, 2002

stitutes no less of an assault on Jewish memory and historical experience. It cynically serves to invert the historical narrative so that Israel is seen an "alien" and "colonial implant" in the region that "usurped" the Palestinian homeland—leading to the conclusion that its people are a "criminal" group of nomadic Jews whose very presence "defiles" Islam, and must be expurgated.

It is not surprising that this revisionist Middle East narrative should lead to the final variant of political antisemitism: the "demonizing" of Israel, or the attribution to Israel of all the evils of the world. This is the contemporary analogue to the medieval indictment of the Jew as the "poisoner of the wells," as Israel—portrayed as *the* metaphor for a human rights violator—is indicted as the "poisoner of the international wells" with no right to exist.

Distinguished British jurist Anthony Julius, often understated in his characterization and critique of antisemitism, summed it up as follows:

To maintain that the very existence of Israel is without legitimacy, and to contemplate with equanimity the certain catastrophe of its dismantling, [...] is to embrace—however unintentionally, and notwithstanding all protestations to the contrary—a kind of Anti-Semitism indistinguishable in its compass and its consequences from practically any that has yet been inflicted on Jews.[7]

3. Ideological Antisemitism:
Antisemitism Under the Cover of Anti-Racism

While the first two indicators are overt, public and clearly demonstrable, ideological antisemitism is much more sophisticated and arguably a more pernicious expression of the new antisemitism. Indeed, it may even serve as an "ideological" support system for the first two indicators, though these are prejudicial and pernicious enough indicators in their own right.

Here, ideological antisemitism finds expression not in any genocidal incitement against Jews and Israel, or overt racist denial of the Jewish people and Israel's right to be; rather, ideological antisemitism disguises itself as part of the struggle *against* racism. Indeed, it marches under the protective cover of the UN and the international struggle against racism.

The first manifestation of this ideological antisemitism was its institutional and juridical anchorage in the "Zionism is Racism" resolution at the UN, a resolution that, as the late US Senator Daniel Moynihan said, "gave the abomination of antisemitism the appearance of international legal sanction." Notwithstanding the fact that the there was a formal repeal of this resolution, "Zionism as Racism" remains alive and well in the global arena, particularly in

7 Anthony Julius, "Don't Panic," *The Guardian*, February 1, 2002.

the campus cultures of North America and Europe, as confirmed by the recent British All-Party Parliamentary Inquiry into Anti-Semitism.

The second manifestation is the indictment of Israel as an apartheid state. This involves more than the simple indictment of Israel as an apartheid state. It also involves the call for the *dismantling* of Israel as an apartheid state as evidenced by the events at the 2001 UN World Conference against Racism in Durban. This indictment is not limited to talk about divestment—it is about the actual dismantling of Israel based upon the notion of apartheid as a crime against humanity.

The third manifestation of ideological antisemitism involves the characterization of Israel not only as an apartheid state—and one that must be dismantled as part of the struggle against racism—but as a Nazi one.

And so it is then that Israel is delegitimized—if not demonized—by the ascription to it of the two most scurrilous indictments of twentieth-century racism—Nazism and apartheid—the embodiment of all evil. These very labels of Zionism and Israel as "racist, apartheid, and Nazi" supply the criminal indictment. No further debate is required. The conviction that this "triple racism" warrants the dismantling of Israel as a moral obligation has been secured. For who would deny that a "racist, apartheid, Nazi" state should not have any right to exist today? What is more, this characterization allows for terrorist "resistance" to be deemed justifiable—after all, such a situation is portrayed as nothing other than *occupation et résistance*, where "resistance" against a racist, apartheid, Nazi occupying state is legitimate, if not mandatory.

There is no more dramatic example of the danger of the "Nazification" of Israel and the inflammatory inversion of the Holocaust than the dual demonizing indictments arising from the recent Israel-Hamas conflict. On the one hand, Jews are blamed for perpetrating a Holocaust on the Palestinians, as in the appalling statement of Norwegian diplomat Trine Lilleng that "The grand-children of Holocaust survivors are doing to the Palestinians exactly what was done to them by Nazi Germany."[8] On the other hand, crowds are incited to another Holocaust against the Jews, as in the chants of protesters who scream "Hamas! Hamas! Jews to the gas!"

What is so disturbing about this ideological Anti-Semitism is not simply the use of these defamatory and delegitimizing indictments to call for the dismantling of the Jewish State itself, but in particular the masking of this ideological antisemitism as if it were part of the struggle against racism, apartheid and

8 Etgar Lefkovitz, "Norwegian envoy equates Israel with Nazis," *Jerusalem Post*, January 21, 2009.

Nazism, thereby transforming an antisemitic indictment into a moral impera-
tive with the imprimatur of international law.

4. 'Legalized Antisemitism': Discriminatory Treatment in the International Arena

If ideological antisemitism seeks to mask itself under the banner of anti-racism,
this fourth indicator of the new anti-Jewishness - legalized antisemitism- is even
more sophisticated and insidious. Here, antisemitism simultaneously seeks to
mask itself under the banner of human rights, to invoke the authority of international law, and to operate under the protective cover of the UN. In a word—and
in an inversion of human rights, language and law—the singling-out of Israel
and the Jewish people for differential and discriminatory treatment in the international arena is "legalized".

The first case study is the 2001 UN World Conference against Racism in
Durban, which became the "tipping point" for the emergence of a new anti-Jewishness. Those of us who witnessed the "Durban Speak" festival of hate in its
declarations, incantations, pamphlets, and marches—seeing antisemitism
marching under the cover of human rights—have forever been transformed by
this experience. "Durban" is now part of our everyday lexicon as a metaphor for
racism and antisemitism.

It should have been otherwise. Indeed, when Durban was first proposed
some ten years ago, I was among those who greeted it with anticipation, if not
excitement. And yet what happened at Durban was truly Orwellian. A World
Conference Against Racism turned into a conference of racism against Israel
and the Jewish people. A conference intended to commemorate the dismantling
of South Africa as an apartheid state resonated with the call for the dismantling of Israel as an apartheid state. A conference dedicated to the promotion
of human rights as the new secular religion of our time, singled-out Israel as
the meta-human rights violator of our day—indeed—as the new anti-Christ of
our time. A conference that was to speak in the name of humanity ended up as
a metaphor for hate and inhumanity. Never have I witnessed the kind of viru-
lence and intensity of anti-Jewishness—mockingly marching under the banner
of human rights—as I found in the festival of hate at Durban.

Another example of legalized antiaemitism occurred annually for over 35
years at the United Nations Commission on Human Rights. The importance
of the Commission's work derived from the fact that the UN exerts enormous
influence around the world. Yet, this influential body consistently began its
annual session with Israel being the only country singled-out for country-spe-

cific indictment—even before the deliberations started—the whole in breach
of the UN's own procedures and principles.[9] In this "Alice in Wonderland"
situation, the conviction and sentence were pronounced even before the hearings commenced. Some thirty percent of all the resolutions passed at the
Commission were indictments of Israel.

It was a hopeful sign when a Reform Panel of eminent persons appointed
by the UN Secretary General Kofi Annan referred to the Commission's "eroding credibility and professionalism" and "legitimacy deficit that casts doubts
on the overall reputation of the United Nations".[10] But after the Commission
was replaced in June 2006 by the UN Human Rights Council, the new body
proceeded to condemn one member state—Israel—in eighty percent of its
twenty-five country-specific resolutions, while the major human rights viola-
tors of our time enjoyed exculpatory immunity. Indeed, five special sessions,
two fact-finding missions, and a high level commission of inquiry have been
devoted to a single purpose: the singling-out of Israel.[11]

These case studies are not the only examples of the international "legal"
character of the new Anti-Semitism. Indeed, an entire paper - if not book—can
be devoted to the systematic, if not systemic, denial to Israel and the Jewish
people of equality before the law and international due process in the international arena. The tragedy is that all this is taking place under the protective
cover of the UN, thereby undermining international law and human rights.
The fact is that there have been more resolutions adopted, committees formed,
deliberations held, speeches made, and resources expended in the condemnation of Israel then on any other state, or combination of states.

5. European Antisemitism on the Rise—Including the Far Right
In speaking of European antisemitism, I do not wish to suggest that
Europe—or any of its countries—is antisemitic. On the contrary, Europe as
a whole is committed to the promotion and protection of democracy, human
rights and the rule of law. But the documentary record in Europe since the
dawn of the new millennium suggests that we are witnessing a serious rise

---

9 See Gregg J. Rickman, "Contemporary Global Anti-Semitism: A Report Provided to the United States
   Congress," United States Department of State, p. 50 & 51: "Resolutions with Negative Country-Specific
   References (2001- 2007) and "Resolutions Criticizing Countries" Human Rights Records (2001-2007).
10 *A more secure world: Our shared responsibility*, report of the High-Level Panel on Threats, Challenges and
   Change, United Nations, 2004.
11 See also Hillel C. Neuer, Statement at a Hearing before the Subcommittee on Africa, Global Human
   Rights and International Operations of the Committee on International Relations—House of
   Representatives, Serial No. 109-221, September 6, 2006.

of antisemitism in Europe almost without parallel or precedent since the Second World War.

Over much of the past decade, governments, international institutions, and NGOs have noted an increase in antisemitic incidents including attacks on Jewish people, property, community institutions, and religious facilities. For example, Resolution 1563 of the Parliamentary Assembly of the Council of Europe noted that "far from having been eliminated, antisemitism is today on the rise in Europe. It appears in a variety of forms and is becoming relatively commonplace."[12]

During my visits to European capitals these past eight years I can personally attest to some of the following events that occurred, all of which were reported upon in the media during these visits:

- Physical assaults upon, and desecration of, synagogues, cemeteries and Jewish institutions;
- Desecration of Holocaust memorials, as in Slovakia, where Jewish memorials were desecrated in what an official described as "the biggest attack on the Jewish community since the Holocaust";
- Attacks upon identifiable Jews, be they orthodox Jews, or Jews wearing a skullcap or Star of David, or other visible Jewish symbols;
- Convergence of the extreme left and the extreme right in public demonstrations calling for "death to the Jews";
- Atrocity propaganda against Israel and Jews, for example, that Israel injects the AIDS virus into Palestinians, as well as the demonizing Nazi and Holocaust metaphors;
- The ugly canard of double loyalty, where in the words of Professor Joel Kotek, of the University of Brussels: "One's position on the Arab-Israeli conflict has become a test of loyalty. Should he express solidarity with Israel he becomes a supporter of a Nazi state?"[13]; and
- The belief—by close to fifty percent of Europeans—that Jews are more loyal to Israel than to their own country and where more than one-third believe Jews have "too much power" in business and finance.[14]

As discussed throughout this paper, there has been an emergence of a new global and virulent antisemitism. It is important also to make note of the strong resurgence of extreme right wing groups, particularly throughout Europe. Extreme

---

12 Resolution 1563: Combating Anti-Semitism in Europe," *Parliamentary Assembly of the Council of Europe* (2007).

13 Daniel Ben Simon, "Haunted by ill winds of the past," *Haaretz Daily Newspaper*

14 ADL Survey in Seven European Countries Finds Anti-Semitic Attitudes Steady; 31 Percent Blame Jews for Financial Crisis,' *Anti-Defamation League*, New York, February 10, 2009.

nationalist parties in some European countries have begun to use—and successfully—antisemitic slogans and ideas that were previously deemed unacceptable.
This antisemitism has even become a central campaign platform by combin-
ing anti-Jewish epithets with a broader message of hatred and exclusion, which
has resulted in violent, hateful and both anti-Jewish and anti-immigrant public demonstrations.

The overt and conscious antisemitism of the old Neo-Nazi groups is easily
identified, and yet it still exists—and thrives—in contemporary society. In the
Netherlands, the *Racism and Extremism Monitor* observed that the contribution
of extreme right-wing participants to racial violence as a whole—particularly
incidents of antisemitism—has risen sharply from 38 incidents in 2005 to 67
in 2006 and is continuing to increase at an exponential rate. "Loosely organized extreme right-wing groups," including informal movements of right-wing
young people (often termed "Lonsdale youth" or skinheads), and neo-Nazi
groups are reportedly gaining ground and influence.[15]

In its November 2007 report, the Dutch monitoring organization Centre
Documentation and Information on Israel expressed concern with the numerous incidents reported on the anniversary of the German surrender in 1945
- May 4 and 5—during which Holocaust monuments were defaced or destroyed.
These actions were seen to be directly related to the rise of the extreme right,
with memorials covered with hate symbols such as swastikas and neo-Nazi slogans. In another example, on December 8, 2007, supporters of the Freedom
Party and the Patriots of Ukraine organization took part in a torchlight march
through Kiev, chanting antisemitic, anti-immigrant, and pro-white power
slogans, including "one race, one nation, one motherland,"[16] frighteningly reminiscent of the hateful slogans of Nazi Germany.

In a response to changing circumstances and challenges, many right-wing
groups have transformed their approaches as a means to incorporate the old,
traditional form of antisemitism into the new, more tolerable antisemitism.
Antisemitic adherents of the far right seek to portray their views as anti-Zionist or anti-Israel, on the grounds that this is more politically acceptable
than open advocacy of Nazi positions. For instance, in its 2007 annual
report on antisemitism, the League for Human Rights of B'nai Brith Canada
cites a bulletin of the neo-Nazi website *Stormfront*, imploring followers to
"remember to say "Zionists" or "Israeli Firsters" instead of "Jews" when making public speeches or writing articles. In this way, the radical right makes

15 "2008 Hate Crime Survey: Anti-Semitism," *Human Rights First*, online
16 Ibid.

explicit the convergence of the old/new antisemitism that remains unspoken in other contexts.

6. Cultural Antisemitism

Cultural antisemitism refers to the *melange* of attitudes, sentiments, innuendo and the like in academia, in Parliaments, among the literati, public intellectuals, and the human rights movement - in a word, *la trahison des clercs*. As UK MP Denis MacShane put it, "The most worrying discovery is that anti-Jewish sentiment is entering the mainstream, appearing in everyday conversations of people who consider themselves neither racist nor prejudiced."[17]

Such antisemitic attitudes include: the remarks of the French Ambassador to the UK questioning why the world should risk another world war because of "that shitty little country Israel"[18]; the observation of Petronella Wyatt that, "Antisemitism is respectable once more, not just in Germany or Catholic-central Europe, but at London dinner tables"[19]; the distinguished British novelist A.N. Wilson dredging up another ugly canard in accusing the Israeli army of "the poisoning of water supplies"[20]; Tom Paulin, Oxford Professor and poet, writing of a Palestinian boy "gunned down by the Zionist SS"[21]; or Peter Hain, a former Minister in the British Foreign Office, stating that the present Zionist state is by definition racist and will have to be dismantled.

Indeed, according to the US State Department Report on Contemporary Antisemitism, drawing comparisons of contemporary Israeli policy to that of the Nazis is increasingly commonplace in intellectual circles, as illustrated by the frequent media images of Israel as a "Nazi-state" during the July 2006 war with Hezbollah,[22] as well as during the more recent war in Gaza, wherein repeated reference was made at the UN Human Rights Council to the "Holocaust perpetrated by the Israelis"; while ADL head Abraham Foxman said "This is the worst, the most intense, the most global that it's been in most of our memories" citing "an epidemic, a pandemic of anti-Semitism."[23]

In summary, antisemitism appears to be "the right and only word," in the words of Gabriel Schoenfeld, for a cultural Anti-Semitism "so one-sided, so

---

17 UK Labour MP Denis MacShane, Chair of the 2006 UK *All-Party Parliamentary Inquiry Into Antisemitism*, as quoted by *The Guardian* on September 7, 2006.

18 "Anti-Semitic' French envoy under fire." BBC Online: *http://news.bbc.co.uk/2/hi/europe/1721172.stm*

19 Petronella Wyatt, "Poisonous Prejudice," in *Spectator*, December 8, 2001

20 A. N. Wilson, "A demo we can"t afford to ignore", *Evening Standard*, April 15, 2002.

21 Tom Paulin, "Killed in Crossfire", *The Observer*, February 18, 2001.

22 This upsurge was documented in the U.S. Department of State's 2006 annual *Country Reports on Human Rights Practices*, as well as its annual *Report on International Religious Freedom*

23 ADL sees 'pandemic of anti-Semitism'. Y-net News: February 7, 2009

eager to indict Israel while exculpating Israel's adversaries, so shamefully adroit in the use of moral double standards, so quick to issue false and baseless accusations and so disposed to invert the language of the Holocaust and to paint Israelis and Jews as evil incarnate."[24] That was six years ago, even before the present pandemic.

7. Discrimination and Exclusion: Globalizing the Boycott

There is a growing incidence of academic, university, trade union and related boycotts and divestments—whose effect in practice, if not in intent—is the singling-out of Israel, Israeli Jews and supporters of Israel for selective opprobrium and exclusion. Indeed, what began as a UK phenomenon has now become a global one—with universities, organizations, and unions from South Africa to Canada, Norway to the United States, and from Turkey to Italy—moving from the boycott of Israeli goods and services to restrictions and bans on Israeli academics. As the UK All-Parliamentary Inquiry into Antisemitism reported: "The singling-out of Israel is of concern. Boycotts have not been suggested against other countries ... The discourse around the boycott debate is also cause for concern, as it moved beyond reasonable criticism into anti-Semitic demonization of Israel."[25]

Labour MP John Mann, chair of the All-Party Parliamentary Group against Anti-Semitism, stressed the motion's discriminatory character against British Jews: "boycotts do nothing to bring about peace and reconciliation in the Middle East but leave Jewish students, academics and their associates isolated and victimized on university campuses."[26]

8. The Old/New *Protocols of the Elders of Zion*

For over one hundred years, the world has been suffused with the most pervasive, persistent and pernicious group libel in history, the *Protocols of the Elders of Zion*—the tsarist forgery proclaiming an "international Jewish conspiracy" bent on "world domination." Today, the "lie that wouldn't die"[27] now underpins the most outrageous of international conspiracy thinking and incitement targeting first Jews and then the "international Zionist conspiracy." So it is, then, that Jews were behind the 9/11 attacks and had forewarning; Jewish doctors are held responsible for inculcating Palestinians with the AIDS virus; that Jewish scientists are responsible for the propagation of the Avian flu; that a Jewish astronaut

24 Gabriel Schoenfeld, "Israel and the Anti-Semites", *Commentary*, June 2002.
25 Report of the All-Party Parliamentary Inquiry into Anti-Semitism," *All-Party Parliamentary Group Against Anti-Semitism* (September 2006), p. 41, pts. 210 & 211
26 Jonny Paul, "Ex-EU Official Condemns UK Academic Boycott Call," *Jerusalem Post,* June 1, 2008.
27 Hadassh ben-Itto, *The Lie that Wouldn't Die.*

is responsible for the explosion of the Columbia space shuttle; that the Jews were behind the publication of the Danish cartoons and the Pope's defilement of Islam; that Jews are responsible for the war in Iraq; that the "genocides" such as in Darfur are orchestrated by the Jews, and so on.

It was not long before the same libelous inheritance from the Jews was transferred to the Jews of Israel—to the international Zionist conspiracy—bringing together the old and new protocols in a conceptual and linguistic symmetry that blamed Israel and Zionists for all the above things that were once blamed on the Jew.

But it is in the Arab and Muslim world that the Protocols have taken hold, not unlike the incitement of the anti-Jewish pogroms in tsarist Russia, or the murders of the Third Reich. The Protocols are propagated in mosques; taught in schools; published by states; sold in bookstores; and, most compellingly, have secured a captive audience in the daily broadcasting media.

9. The Resurgence of Global Antisemitism: Evidentiary Data

The data unsurprisingly confirm that antisemitic incidents are very much on the rise. Still, the available figures only show half the picture—they demonstrate an increase in this old/new antisemitism by concentrating on the traditional antisemitic paradigm targeting individual Jews and Jewish institutions, while failing to consider the new antisemitic paradigm targeting Israel as the Jew among nations and the fallout from it for traditional antisemitism. This caveat is important—for the rise in traditional antisemitism cannot be viewed solely in the context of the traditional paradigm. Rather, the rise in traditional antisemitism should be seen as a complement to—and consequence of—the rise in the new antisemitism, insidiously buoyed by a climate receptive to attacks on Jews because of the attacks on the Jewish state.

- For instance, a trend can be noted in the statistical data of a rise in antisemitic incidents correlating with the situation in the Middle East, particularly with respect to the Arab-Israeli conflict. Data from the 2007 Report of Tel Aviv University's Stephen Roth Institute for the Study of Contemporary Antisemitism and Racism illustrate an upsurge in violence and related antisemitic crimes in the years 2000 and 2006 that correspond with the beginning of the Second Intifada and the Israel-Hezbollah War.[28] More recent reports, such as from the ADL, have shown a major increase in anti-Jewish and anti-Israel attacks and demonstrations since the recent 2009 Israel-Hamas war, which have even been characterized as a "pandemic".[29]

---

28 Dina Porat & Esther Webman (eds.) "Anti-Semitism Worldwide 2007: General Analysis," The Stephen Roth Institute for the Study of Contemporary Anti-Semitism and Racism, Tel Aviv University (in cooperation with the World Jewish Congress): *http://www.tau.ac.il/Antisemitism/*

29 Supra. At 25.

- The 2006 Pew Global Attitudes Project Poll noted that the percent of people polled with an unfavourable view of Jews in various Muslim countries was exceptionally high. In Egypt it was as high as ninety-seven percent and in Jordan ninety-eight percent.[30] In 2007, overall levels of violent antisemitic attacks against persons increased in Canada, Germany, Russia, Ukraine, and the United Kingdom according to official statistics and reports of nongovernmental monitors. Indeed, there is a trend that antisemitic incidents increasingly take the form of physical attacks on individuals; a "constant pressure to conceal one's [Jewish] identity" has been noted, while Jewish leaders have been singled out for violence.[31]

- A disturbing number of victims of antisemitic attack are school students. Children and young people have been assaulted and threatened in the streets, on public transport, and even in and around their schools. Physical assaults have taken place in France, Germany, Russia, the United Kingdom and the United States; children on playgrounds have been pelted with stones. With respect to universities, Jewish students and student centers, dormitories and Jewish clubs have been assaulted.[32] For example, just days ago, one hundred anti-Israel activists descended upon the York University Hillel student club shouting slogans such as "Zionism is racism," threatening and intimidating Jewish students.[33]

- Jewish institutions have been particularly susceptible to attacks as "centers of Jewish life became the main targets for those seeking to express their hatred and strike a symbolic blow against Jews as a people."[34] Synagogues, cemeteries and/or Holocaust memorials have been reported vandalized and desecrated in no less than 26 different countries.[35]

- The report from Human Rights First noted that "in some countries, the frequency and severity of attacks on Jewish places of worship, community centers, schools, and other institutions resulted in a need for security measures by representatives of both the Jewish community and local or national government." The human rights NGO credited such "enhanced security"—and not a decrease in anti-Semitic sentiment—with reducing

---

30 2005 to 2006 Pew Global Attitudes Project Poll on Anti-Semitic Attitudes in Selected Muslim Countries.

31 "2008 Hate Crime Survey: I. Anti-Semitism" *Human Rights First*, see
http://www.humanrightsfirst.org/discrimination/reports.aspx?s=antisemitism&p=index

32 Ibid

33 "An eyewitness account of this week's aggressive intimidation of Jewish students at York University." Jonathan Kay. National Post: February 12, 2009.

34 Supra. At 33

35 Ibid.

serious attacks, commenting that "the reality in which such protection is required on an everyday basis is, however, perhaps the truest indicator of just how far the revival of Anti-Semitism has progressed since 2000."[36]

- In 2007, 1,042 antisemitic incidents were reported to the League for Human Rights of B"nai Brith Canada, constituting an overall increase of 11.4% from the previous year. A five-year view shows that the number of incidents has almost doubled since 584 incidents were reported in 2003, while a ten-year view shows a dramatic upward trend with incidents multiplying more than four-fold since 1998, when there were 240 reported cases.[37]

Conclusion

The thesis of this paper, on the state of global antisemitism as an assault on human rights, is that we are witnessing today an old/new escalating, sophisticated, global, virulent, and even lethal antisemitism. In its benign (if it can be called benign) form the old/new Anti-Semitism refers to increased hostility towards and attacks on: Jewish people and property, and Jewish communal, educational and religious institutions; "the mendacious, dehumanizing, or stereotypical allegations about Jews or the powers of Jews as a collective";[38] Holocaust denial and inversion; conspiracy theories where Jews and Israel are blamed as "poisonors of the wells"; boycotts of Jews and Israeli nationals; accusations of dual loyalty; and the singling-out of Israel and the Jewish people for differential and discriminatory treatment in the international arena, and denial of fundamental rights. In its more virulent and lethal form it refers to the delegitimization and demonization of the Jewish people—of the emergence of Israel as the collective Jews among the nations—and to state-sanctioned genocidal antisemitism which constitutes a contemporary warrant for genocide. It is this escalation and intensification of antiemitism that underpins—indeed, necessitates—the establishment of an International Parliamentary Coalition to confront and combat this oldest and most enduring of hatreds. Silence is not an option. The time has come not only to sound the alarm—but to act. For as history has taught us only too well: while it may begin with Jews, it does not end with Jews. Antisemitism is the canary in the mineshaft of evil, and it threatens us all.

---

36 Ibid.

37 Ruth Klein & Anita Bromberg, "2007 Audit of Anti-Semitic Incidents: Patterns of Prejudice in Canada," *League for Human Rights of B'nai Brith Canada*, p. 2.

38 As stated by the European Monitoring Center of Racism and Xenophobia (EUMC), in Gregg J. Rickman "Contemporary Global Anti-Semitism: A Report Provided to the United States Congress," United States Department of State, p. 19.

Reverend Majed El Shafie

Reverend Majed El Shafie, President and Founder of OFWI, was born in Egypt to a prominent Muslim family of judges and lawyers. He was detained and severely tortured by Egyptian authorities after he converted to Christianity and began advocating equal rights for Egyptian Christians. Sentenced to death, he fled Egypt by way of Israel and settled in Canada in 2002, establishing OFWI to share a message of freedom, hope, and tolerance for religious differences and to promote human rights in this area through advocacy and public education. Rev. El Shafie has testified twice before the Subcommittee on International Human Rights of the Standing Committee on Foreign Affairs and International Development and has provided expert reports or expert testimony in numerous refugee proceedings in Canada and the United States. OFWI supports religious freedom without regard to the victims' religion or creed. Accordingly, it also stands against antisemitism and has organized several inter-faith events in cooperation with B'nai Brith Canada. It has an extensive network of local sources in Muslim and communist countries and cooperates with other human rights observers and organizations. More information is available on the OFWI website at www.onefreeworldinternational.org.

I. Introduction

Antisemitism is an abhorrent attitude that has led to untold suffering through-out the ages. It dehumanizes the Jewish people thus justifying discrimination, exploitation, abuse, and even murder. Its inevitable end is attempted destruction of the Jewish people as in the Nazi Holocaust.

While we would like to believe that antisemitism is only an historical issue and no longer relevant, it is on the increase in Canada and worldwide. It continues to surface in traditional ways with open verbal, symbolic, or physical attacks against Jewish individuals or symbols. A new, contemporary antisemitism couches itself in the cloak of anti-zionism, spun as "legitimate" criticism of the State of Israel.

The frame of reference for this Parliamentary Inquiry relates to antisemitism in Canada. However, antisemitism in Canada today cannot be viewed in isolation from its broader historical and international context or from its relationship to the treatment of other religious minorities around the world. Since most contributors to this Inquiry are expected to focus on Canada, the present submissions will focus on the broader view, relating it to the Canadian context. More information about the incidents mentioned herein can be obtained by contacting OFWI.

II. Antisemitism: History

The history of antisemitism and its culmination in the horrors of the Holocaust are well-known. Yet we must not take such knowledge for granted, but must continue to tell the story in order to educate new generations and so we would not forget or become complacent.

From the exile of the Jews by the Romans after the destruction of the Temple in Jerusalem to the Spanish Inquisition and from the pogroms of Russia to the Edicts of Expulsion (Spain and England, among others) and finally to the horrors of the Nazi gas chambers, Jews have been harassed, discriminated, oppressed, persecuted, and killed, simply because they were Jews. The sixty-odd years since the end of the Second World War and the establishment of the State of Israel have provided the Jewish people with a rare moment of reprieve from the constant onslaught of antisemitism. Yet even that precarious respite has begun to show distinct signs of running out, especially over the last decade.

Canada is not free from the stain of antisemitism despite our history of openness, tolerance, and welcoming immigration. Historically we must acknowledge, for example, a strong climate of antisemitism in the period before and into the Second World War. Canada's immigration policy was extremely restrictive toward Jewish immigrants and refugees. Even in 1939 when the nature of Nazi policies was already apparent, Canada sent over 900 Jewish refugees on the St. Louis ship back to Europe where many perished in Nazi death camps.

As the full horrors of the Holocaust were revealed in the aftermath of the Second World War, entire generations were traumatized by the evidence of human capacity for evil against their fellow human beings and swore, "Never again".

III. Antisemitism: Contemporary Manifestations and Nature

While there are no Nazi death camps today, traditional antisemitism persists. Fascism of the 20th century has given way to a self-righteous, nefarious antisemitism from the left of the political spectrum which shares the field with various forms of neo-fascist ideology on the extreme right. Manifestations include attacks on Jewish individuals, businesses, synagogues, schools, and other identifiable Jewish targets. In Europe Jewish cemeteries are defaced and in Paris a young Jewish man was kidnapped and brutally tortured for 24 days before being killed in unimaginable horror by 23 people with the indirect involvement or wilful blindness of dozens of others. Closer to home, synagogues and schools have been vandalized or firebombed from Montreal and Quebec City to Kelowna, while university students conceal their Jewish identity to avoid harassment and intimidation on campus amid hostile protests and "academic" conferences that are little more than anti-Israel propaganda sessions.

Contemporary antisemitism typically masquerades as anti-zionism. Various examples include, for example, op-eds and editorials harshly critical of Israel; comparisons between Israeli policies and apartheid or Nazi Germany; biased and even falsified news reporting in such unexpected places as Sweden, with the support of the government moreover; Israeli athletes and sports teams excluded from sporting events or welcomed with Nazi greetings; vicious anti-Israel demonstrations; and calls for boycotts. In Canada, only a few weeks ago the United Church of Canada rejected a resolution mandating a concerted boycott of Israel, but passed one encouraging individual groups and churches to examine the issue and take appropriate measures.

There is no question that Israel can and should be evaluated and critiqued on its policies just like any other state as long as such criticism is based on facts and truth. Anti-zionism, however, goes beyond legitimate criticism and transfers antisemitic thought patterns from the people to the state. Where it is morally reprehensible to question the right of Jews to exist as individuals and as a people, questioning the legitimacy of the State of Israel or its right to defend itself seems superficially acceptable and does not attract the same censure. Yet the same antisemitic logic operates as is plainly obvious if one tries to apply the same critiques to other states. Consequently, antisemitism in this paper is understood to include anti-zionism.

The rise of contemporary antisemitism is of particular concern because of its ready acceptance in academia, the media, and among the political classes in many countries and the influence these have on the mainstream. Antisemitism in academia benefits from the air of legitimacy associated with scholarship and leaves an indelible impact on future generations of decision-makers causing damage far beyond proportion. In the news media antisemitism directly influences the "man-in-the-street". Yet media "objectivity" has somehow come to mean, not the dispassionate reporting of facts, but presenting a balance between competing positions, regardless of their relative merits or moral strengths. This has resulted in imputing moral equivalence to Israel's actions of self-defence and those of terrorists attacking innocent Israelis, which can only be described as bias. Finally, antisemitism in political classes leads to antisemitism in the community being downplayed, anti-Israel slugfests like the Durban conference on racism, and blatantly one-sided resolutions at the United Nations.

Another concern is the increasingly public nature of antisemitic acts and the recurrent theme of onlookers doing nothing to protect victims. To the extent that the general public is indifferent or condones antisemitic actions even after decades of public education campaigns about human rights and the horrors to which antisemitism can lead, the future is bleak indeed.

IV. Antisemitism and Other Religious Minorities

While the effect of antisemitism on Jews as fellow human beings is sufficient reason to be concerned, it is not the only reason. Despite increases in antisemitism, historically speaking Jews still live and worship relatively freely in the West and have some safety in the protection of the State of Israel. On the other hand, human nature has not changed, as evidenced in the genocide of Rwanda in the 1990s. In the 21st century, black African Muslims in Darfur are brutalized by their Arab Muslim countrymen, converts from Islam are pursued by the death penalty across the Muslim world, and any Christians discovered in North Korea and unregistered church leaders in China are imprisoned, put to forced labour, and often tortured, particularly in the former.

These are only a minuscule sampling of events taking place today around the world, or even in the countries mentioned. But what do they have to do with antisemitism in Canada? The answer is - nothing on the surface, and yet every-thing. Where human beings think little or nothing of oppressing their fellow human beings, whether because of the colour of their skin or their religious beliefs or rites, the identity of the victim matters little. In fact, the only reason we do not hear of Jews persecuted in many of these countries despite rampant antisemitism is that any Jewish community that may once have existed is now either virtually or actually non-existent. The following examples demonstrate how antisemitism and persecution of other religious minorities coexist.

Despite a peace agreement with Israel committing it to abstain from hostile propaganda or incitement, Egypt's state-run media are full of grossly antise-mitic and anti-Israel political cartoons, editorials, and television programs; school textbooks omit Israel on maps and declare that Israel remains the enemy and that war can break at any moment; and authorities close their eyes to ter-rorists smuggling weapons to Gaza. At the same time, Christians, Bahá'í's and others are discriminated and fear forcible conversion, imprisonment, and pos-sible torture, while converts are often tortured or killed even by their own family-members.

The President of Iran rants against Israel threatening its destruction, pursues nuclear weapons, and Iranian Jews, and often Bahá'í's, are charged with spying for Israel. Meanwhile Iranian Christians and Bahá'í's are frequently arrested and held without charge, and converts are tortured to extract the names of other converts or information about house churches.

In Pakistan, despite the absence of any apparent Jewish community, antisemitism and anti-zionism are widespread. In the meantime, impover-ished Christians are lured into enslavement in this country where a two-year old Christian girl can be raped because her father refuses to convert to Islam. Christians, Hindus, and others are killed arbitrarily with vague and draconian Blasphemy Laws serving as pretext, and Ahmadis, considered heretics, are pro-hibited under threat of criminal sanction by anti-Ahmadi laws from presenting themselves as Muslims or publicly observing rites.

Saudi Arabia officially prohibits entry to Israelis or those with Israeli stamps in their passports and unofficially bans Jews. In 2005 a teacher who had spo-ken positively about Jews and the Bible was sentenced to almost three and a half years in penitentiary and 750 lashes before OFWI intervention led to his release. At the same time, the Muslim Shi'a minority faces discrimination, all public non-Muslim religious practice is forbidden and religious police peri-odically raid even the private religious gatherings of foreigners imprisoning participants and confiscating Bibles.

Problems with "media objectivity" apply here as much as to antisemitism. For example, in a recent Canadian news report, an American-born girl who fled home claiming her father had threatened to kill her for converting from Islam to Christianity was characterized as a normal rebellious teenager afraid of "punishment", omitting any mention of death threats. Such attitudes and reporting make any resolution of the human rights issues involved impossible as the first victim of this false objectivity is the truth. However, the real victims of such distortion are Jews and others whose religious beliefs make them a target.

Just like in Nazi Germany, wherever antisemitism flourishes other religious or ethnic minorities, the disabled, homosexuals, and others eventually face persecution, and other basic human rights, such as women's rights, freedom of expression, etc., are or soon will be threatened. If left unchecked such attitudes and oppression will spread like poison and affect Jews and other minorities alike worldwide. Even if they do not result in wide-scale antisemitism or anti-religious behaviours in Canada, the potential for a cataclysmic and costly world war to protect our freedoms is very real and the results not a foregone conclusion. As a result, it is our responsibility to speak out, to come to the aid of victims, and to ensure that such attitudes are not permitted to flourish in Canada or anywhere else in the world.

V. Conclusion and Recommendations

History teaches us that if we do not remember and learn from our history we are destined to repeat our mistakes. There is perhaps no lesson more important than that of antisemitism, the Holocaust, and genocide, yet we do not seem to learn this lesson. The Rwandan genocide, the greatest example of an entirely avoidable evil since the Holocaust, took place despite clear warning signs that the world simply chose to ignore. In the meantime, antisemitism simmers.

If the rise of antisemitism is permitted to go unchecked, the result will be another holocaust more destructive, more barbaric, and more unthinkable than that unleashed by the Nazis in the 1930s and 1940s. The spirit of hatred and intolerance will not rest with the destruction of the Jewish state and elimination of all Jews, but will endanger all freedom-loving peoples.

We have plenty of laws in place to protect individuals and property from generic and antisemitic crimes. We do not need more laws or regulations. We need the political will to enforce those laws that already exist. We need leaders in and out of government with the moral strength to speak truth boldly, loudly, and clearly to those, individuals, governments, or media, who would hide behind false notions of political correctness, self-righteous politics whether of the extreme right or left, or the false cover of a disingenuous concept of anti-zionism. We must also encourage other governments to do the same, for example showing the Swedish government that it is possible to support freedom of the press while still condemning vile content. Finally, we must not be afraid to clearly state the connection where it exists between incidents such as the Paris torture case and extremist Islamic teachings.

If we do not speak out on behalf of the Jewish people and against antisemitism today, who will speak out tomorrow for the Christians, or Bahá'í's, Uyghur or Darfur Muslims, Tibetan Buddhists, or Ahmadis, to mention only a few? Antisemitism is everyone's issue and we must not be silent.

Karen Eltis

Professor Karen Eltis is a tenured law Professor (Professeur agrégé), at the Faculty of Law of the University of Ottawa Canada (Section de droit civil) and a member of the Center for Law, Technology and Society. A past director of the Human Rights Centre and of the Bijuridical & National Programme, Karen Eltis specializes in internet law, policy and ethics, and comparative law. She served as Senior Advisor to the National Judicial Institute and worked with the Department of Justice (Canada). She is also an Adjunct Associate Professor at Columbia Law School, where she teaches Internet and Comparative Constitutional Law. She is Fluent in French, English, Hebrew, and Spanish and holds law degrees from McGill University, the Hebrew University of Jerusalem and Columbia Law School (Harlan Fiske Stone Scholar). She clerked for Chief Justice Aharon Barak of the Supreme Court of Israel. Prior to joining the faculty at the University of Ottawa, Karen was a litigation associate in New York City, focusing on International Dispute Resolution. Her latest book is titled *Courts, Litigants and the Digital Age* (Irwin Law, 2012).

Karen Eltis*

Associate Professor of Law, University of Ottawa
Past Director, Centre for Research and Education in Human Rights

Oral Testimony of Professor Karen Eltis, University of Ottawa Law School. Delivered to the Canadian Parliamentary Coalition to Combat Antisemitism on 7 December 2009.

The global phenomenon of antisemitism that draws on traditional motifs but extends from the individual to the collective Jew, Israel, is spilling over into Canadian campuses and creating a hostile environment of intimidation, fear, and demonization, in which violence, both psychological and even physical, is increasingly extended legitimacy. Worse, for me as a jurist, it is alarming that it is increasingly couched in the language of human rights.

Most obvious among others in this context is the so-called Israel Apartheid Week, during which the Jewish state is attributed all of the world's evils and effectively equated with what we most loathe: racism, apartheid, and even Nazism. I believe that Robert Wistrich, who you heard not long ago, discussed the morphing of antisemitism to correspond with the zeitgeist, the spirit of the time. The Jewish state, its citizens, and its supporters—which of course includes students and faculty—not surprisingly become legitimate targets for demonization and violence, and the political entity that they may be associated with—I, for instance, am a dual citizen— becomes a target for eradication, in fact.

In a word—and this is what concerns me—racist affirmations, incredulously but frighteningly, are proffered and, indeed, made palatable to us and virtually unassailable when they are couched in human rights rhetoric.

Essentially, the bottom line is that Jews are not here asking for special treatment when they rise against the old antisemitism or the new antisemitism. We are asking for equal treatment.

There is a normative framework already in place in Canada that is in fact the envy of many places in the world. It is already instituted and is well equipped to deal with this problem. It is only a question, not of reinventing the wheel, but of extending this framework to what has become an unpopular group: Israelis and, by extension, Jews.

Universities and societies as a whole have recognized the harms of harassment on enumerated and analogous grounds. We have recognized the impact

---

* The testimony of Professor Eltis is comprised of both an oral submission presented to the Canadian Parliamentary Inquiry into Antisemitism on 7 December 2009, and an untitled written submission presented to the Panel outlining the nature of antisemitism on Canadian university campuses. Full unabridged transcripts of Professor Bauer's testimony can be found at *http://www.cpcca.ca/inquiry.htm.*

of degrading speech on women's and minorities' equality and psychological well-being. We therefore consciously balance what is called "negative freedom of speech"- meaning the freedom from state interference to express ourselves— with what is known in Berlinian terms as "positive freedom of speech", that is to say, the right to express yourself in society, to have the tools where you feel comfortable enough and are unafraid to express yourself. Positive freedom of expression is increasingly recognized by the courts.

We also recognize equality as a countervailing value, and we regularly, in Canada, limit offensive and oppressive speech, be it on campus, at the workplace, or elsewhere. This limiting is not considered antithetical to Canadian values provided that the proper balancing of values is applied.

On the contrary, it is considered a promotion of Canadian values to allow historically vulnerable groups to express themselves and to promote their equality and dignity. Accordingly, many workplaces and many universities define discriminatory harassment as "objectionable and unwelcome comment, conduct, display, communication in any form based on any of the prohibited grounds listed. It is behaviour which would be reasonably perceived to demean, humiliate or cause offence," etc.

There are even cracks in the U.S. model. I have just returned now from the U.S. where freedom of expression is sacrosanct. A recent book by Harry R. Lewis, a Harvard professor and one of the great pioneers of freedom of expression, notes that in the Internet age one needs to reconsider an absolute stance of freedom of expression. I think the so-called anti-Zionist or antisemitic rhetoric that I refer to in my report fits the bill.

Jewish students and other vulnerable minorities deserve no less—that is to say, an extension to them of the protection of the normative framework already in place—yet somehow and unfortunately, a double standard prevails. Somehow, in some environments, including some campuses, targeting Jews or targeting Israelis is acceptable despite the fact that these same entities do not hesitate in limiting certain forms of speech when they are offensive—and I'm glad for that—for instance, to women or other minorities.

This led Professor Shalom Lappin to remark, "If one group of students is permitted to engage in violent harassment of another without the decisive intervention of the University's administration, then the conditions for a free and unfettered exchange of ideas are completely undermined, and the primary purpose of university life is betrayed." That is to say, if they are afraid to express themselves, they do not benefit from freedom of expression. So it is not a question of rights versus some other value; it is a question of rights versus rights.

Examples abound of the double standard where the normative framework that is in place to protect vulnerable minorities is not applied to Jews. Excluding more cynical explanations, I think I would attribute this to the fear of suppressing legitimate political expression.

The continued discussion of where we distinguish between antisemitism and anti-Zionism has been a constant preoccupation and, perhaps, legitimately so. This is why, as a practical recommendation, I propose that we incorporate by reference clear indicia, such as the EUMC working definition, which I believe you have in your packages, and other indicia that have been elaborated by scholars, in order to do away with the tautology of antisemitism versus anti-Zionism and to do away with the danger of ad hoc responses.

Doing so—that is to say, incorporating by reference indicia such as those in the EUMC and others that I mention in my report—will also help to promote transparency. Thus, for instance, the EUMC cites contemporary manifestations of antisemitism in public life as including: denying the Jewish people their right to self-determination by claiming that Israel is a racist endeavour; using the symbols of classic antisemitism to demonize Israel; and applying a double standard to the Jewish state. This is precisely what Israel Apartheid Week and other such events do.

Again, many indicia can be used. Most come back to the question of demonization and a double standard to distinguish between legitimate political expression and unacceptable antisemitism in its new form. Delinking the Jewish people from their homeland can amount to a denial of the very identity of the Jewish people and, indeed, exogenously impose versions of identity. Time does not permit me to go into details of what distinguishes antisemitism from anti-Zionism. In my text I refer to a number of definitions that would be helpful in that endeavour.

To summarize my comments, Jews are not asking in this context for special treatment, but for equal treatment; that is to say, to have the legal framework that is already in place extended to protect them, Jewish students, Jewish faculty, and Jewish workers, from the type of hostile environment that prevents them from taking an equal place in society and prevents them from expressing themselves. It is a question of balancing freedom of expression of anti-Zionists or even antisemites with the freedom to express themselves and the dignity and equality of Jews, Israelis and others.

Finally, in order to promote transparency, prevent ad hoc responses, and help us do away with the tautology of antisemitism versus anti-Zionism, I propose the adoption of criteria such as the EUMC definition and others incorporated by reference into the relevant documents.

Written Submission Prepared by Professor Eltis for the Canadian Parliamentary Coalition to Combat Antisemitism.

A Jewish student threatened with beheading at the University of Toronto; another grabbed by the neck and verbally assaulted during an "anti-Israel" event at the same institution; Jewish students trapped at Hillel (Jewish Center) for fear of physical attack while the doors are pounded on and racial slurs shouted at York; verbal and physical attacks on Jewish students reported at Carleton.[1] These incidents—a mere sampling of a growing phenomenon of intimidation increasingly prevalent on Canadian campuses, rarely (if ever) met with decisive condemnation let alone concerted action[2]—seem to confirm Pierre-Andre's Taguieff's observation that "not since the Second World War have we witnessed such a rash of anti-Jewish acts, which have met with such limited intellectual and political resistance."[3]

This is, indeed, a time when historical truth and values such as equality struggle to endure in the face of increasing attacks on Jews, insidiously couched in human rights rhetoric. Thus, for instance, Iran's president Mahmoud Ahmadinejad's recurring and unequivocal assertions that Israel "should be wiped off the map," and his incitement of students to ultimately commit genocide, chanting "death to the Jews" at a government-sponsored conference[4] was tactically justified in terms of human rights, namely, free speech and open debate.

These occurrences are by no means isolated nor are they far removed from Canadians. Instead, as noted above, they echo similar calls for incitement to violence against Jews (including but not limited to chants for "death to Jews") at so-called "anti-Israel" rallies in Montreal, Toronto and Calgary earlier this year.[5]

---

1 See e.g. "Students Threatened with beheading at U of T's Israeli Apartheid Week" *The Jewish Tribune* (10 March 2009), online: *http://www.jewishtribune.ca/TribuneV2/index.php/200903101454/Student-threatened-with-beheading-at-U-of-T-s-Israeli-Apartheid-Week.html.* For a more detailed report of such incidents on Canadian campuses see e.g. *www.peaceoncampus.ca.*

2 See e.g. Shlomo Lapin's critique infra Note 15.

3 Pierre-Andre, Taguieff, *The New Judeophobia* (Editions Mille et une nuits, 2002).

4 See e.g. BBC News *http://news.bbc.co.uk/2/hi/middle_east/8010702.stm.*
Transcript of speech available at *http://www.haaretz.com/hasen/spages/1024097.html*
See also Ewen MacAskill & Chris McGreal, "Israel Should Be Wiped off Map, Says Iran's President, Guardian" The Guardian (27 October 2005), online: *http://www.guardian.co.uk/world/2005/oct/27/israel.iran.*

5 See e.g. Paul Lugen, "Police asked to Investigate Anti-Israel Protest" *The Canadian Jewish News* (22 January 2009), online:*http://www.cjnews.com/index.php?option=com_content&task=view&id=16092&Itemid=86/*
In a video released by the Canadian Jewish Congress (Canadian Jewish Congress, News release, "CJC exposes incitement to hatred and violence at pro-Hamas rallied" (14 January 2009), online: *http://cjc.ca/template.php?action=news&story=1003):* "some protesters are heard repeating the medieval anti-Semitic libel that Jews drink blood. One woman is seen yelling, "Jewish child, you're going to f***ing die, Hamas is coming for you." At a rally in Calgary men were photographed giving the Nazi salute ...". The calls effectively mimic those housed within the Hamas covenant, which—interestingly for our purposes—frames its demand for the "obliteration from existence" of the Jewish state as a "religious right". Covenant is available at: *http://avalon.law.yale.edu/20th_century/hamas.asp.*

Blatantly antisemitic rhetoric, masking as the exercise of constitutionally enshrined rights is widespread at Canadian Universities, epitomized by recurring high-profile events such as "Israel Apartheid Week". Its disturbing but clear implication is that Israel is a racist entity that must be dismantled.[6] The campaign further suggests that the Jewish state's supporters (including Jewish and certainly Israeli students and faculty who have not disowned their heritage) must be greeted with opprobrium as proponents of vile racism by any peace-loving Canadian.

Most disturbingly, perhaps, the anti-Semitic or even genocidal affirmations (and I do not use this term lightly) voiced on Canadian campuses in the context of these events and beyond, not only serve to intimidate and silence Jews on campus but are progressively cloaked in human rights discourse. In a word, classic anti-Jewish motifs are made palatable to the Canadian ear when craftily phrased in terms of freedom of expression or a right of the oppressed to self-determination. This racist rhetoric, evoking familiar themes of Jewish power and domination (e.g. posters on campus often evoke blood libels with Palestinian children substituting their Christian counterparts …)[7] are often preceded by the denial of atrocities perpetrated against the vilified group and veiled in rights rhetoric.

From the General to the Specific

This phenomenon is particularly worrisome in the context of a niversity, whose mission is generally "to promote the advancement of learning and the dissemination of knowledge" and whose responsibility is to "foster an environment of respect, conducive to the sharing of knowledge free from harassment, verbal or other violence and fear of reprisals." This new anti-Jewishness (or so called "antizionist" discourse)[8] not only significantly impacts on Jewish students' ability to learn and share as equal members of the campus community but also affects their psychological health and well-being. Plainly put, many Jewish and Israeli students are intimidated and even afraid. They are afraid to reveal their

6 See the Hon. Irwin Cotler's statement on point. More generally (focusing on U.S. campuses) see also Khaled Abu Toameh, "On Campus: The Pro-Palestinians' Real Agenda" (24 March 2009), online: The Hudson New York Briefing Council
http://www.hudsonny.org/2009/03/on-campus-the-pro-palestinians-real-agenda.php

7 See e.g, SPHR poster . The image and an article on the subject have been made available at the Fulcrum online at *http://www.scribd.com/doc/12845977/Fulcrum-022609*. See also Gerald M. Steinberg & Sarah Mandel, "Watching the Watchers" (2006) 43 Justice 24 at 26 (chronicling the inversion of human rights narratives by various "human rights" NGOs. "In Belgium, the local branch of Oxfam, which was headed for many years by a radical socialist named Pierre Galand, distributed an anti-Semitic poster in 2003 based on the theme of the blood libel, in promoting a campaign to boycott Israeli goods and Israelis themselves").

8 In order to avoid tautological debate regarding antisemitism versus antizionism, I proposed elsewhere that the EUMC Working Definition of Anti-Semitism (available at *http://eumc.eu.int/eumc/material/pub/AS/AS-WorkingDefinition-draft.pdf*) be incorporated by reference in campus codes of conduct respecting harassment.

Jewishness, their support for Israel, or to engage in discussion and debate in what is an ever hostile and aggressive environment for anyone who dares to challenge engrained views concerning Jews and the Jewish state (be it in the classroom or outside). Some are even ashamed of their identity, having internalized the vilification repeatedly directed at them and been regularly exposed to hateful discourse and symbols (i.e. Jewish star alongside swastika ...). All this is shamelessly cloaked as an exercise of the right to legitimate political protest with regard to the situation in the Middle East.

Significantly, this harassment and incremental demonization[9] is not without long-term consequence and sequel for young Jewish students in particular. As Engel explains more generally: "Harassment can wear down a person's defenses and resistance over time ... tiring them out and making them insecure and anxious. It is another powerful form of psychological violence."[10]

It is in fact, as a US court dealing with antisemitic comments in the workplace context recently opined, the *accumulation* of vilifying and derogatory comments that create an atmosphere of fear, silencing and shame for its victims exposed to this propaganda.[11] *A fortiori* for the campus environment, which unlike the workplace, also serves as a home for many students, this exacerbates the effects of intimidation.

Affirmative or positive right to expression

The human rights narrative disturbingly co-opted by proponents of traditional antisemitic discourse misleadingly suggests that the only rights at stake and worthy of protection are their own—to the exclusion of the rights of the Jewish campus community members to an environment free of harassment.

In other words, the human rights rhetoric in this context rests on the premise that restraints on speech alone pose a threat to this constitutionally protected value. Instead —and in line with the Canadian Supreme Court's decision in *Keegstra*[12] and elsewhere—it should be argued that if permitted to proceed uninhibited, certain forms of speech, particularly racist and harassing rhetoric such as "Israel Apartheid" serves not only to undermine Jews' equality

---

9 Recently described in this context by Natan Sharansky as "comparisons of Israelis to Nazis and Palestinian refugee camps to Auschwitz" applying a double standard, singling out Israel for human rights abuses "when countries like China and Syria are ignored". See Mike King, "Anti-Semites Focus on Israeli State: Sharansky" *The Gazette* (15 March 2004).

10 Engel: 1998, 44.

11 See *Cutler v. Dorn* 196 N.J. 419, 955 A.2d 917 available at: *http://lawlibrary.rutgers.edu/courts/supreme/a-51-07.opn.html*. Held the court, "The threshold for demonstrating a religion-based, discriminatory hostile work environment is no more stringent than the threshold that applies to sexually or racially hostile workplace environment claims".

12 *R. v. Keegstra*, [1990] 3 S.C.R. 697.

and dignity on campus but effectively threatens to muzzle them and prevent them from participating in campus community life.[13]

Other than being antithetical to Canadian values such as tolerance, multi-culturalism and equality, and to the university mission, this is an Orwellian inversion manipulated to promulgate hate, and to undermine the above stated values.

It stands to reason, therefore, that universities and, indeed, society are duty-bound to take corrective action to protect not only the "Anti-Israel" protesters' freedom *from* infringements on free speech—as they have done already—but Jewish victims' positive[14] or affirmative rights *to* expression, dignity and equality. In this case and in the balance of rights, the latter must prevail. Professor Shalom Lapin (who declined an invitation to speak at York University by reason of its failure to address the lamentable Hillel incident cited above) writes: "If one group of students is permitted to engage in violent harassment of another without the decisive intervention of the University's administration, then the conditions for a free and unfettered exchange of ideas are completely undermined, and the primary purpose of university life is betrayed."[15] For surely the purpose of protecting speech "is not to carve out a private, solipsistic sphere but, rather, to protect our efforts to communicate with other people. Freedom of expression should not be seen as a solely nega-tive right whose only function is to protect us against interference and not to give us any right to positive assistance in our endeavour to communicate with others ..."[16]

A Final Word

Incredulously, constitutionalism—the anticipated safeguard against the devas-tation of democracy from within—may itself, it seems, be co-opted for that very purpose. Once issues are proffered "in terms of conflict of right as opposed to conflicts of interest" the balance of power inevitably changes as the person(s)

---

13 I will refrain from cataloguing the incidents on Canadian campuses, which have been well-documented elsewhere. See also www.peaceoncampus.ca.

14 To employ Isaiah Berlin's Two Conceptions of Liberty (Four Essays on Liberty, 1969) at 118.
See also J.F. Gauldrault-Desbiens, "From Sisyphus's Dilemma to Sisyphus's Duty? A Meditation on the Regulation of Hate" (2001) 46 McGill L. J. 1117-1137. He argues that "this dilemma [of inhibiting speech] becomes *a duty to regulate against abusive forms of expression*, because a constitutional democracy cannot tolerate radical denials of the humanity of some of its citizens ...".

15 See Professor Lapin's letter to the President and Vice-Chancellor of York University available at: http://www.peaceoncampus.ca/articles/articles-detailed.php?artclid=1&artname=Letter-to-the-President-and-Vice-Chancellor-of-York-University-from-Professor-Shalom-Lappin-after-canceling-his-appearance-to-lecture-due-to-the-lack-of-response-to-student-intimidation-

16 See *inter alia* Denise Meyerson, "The Legitimate Extent of Freedom of Expression" (2002) 52 U. Toronto L.J.

invoking 'rights' is presumed to be of higher moral caliber—a "Constitutional Warrior" fighting injustice—even if it is a genocide denier or a proponent of racist doctrines.

As to the 'slippery slope' argument, or the 'hate speech' conundrum respecting where the proper line is to be drawn, I have argued elsewhere[17] in favour of incorporating the EUMC *Working Definition of Anti-Semitism*[18] by reference into various university policies regarding hostile speech/harassing behaviour on campus in order to prevent the need for problematic ad hoc responses. I submit further that the "set of indices" that the Hon. Irwin Cotler proposes, by which we can, in his words, "identify, and pour content into, the nature and meaning of the new anti-Jewishness"[19], serve to demarcate legitimate criticism of Israel from blatant antisemitism, masking as such.

The danger of hijacking human rights narratives towards racist incitement is not unprecedented. The lessons of France's Vichy regime are most informative where, as Richard Weisberg demonstrated, appropriated legal language associated with profound pre-existing social values subverted those very principles and layed the foundation for their destruction. If constitutionalism is to serve the purpose for which it was intended—that is to safeguard substantive democracy - we must not be fooled by the cynical invocation and manipulation of human rights values. History teaches the importance of the precautionary principle as it relates to incitement to hatred against historically vulnerable groups. The Canadian Supreme Court has embraced this view by upholding carefully drafted anti-hate provisions. It bears repeating that in Canada the willful promotion of hatred under certain circumstances is deemed a justifiable and proportional limit on free expression in light of its deleterious effects upon the dignity and equality of the vulnerable and society as a whole[20]. The hope here is to raise awareness of the problem and to prompt meaningful intervention. The challenge for political leaders, university administrators, the media and particularly

---

17 As the context of this report does not allow for further elaboration. See e.g. CAFI conference "Emerging trends in anti-Semitism" (unreported). CAFI website: *http://caficonference.com/*

18 *http://eumc.eu.int/eumc/material/pub/AS/AS-WorkingDefinition-draft.pdf.*

19 See Irwin Cotler, "Human Rights and the New Anti-Jewishness" 38 Justice 24 (2004), available at *http://www.intjewishlawyers.org/docenter/frames.asp?id=9285*; see also Irwin Cotler, Human Rights and the New Anti-Jewishness, FrontPageMagazine.com, *http://www.frontpagemag.com/Articles/ReadArticle.asp?ID=12191* (referring to "genocidal or existential anti-Semitism"). See also e.g. Ruth Wisse, "Why Anti-Semitism Succeeds,"

20 While it is beyond the scope of this report to elaborate on the legal or jurisprudential framework see e.g. R. v. Keegstra, [1990] 3 S.C.R. 697, where the Court recognized the role of words in ushering in violence. See also Mugesera v. Canada (Minister of Citizenship and Immigration), [2005] SCC 40 § 8, available at for the potential of abuse of the protected human rights guarantees.

civil society now is not to let constitutionalism be undermined by the very narrative it conceived.

Manfred Gerstenfeld

Dr. Manfred Gerstenfeld holds a PhD in environmental studies from Amsterdam University. Dr. Gerstenfeld is a chemist (Amsterdam University) and an economist (Amsterdam and Rotterdam Universities). He also holds a high-school teaching degree from the Dutch Jewish Seminary. For more than forty years he has been an international consultant, specializing in business strategy. Dr. Gerstenfeld has been a non-executive board member of the Israel Corporation (one of Israel's largest investment companies) and various other Israeli public companies.

Dr. Gerstenfeld is currently, inter alia, Chairman of the Board of Fellows of the Jerusalem Center for Public Affairs; an editor of *The Jewish Political Studies Review*, co-publisher of the *Jerusalem Letter/Viewpoints, Post-Holocaust and Anti-Semitism and Changing Jewish Communities*. He has authored ten books, most recently *The Abuse of Holocaust Memory: Distortions and Responses* (2009) and has edited four other books.. He has also published articles in leading papers and journals in various countries on political, economic, environmental, religious and historical subjects; a number of these concern Holocaust related, post-Holocaust and antisemitism issues. He has given invited lectures at a number of universities, many international symposia and congresses.

His past public affairs activities include Chairman, World Union of Jewish Students (1963-1967); Member, European Executive of World Jewish Congress (1964-1967); Trustee, Memorial Foundation for Jewish Culture (1964-1967); Council Member, World University Service (1964-1968); Vice-chairman of the Dutch Immigrants' Association, Jerusalem branch (1974-5); Member of the Executive of the Democratic Movement for Change (1976-1980)—at the time, Israel's third largest party; Member of the Council of the World Zionist Organization (1977-1981); Member of Israel Government Committee for

131

appointing auditors to public companies (1978-1988); Vice-Chairman of the Council of the Foundation for Research of Dutch Jewry; Member of the national executive of the Dutch Immigrant's Association (1990-1992).

Jerusalem Center for Public Affairs

The Jerusalem Center for Public Affairs is an independent policy institute, established in 1976, devoted to the analysis of key issues concerning Israel and the Jewish people. The Center's fellows are leading scholars and experts from various continents. The Post-Holocaust and Antisemitism program of the Jerusalem Center's Institute for Global Jewish Public Affairs has a wide ranging agenda of in depth analysis of the main trends in contemporary antisemitism.

Dr. Manfred Gerstenfeld*

Director of the Post-Holocaust & Antisemitism Program, Jerusalem Centre for Public Affairs

Oral Testimony of Dr. Manfred Gerstenfeld, Director of Post-Holocaust & Antisemitism Program, as an Individual. Delivered to the Canadian Parliamentary Coalition to Combat Antisemitism via teleconference on 16 November 2008

Mr. Chairman, I first would like to express my appreciation for being given this opportunity to make a number of observations on anti-Semitism.

You will find, in the documents that we've presented to you, our detailed, footnoted presentation on global antisemitism. It analyzes the main characteristics of this global antisemitism, including the main originators of anti-Jewish hatred, the instruments they use, and the impacts of the antisemitic process. We have also included specific recommendations on what we think your committee should recommend.

I cannot, in the limited time available, deal with the large number of topics that are in the document we've submitted to you. I will focus on two issues that I consider particularly important. First, if we speak about Canadian antisemitism, what are my associations as somebody who analyzes global antisemitism? My second focus concerns what I hope will be the main recommendations of your commission.

Now, if we speak about Canada and antisemitism among experts of international antisemitism abroad, it is first and foremost campus antisemitism. Among democratic countries, Canada and the United Kingdom are the international pioneers in this field, followed by the United States and Norway.

Seven years ago, we at the Jerusalem Center for Public Affairs, where I am the chairman of the board, initiated a research program into global academic

First, we had a Canadian intern student who had been physically attacked at Concordia University because of her pro-Israeli views. That same year, our attention was drawn to a lecture by Ted Honderich, a British professor of Canadian origin, at the University of Toronto. He said there that the Palestinians had a "moral right" to blow up Jews. He even encouraged them to do so.

These two cases of antisemitic incitement in Canada led to the beginning of our research program on global antisemitism on campus.

---

* The testimony of Dr. Gerstenfeld is comprised of both an oral submission presented tot eh Canadian Parliamentary Inquiry into Antisemitism on 16 November 2008 and a subsequent written submission discussing the origins and characteristics of contemporary antisemitism. A full unabridged transcripts of the found at *http://www.cpcca.ca/inquiry.htm*.

Regretfully, our knowledge of Canadian campus antisemitism has grown very much since then. I'll just mention a few incidents with which you're probably familiar.

There has been more violence at Concordia. The hate program of Israeli Apartheid Week began at the University of Toronto in 2004. It has spread from Toronto, nationally and internationally.

There was a call for a boycott by anti-Israeli academics in January 2009 by Sid Ryan, president of the Ontario branch of the Canadian Union of Public Employees.

During a visit I made to Canada this past summer, I was told by several professors and students that Jewish students are increasingly avoiding York University because of problems there. In February, Jewish students were confronted on the York campus by murderous antisemitic threats. A conference at York campus that demonized Israel took place there in June this year.

I recall that when I published my book Academics Against Israel and the Jews in 2007, I included, among the 17 case studies, two on Canada, because I considered it particularly important. I had a third chapter prepared that was dedicated to York University, but the author was too late with the corrections. Otherwise, three out of 18 case studies would have been Canadian. This is a further indication of the relative importance of campus antisemitism in Canada from a global viewpoint.

I think your country's image is being increasingly tainted abroad by both the incidents of antisemitic hatred on a number of your campuses and the poor reaction of campus administrations against it. I have not seen, over seven years, any indications of a decline in the hate phenomena on your campuses. The testimonies of Jewish students on Canadian campuses—you can find them in the preparatory material that's been submitted to you for today—will further confirm my opinion.

Now, campus antisemitism in Canada and elsewhere is an indicator of much more widespread problems in academia. Jews and Israel are often the first to be attacked, but it's only a matter of time until others will be targeted. You cannot explain this problem away by saying that academic freedom is too loosely interpreted and many administrators of universities are weak personalities. In his novel Nineteen Eighty- Four, George Orwell introduced three famous slogans: "War is Peace", "Slavery is Freedom", and "Ignorance is Strength". I think that had Orwell lived today and written about some universities—not only Canadian ones—he might have added these: "Propaganda is Advancing Knowledge", "Indoctrination is Higher Education", and "Incitement promotes Scholarship".

I have worked for forty years as a strategic adviser to a variety of the world's largest corporations. I have never seen, during those years, any self-ruling body that after a certain time didn't become morally corrupt, be that in the business world or elsewhere, such as in academia.

There may well be a necessity for a much more general inquiry into the functioning of Canadian universities. A first step could be that complaints concerning antisemitism on campus should not be investigated by the universities themselves, which tend to whitewash them, but by outside bodies.

There are, beside campus antisemitism, other aspects of Canadian antisemitism. Just to mention one, classic versions of protestant antisemitism have mutated into anti-Israelism in parts of the United Church of Christ in Canada. However, none of the other issues equal in importance Canadian campus antisemitism.

That is the first issue.

The second issue I want to address is what I hope will be the main recommendations of your commission. Canada was the first country to withdraw from Durban II. I think it should also be the first country to bring an interstate complaint against Iran before the International Court of Justice. Both Iran and Canada are parties to the genocide convention, and Iran has criminally violated this genocide treaty. I think your former justice minister, Professor Cotler, can explain this much better than I can.

As for the second recommendation, there is a dramatic shortage in the world of think tanks and university institutions that study national and global antisemitism. Canada became an international leader in the field of national Jewish studies when its government of the time funded chairs in Canadian Jewish studies at both Concordia University and York University. By funding institutions for the study of antisemitism, it can become an international leader in this field as well, and the analysis of campus antisemitism should be a high priority for such institutions.

My third recommendation is that there is a need for perfected methods of monitoring and analyzing antisemitic incidents deriving from the three main variants of antisemitism over the past 2,000 years: first, religious antisemitism; second, ethnic or nationalist antisemitism; and third, anti-Israelism. This also must include antisemitism on the Internet. If you charge an institution with establishing criteria, sophisticated methodologies, and a data bank, as well as ongoing monitoring, you may make Canada an international leader in this area, from which many others may be able to learn a lot.

I should underline that no work can be done without an accepted definition of what antisemitism is. It is therefore important to accept such a definition, and the best available for this purpose is the one adopted by the EUMC.

My other recommendations are contained in the document that I presented earlier to your commission. Our centre will gladly assist you in bringing these recommendations closer to implementation.

Thank you for your attention.

Written Submission Prepared by Dr. Manfred Gerstenfeld and the Jerusalem Center for Public Affairs for the Canadian Parliamentary Coalition to Combat Antisemitism.

Global Antisemitism:

Originators, Instruments, Impacts and Recommendations

Introduction

Contemporary antisemitism has an increasingly global character. Any inquiry into a national situation therefore requires a broad background understanding of developments and trends in global antisemitism. This presentation provides an overview of the main characteristics and tendencies of contemporary antisemitism.

Characteristics of Contemporary Antisemitism

Contemporary antisemitism uses a number of major hate motifs, which have recurred in various forms over more than two thousand years. They derive from one core motif: the Jews—and nowadays also Israel—embody absolute evil. This motif recurs in a large number of ways, many of which are less explicit and more diluted.

The 2001 United Nations Anti-racism Conference in Durban, South Africa widely revealed the global re-intensification of such antisemitism. As contemporary antisemitism has so many aspects, we refer in this article to a large number of sources. Many are original publications of the Post-Holocaust and Antisemitism program of the Jerusalem Center for Public Affairs. We recommend them for lecture by the staff of the inquiry commission in order to get a fuller picture of the issues treated in this presentation.

This core motif of antisemitism breaks down into a number of hate sub-motifs, of which the main ones are the Jews' alleged lust for power (including money), the Jews' alleged lust for killing (including the alleged responsibility for killing Jesus which was determined and executed by the Romans, thirst for blood, in particular of children) and claiming that the Jews are sub-human.

As has been said earlier, antisemitism presents itself in extreme forms as well as in less explicit and more diluted ones. The most extreme hate-incitements against the Jews express themselves differently in the three main types of antisemitism—religious, nationalistic-ethnic, and anti-Zionism.

In Christian religious antisemitism the Jews are accused of being Christ killers. In Muslim religious antisemitism the Jews are inter alia considered animals. Some Muslim traditions, currently quoted, call for the murder of all Jews. In nationalist, ethnic antisemitism Jews are charged of belonging to a genetically inferior ethnicity. In anti-Zionism, Israel is accused of being a Nazi state, which has no right to exist. A thorough mapping of hate bodies and the collaboration among them has never been undertaken.

Stages of Antisemitism

The various types of antisemitism have three stages in common: *demonization, exclusion*, and *expulsion or extermination*.[1] In anti-Zionism the demonization stage manifests itself as concentrated criticism against Israel, while other states, whose human rights record is far worse, are criticized much less or not at all. An example of exclusion is the boycott campaigns against Israel. The expulsion or extermination threats manifest themselves mainly in Muslim states and the Palestinian Authority. They can also be found however among Neo-Nazis and some Muslims in Western countries

The multiple ongoing attacks on Israel and the Jews in the new century combine into a system, *as if controlled by an invisible hand*. Its sum total is similar to a *"postmodern total war"* against Israel and the Jews.[2][3] This complex whole is of a different nature than the "modern war" of the Nazis against the Jews in the previous century. (One might compare this with hate pollution coming out of many exhausts, as opposed to hate pollution coming mainly out of a huge chimney, which spreads it over the whole globe.)

The combination of a great variety of hate originators using multiple instruments leads to new global and national anti-Semitic environments. In it anti-Israelism or anti-Zionism and classic antisemitism overlap to a large extent as can be seen from a detailed analysis made of opinion polls, written texts, and cartoons.[4]

The use of a common definition of antisemitism can play an important role in the battle against this hate propagation. As such we recommend the Working Definition of Antisemitism of the European Union Monitoring Centre on Racism and Xenophobia.[5]

---

1 Manfred Gerstenfeld, "Anti-Semitism and Jewish Defense at the United Nations World Summit on Sustainable Development, 2002 Johannesburg, South Africa," interview with Shimon Samuels, *Post-Holocaust and Anti-Semitism*, No. 6, 2 March 2003. *http://www.jcpa.org/JCPA/Templates/ShowPage.asp?DRIT=3 &DBID=1&LNGID=1&TMID=111&FID=624&PID=0&IID=737&TTL=Anti-Semitism_and_Jewish_Defense_at_the_ United_Nations_World_Summit_on_Sustainable_Development,_2002_Johannesburg,_South_Africa*

2 Manfred Gerstenfeld, "The Twenty-first-century Total War Against Israel and the Jews: Part One," *Post-Holocaust and Anti-Semitism*, No. 38, 1 November 2005. *http://www.jcpa.org/JCPA/Templates/ShowPage. asp?DRIT=3&DBID=1&LNGID=1&TMID=111&FID=624&PID=0&IID=584&TTL=The_Twenty-first-century_Total_War_ Against_Israel_and_the_Jews_Part_One*

3 Manfred Gerstenfeld, "The Twenty-first-century Total War Against Israel and the Jews: Part Two," *Post-Holocaust and Anti-Semitism*, No. 56, 1 December 2005. *http://www.jcpa.org/JCPA/Templates/ShowPage. asp?DRIT=3&DBID=1&LNGID=1&TMID=111&FID=624&PID=0&IID=583&TTL=The_Twenty-first-century_Total_War_ Against_Israel_and_the_Jews_Part_Two*

4 Manfred Gerstenfeld, "Anti-Israelism and Anti-Semitism: Common Characteristics and Motifs," *Jewish Political Studies Review* 19:1-2, Spring 2007. *http://www.jcpa.org/JCPA/Templates/ ShowPage.asp?DRIT=3&DBID=1&LNGID=1&TMID=111&FID=625&PID=1666&IID=1673&TTL=A nti-Israelism_and_Anti-Semitism:_Common_Characteristics_and_Motifs*

5 Michael Whine, "Progress in the Struggle Against Anti-Semitism in Europe: The Berlin Declaration and the European Union Monitoring Centre on Racism and Xenophobia's Working Definition of Anti-Semitism," *Post-Holocaust and Anti-Semitism*, No. 41, 1 February 2006. *http://www.jcpa.org/JCPA/Templates/ ShowPage.asp?DRIT=3&DBID=1&LNGID=1&TMID=111&FID=624&PID=0&IID=580&TTL=Progress_in_the_ Struggle_Against_Anti-Semitism_in_Europe:_The_Berlin_Declaration_and_the_European_Union_Monitoring_ Centre_on_Racism_and_Xenophobia%27s_Working_Definition_of_Anti-Semitism*

Originators of Antisemitism in the 21st Century

At present a number of major originators of antisemitism exist.

(1) *Antisemitism emanating from Muslim countries:*[6] Antisemitism is widely spread in Arab and other Muslim countries. Extreme antisemitic incitement comes from many sources in the Muslim world including from governments of countries who are at peace with Israel. The most extreme hate manifestation originates in Iran, whose president Mahmoud Ahmadinejad is a genocide promoter. This has not prevented Western government officials, religious leaders and academics to host him in their countries. Palestinian antisemitism has many genocidal elements.

(2) *Antisemitism from Muslim communities in the Western world:*[7] The mass immigration to Western countries from the Muslim world has also meant the arrival among these of a significant numbers of extreme antisemites of a type often unknown previously in those states. One example is the public calls, mainly by Muslim, of 'Death to the Jews'

6 David Cook, "Anti-Semitic Themes in Muslim Apocalyptic and Jihadi Literature," *Post-Holocaust and Anti-Semitism*, No. 56, 1 May 2007. http://www.jcpa.org/JCPA/Templates/ShowPage.asp?DRIT=0&DBID=1&LNGID=1&TMID=111&FID=624&PID=0&IID=1554&TTL=Anti-Semitic_Themes_in_Muslim_Apocalyptic_and_Jihadi_Literature

Itamar Marcus and Barbara Crook, "Anti-Semitism among Palestinian Authority Academics," *Post-Holocaust and Anti-Semitism*, No. 69, 1 June 2008.http://www.jcpa.org/JCPA/Templates/ShowPage.asp?DRIT=3&DBID=1&LNGID=1&TMID=111&FID=624&PID=0&IID=2205&TTL=Anti-Semitism_among_Palestinian_Authority_Academics

Manfred Gerstenfeld, "Major Anti-Semitic Motifs in Arab Cartoons," interview with Joël Kotek, *Post-Holocaust and Anti-Semitism*, No. 21, 1 June 2004. http://www.jcpa.org/JCPA/Templates/ShowPage.asp?DRIT=3&DBID=1&LNGID=1&TMID=111&FID=624&PID=0&IID=644&TTL=Major_Anti-Semitic_Motifs_in_Arab_Cartoons

Manfred Gerstenfeld, "The Development of Arab Anti-Semitism," interview with Meir Litvak, *Post-Holocaust and Anti-Semitism*, No. 5, 2 February 2003. http://www.jcpa.org/JCPA/Templates/ShowPage.asp?DRIT=3&DBID=1&LNGID=1&TMID=111&FID=624&PID=0&IID=741&TTL=The_Development_of_Arab_Anti-Semitism

7 Mikael Tossavainen, "Arab and Muslim Anti-Semitism in Sweden," *Jewish Political Studies Review* 17:3-4, Fall 2005. http://www.jcpa.org/JCPA/Templates/ShowPage.asp?DRIT=5&DBID=1&LNGID=1&TMID=111&FID=610&PID=861&IID=1028&TTL=Arab_and_Muslim_Anti-Semitism_in_Sweden

Mikael Tossavainen, "Jewish-Muslim Relations in Sweden," *Changing Jewish Communities*, No. 40, 15 January 2009. http://www.jcpa.org/JCPA/Templates/ShowPage.asp?DRIT=4&DBID=1&LNGID=1&TMID=111&FID=610&PID=0&IID=2746&TTL=Jewish-Muslim_Relations_in_Sweden

Simon Erlanger, "Muslims and Jews in Switzerland," *Changing Jewish Communities*, No. 37, 15 October 2008. http://www.jcpa.org/JCPA/Templates/ShowPage.asp?DRIT=0&DBID=1&LNGID=1&TMID=111&FID=610&PID=0&IID=2606&TTL=Muslims_and_Jews_in_Switzerland

Manfred Gerstenfeld, "Muslim-Jewish Interactions in Great Britain," interview with Michael Whine, *Changing Jewish Communities*, No. 32, 15 May 2008. http://www.jcpa.org/JCPA/Templates/ShowPage.asp?DRIT=4&DBID=1&LNGID=1&TMID=111&FID=610&PID=0&IID=2200&TTL=Muslim-Jewish_Interactions_in_Great_Britain

Manfred Gerstenfeld, "Muslim-Jewish Relations in Australia: Challenges and Threats," interview with Jeremy Jones, *Changing Jewish Communities*, No. 45, 15 June 2009. http://www.jcpa.org/JCPA/Templates/ShowPage.asp?DRIT=4&DBID=1&LNGID=1&TMID=111&FID=610&PID=0&IID=2974&TTL=Muslim-Jewish_Relations_in_Australia:_Challenges_and_Threats

Manfred Gerstenfeld, "Muslim-Jewish Interaction in the Netherlands," *Changing Jewish Communities*, No. 26, 15 November 2007. http://www.jcpa.org/JCPA/Templates/ShowPage.asp?DBID=1&TMID=111&LNGID=1&FID=623&PID=0&IID=1897

or similar slogans in anti-Israeli demonstrations including, for the first time since the war, in Germany. European governments often try to avoid the subject of extreme racism among minorities coming to the surface or getting the required public attention. Parts of the European elites falsely claim that only white people can be racists.

(3) *State sponsored antisemitism:*[8] Since the fall of communism, state-promoted or state-sponsored antisemitism to varying degrees mainly occur in Arab and Muslim countries. However, in a number of other countries the anti-Israeli positions of governments create a societal climate inductive to antisemitism. Venezuela is one such example. To a much lesser extent the phenomenon also exists with the current Labor party dominated government of Norway.

(4) *The extreme Right:*[9] The antisemitic extreme right presently has a revival in Europe. In Eastern European countries this is partly stimulated by reactions to communism and economic problems. In Western Europe the problems related to mass immigration, poor integration of immigrants, as well extreme anti-Western racism among some immigrant groups are enhancing this development.

(5) *The far Left and currents in socialist parties:*[10] Politicians of the extreme left and sometimes also those of socialist parties play a major role in the demonization of Israel. During the recent Gaza war for instance, Swedish Social Democrat politicians participated in demonstrations in which there were shouts of 'Death to the Jews', swastikas, and banners of Arab terror movements calling for the genocide of Israel. In Norway, even a government minister participated in such a demonstration.[11]

---

8 Manfred Gerstenfeld, "Ahmadinejad Calls for Israel's Elimination and Declares War on the West: A Case Study of Incitement to Genocide," Jerusalem Viewpoints, No. 536, 1 November 2005. *http://www.jcpa.org/jl/vp536.htm*

Manfred Gerstenfeld, "Another Year of Anti-Semitism and Anti-Israelism in Norway," Post-Holocaust and Anti-Semitism, No. 82, 1 July 2009. *http://www.jcpa.org/JCPA/Templates/ShowPage.asp?DRIT=3&DBID=1&LNGID=1&TMID =111&FID=624&PID=0&IID=3000&TTL=Another_Year_of_Anti-Semitism_and_Anti-Israelism_in_Norway*

9 Thomas Haury, "Current Anti-Semitism in East Germany," *Post-Holocaust and Anti-Semitism*, No.59, 1 August 2007. *http://www.jcpa.org/JCPA/Templates/ShowPage.asp?DRIT=0&DBID=1&LNGID=1&TMID=111 &FID=624&PID=0&IID=1612&TTL=Current_Anti-Semitism_in_East_Germany*

10 Ben Cohen, "The Persistence of Anti-Semitism on the British Left," Jewish Political Studies Review 16:3-4, Fall 2004. *http://www.jcpa.org/JCPA/Templates/ShowPage.asp?DRIT=3&DBID=1&LNGID=1&TMID=111&FID=625 &PID=863&IID=1075&TTL=The_Persistence_of_Anti-Semitism_on_the_British_Left*

Dave Rich, "Holocaust Denial as an Anti-Zionist and Anti-Imperialist Tool for the European Far Left," Post-Holocaust and Anti-Semitism, No. 65, 1 February 2008. *http://www.jcpa.org/JCPA/Templates/ShowPage. asp?DRIT=3&DBID=1&LNGID=1&TMID=111&FID=624&PID=0&IID=2011&TTL=The_Holocaust_as_an_Anti-Zionist_ and_Anti-Imperialist_Tool_for_the_Left*

11 Manfred Gerstenfeld and Tamas Berzi, "The Gaza War and the New Outburst of Anti-Semitism," *Post-Holocaust and Anti-Semitism*, No. 79, 1 April 2009. *http://www.jcpa.org/JCPA/Templates/ShowPage.asp?DRIT=3 &DBID=1&LNGID=1&TMID=111&FID=624&PID=0&IID=2895&TTL=The_Gaza_War_and_the_New_Outburst_of_ Anti-Semitism*

(6) *Media:*[12] Media often report about the Middle East in a one-sided anti-Israeli manner. They ignore context and often underline real or perceived negative acts of Israel, while regularly omitting information about far more negative events in the Arab or Muslim world, including Palestinian society. For many Muslim immigrants in Western countries in particular, but also for others, there is often no distinction between Jews and Israel. The biased media information thus indirectly leads to physical and verbal attacks on local Jews as well. Media are both originators and instruments of classic anti-Semitism and anti-Israelism.

(7) *Academics:*[13] Anti-Israeli and antisemitic actions in academia manifest themselves in biased teaching, boycott proposals, divestment initiatives,

---

12 Manfred Gerstenfeld, "The Muhammad Al-Dura Blood Libel: A Case Analysis," interview with Richard Landes, *Post-Holocaust and Anti-Semitism*, No. 74, 1 November 2008. *http://www.jcpa.org/JCPA/Templates/ShowPage.asp?DRIT=3 &DBID=1&LNGID=1&TMID=111&FID=624&PID=0&IID=2658&TTL=The_Muhammad_Al-Dura_Blood_Libel:_A_ Case_Analysis*

Manfred Gerstenfeld, "CAMERA: Fighting Distorted Media Coverage of Israel and the Middle East," interview with Andrea Levin, *Post-Holocaust and Anti-Semitism*, No. 33, 1 June 2005. *http://www.jcpa.org/JCPA/ Templates/ShowPage.asp?DRIT=3&DBID=1&LNGID=1&TMID=111&FID=624&PID=0&IID=607&TTL=CAMERA:_ Fighting_Distorted_Media_Coverage_of_Israel_and_the_Middle_East*

Joel Fishman, "The Big Lie and the Media War Against Israel: From Inversion of the Truth to Inversion of Reality," *Jewish Political Studies Review* 19:1-2, Spring 2007.*http://www.jcpa.org/JCPA/Templates/ShowPage. asp?DRIT=3&DBID=1&LNGID=1&TMID=111&FID=624&PID=0&IID=1704&TTL=The_Big_Lie_and_the_Media_ War_Against_Israel:_From_Inversion_of_the_Truth_to_Inversion_of_Reality*

Joel Fishman, "The Big Lie and the Media War Against Israel: From Inversion of the Truth to Inversion of Reality," *Jewish Political Studies Review* 19:1-2, Spring 2007. *http://www.jcpa.org/JCPA/Templates/ShowPage. asp?DRIT=3&DBID=1&LNGID=1&TMID=111&FID=624&PID=0&IID=1704&TTL=The_Big_Lie_and_the_Media_ War_Against_Israel:_From_Inversion_of_the_Truth_to_Inversion_of_Reality*

13 Tammi Rossman-Benjamin, "Anti-Zionism and the Abuse of Academic Freedom: A Case Study at the University of California, Santa Cruz," *Post-Holocaust and Anti-Semitism*, No. 77, 1 February 2009. *http://www.jcpa.org/JCPA/ Templates/ShowPage.asp?DBID=1&LNGID=1&TMID=111&FID=624&PID=0&IID=2812*

Manfred Gerstenfeld, "2007-2008: Another Year of Global Academic Anti-Semitism and Anti-Israelism," *Post-Holocaust and Anti-Semitism*, No. 73, 1 October 2008. *http://www.jcpa.org/JCPA/Templates/ShowPage. asp?DRIT=3&DBID=1&LNGID=1&TMID=111&FID=624&PID=0&IID=2518&TTL=2007-2008:_Another_Year_of_ Global_Academic_Anti-Semitism_and_Anti-Israelism*

Manfred Gerstenfeld, "Recent Developments on the Academic Boycott: A Case Study," *Post-Holocaust and Anti-Semitism*, No. 61, 1 October 2007. *http://www.jcpa.org/JCPA/Templates/ShowPage.asp?DRIT=3&DBID=1&LNGID=1 &TMID=111&FID=624&PID=0&IID=1832&TTL=Recent_Developments_on_the_Academic_Boycott:_A_Case_Study*

Manfred Gerstenfeld, "How to Fight Anti-Israeli Campaigns on Campus," *Post-Holocaust and Anti-Semitism*, No. 51, 1 December 2006. *http://www.jcpa.org/JCPA/Templates/ShowPage.asp?DRIT=3&DBID=1&LNGID=1&TMID=111 &FID=624&PID=0&IID=1255&TTL=How_to_Fight_Anti-Israeli_Campaigns_on_Campus*

Ronnie Fraser, "The Academic Boycott of Israel: Why Britain?," *Post-Holocaust and Anti-Semitism*, No. 36, 1 September 2005. *http://www.jcpa.org/JCPA/Templates/ShowPage.asp?DRIT=3&DBID=1&LNGID=1&TMID=111 &FID=624&PID=0&IID=603&TTL=The_Academic_Boycott_of_Israel:_Why_Britain?*

Yves Pallade, "New Anti-Semitism in Contemporary German Academia," *Jewish Political Studies Review* 21:1-2, Spring 2009. *http://www.jcpa.org/JCPA/Templates/ShowPage.asp?DRIT=3&DBID=1&LNGID=1&TMID=111 &FID=624&PID=0&IID=3018&TTL=%22New%22_Anti-Semitism_in_Contemporary_German_Academia*

Avi Weinryb, "The University of Toronto - The Institution where Israel Apartheid Week was Born," *Jewish Political Studies Review* 20:3-4, Fall 2008. *http://www.jcpa.org/JCPA/Templates/ShowPage.asp?DBID=1&LNGID=1 &TMID=111&FID=624&PID=0&IID=2778*

discrimination of Jews identifying with Israel and sometimes classic antisemitic acts. Such initiatives recur on a number of campuses in countries among which the main ones are Great Britain, Canada, and the United States. Anti-Israeli teachers are often also clustered worldwide in some disciplines, such as Middle Eastern studies and linguistics. These and other hate phenomena have been analyzed in detail in a book titled *Academics against Israel and the Jews* published by the Jerusalem Center for Public Affairs.[14]

(8) *NGOs:*[15] Non-governmental organizations are in the forefront of attacks on Israel, many of which according to the EUMC working definition have an antisemitic character.

(9) *Several Christian movements:*[16] Several Christian movements, in the United States, Canada, some European countries and a variety of developing countries, play an important role in anti-Israeli actions with a strong antisemitic character. Many among these are mainstream Protestants. They propose discriminatory measures against Israel, without taking similar positions against other countries, which are extreme human rights abusers. Theological reasons sometimes play a major role in antisemitic actions. While a number of activities of originators of

Alain Goldschläger, "The Canadian Campus Scene" In: Manfred Gerstenfeld (ed.), *Academics against Israel and the Jews* (Jerusalem: Jerusalem Center for Public Affairs, 2007). http://www.jcpa.org/JCPA/Templates/ShowPage. asp?DRIT=3&DBID=1&LNGID=1&TMID=111&FID=624&PID=0&IID=2614&TTL=The_Canadian_Campus_Scene

Corinne Berzon, "Anti-Israeli Activity at Concordia University 2000-2003" In: Manfred Gerstenfeld (ed.), *Academics against Israel and the Jews* (Jerusalem: Jerusalem Center for Public Affairs, 2007). http://www.jcpa.org/ JCPA/Templates/ShowPage.asp?DRIT=3&DBID=1&LNGID=1&TMID=111&FID=610&PID=0&IID=2638 &TTL=Anti-Israeli_Activity_a_Concordia_University_2000-2003

14 Manfred Gerstenfeld (ed.), *Academics against Israel and the Jews* (Jerusalem: Jerusalem Center for Public Affairs, 2007).

15 Gerald Steinberg, "The Centrality of NGOs In Promoting Anti-Israel Boycotts And Sanctions," *Jewish Political Studies Review* 21:1-2, Spring 2009. http://www.jcpa.org/JCPA/Templates/ShowPage.asp?DRIT=3&DBID=1 &LNGID=1&TMID=111&FID=624&PID=2959&IID=2957&TTL=The_Centrality_of_NGOs_In_Promoting_Anti-Israel_ Boycotts_And_Sanctions

16 Dexter Van Zile, "Mennonites against Israel," *Post-Holocaust and Anti-Semitism*, No. 83, 1 August 2009. http://www.jcpa.org/JCPA/Templates/ShowPage.asp?DRIT=3&DBID=1&LNGID=1&TMID=111&FID=624&PID=0 &IID=3023&TTL=Mennonites_against_Israel

Manfred Gerstenfeld, "Christian Friends and Foes of Israel," interview with David Parsons, *Post-Holocaust and Anti-Semitism*, No. 78, 1 March 2009. http://www.jcpa.org/JCPA/Templates/ShowPage.asp?DRIT=3 &DBID=1&LNGID=1&TMID=111&FID=624&PID=0&IID=2877&TTL=Christian_Friends_and_Foes_of_Israel

Manfred Gerstenfeld, "The Historical Roots of the Anti-Israel Positions of Liberal Protestant Churches," interview with Hans Jansen, Post-Holocaust and Anti-Semitism, No. 57, 1 June 2007. http://www.jcpa.org/JCPA/Templates/ShowPage.asp?DRIT=0&DBID=1&LNGID=1&TMID=111&FID=624&PID=0& IID=1565&TTL=The_Profound_Historical_Roots_of_Protestant_Anti-Semitism

Eugene Korn, "Divestment from Israel, the Liberal Churches, and Jewish Responses: A Strategic Analysis," Post-Holocaust and Anti-Semitism, No. 52, 1 January 2007. http://www.jcpa.org/JCPA/Templates/ ShowPage.asp?DBID=1&LNGID=1&TMID=111&FID=624&PID=0&IID=1421&TTL=Divestment_from_Israel,_the_ Liberal_Churches,_and_Jewish_Responses:_A_Strategic_Analysis

antisemitism in various fields—such as media, academics, NGOs and
the United Nations—are monitored by various bodies, this is not the
case for Christian antisemitism.

(10) **Trade unions:**[17] In some countries, trade unions are in the forefront
of the anti-Israeli battle. They promote discriminatory actions against
Israel, while avoiding such actions against extreme offenders of human
rights. The main such trade unions are in the United Kingdom and
Ireland. Other countries where these have manifested themselves
include Canada, South Africa, Norway, and Denmark.

(11) **United Nations:**[18] The United Nations is both an originator and an
instrument of antisemitism. One extreme form in which this manifests itself is the multiple anti-Israeli resolutions of the UN General
Assembly. Another is the multiple discriminatory resolutions of the
United Nations Human Rights Council.

(12) **Jewish Antisemites:**[19] Anti-Israeli and self-hating Jews are often in the
forefront of the anti-Israel battle. They may not be very numerous, but

---

17 Ronnie Fraser, "Trade Union and Other Boycotts of Israel in Great Britain and Ireland," *Post-Holocaust and Anti-Semitism*, No. 76, 1 January 2009. *http://www.jcpa.org/JCPA/Templates/ShowPage.asp?DRIT=0 &DBID=1&LNGID=1&TMID=111&FID=624&PID=0&IID=2717&TTL=Trade_Union_and_Other_Boycotts_of_Israel_in_ Great_Britain_and_Ireland*

18 Alfred H. Moses, "From Durban I to Durban II: Preventing Poisonous Anti-Semitism," *Post-Holocaust and Anti-Semitism*, No. 71, 1 August 2008. *http://www.jcpa.org/JCPA/Templates/ShowPage.asp?DRIT=3&DBID=1 &LNGID=1&TMID=111&FID=624&PID=0&IID=2312&TTL=From_Durban_I_to_Durban_II:_Preventing_Poisonous_ Anti-Semitism*

Hillel C. Neuer, "The Struggle against Anti-Israel Bias at the UN Commission on Human Rights," *Post-Holocaust and Anti-Semitism*, No. 40, 1 January 2006. *http://www.jcpa.org/JCPA/Templates/ShowPage. asp?DRIT=3&DBID=1&LNGID=1&TMID=111&FID=624&PID=0&IID=581&TTL=The_Struggle_against_Anti-Israel_ Bias_at_the_UN_Commission_on_Human_Rights*

Manfred Gerstenfeld, "Europe's Consistent Anti-Israeli Bias at the United Nations," interview with Dore Gold, *Post-Holocaust and Anti-Semitism*, No. 34, 1 July 2005. *http://www.jcpa.org/JCPA/Templates/ ShowPage.asp?DRIT=3&DBID=1&LNGID=1&TMID=111&FID=624&PID=0&IID=615&TTL=Europe%27s_Consistent_ Anti-Israeli_Bias_at_the_United_Nations*

Manfred Gerstenfeld, "The United Nations: Leading Global Purveyor of Anti-Semitism," interview with Anne Bayefsky, *Post-Holocaust and Anti-Semitism*, No. 31, 1 April 2005. *http://www.jcpa.org/JCPA/ Templates/ShowPage.asp?DRIT=3&DBID=1&LNGID=1&TMID=111&FID=624&PID=0&IID=612&TTL=The_United_ Nations:_Leading_Global_Purveyor_of_Anti-Semitism*

Manfred Gerstenfeld, "Anti-Semitism and Jewish Defense at the United Nations World Summit on Sustainable Development, 2002 Johannesburg, South Africa," interview with Shimon Samuels, *Post-Holocaust and Anti-Semitism*, No. 6, 2 March 2003. *http://www.jcpa.org/JCPA/Templates/ShowPage.asp?DRIT=3 &DBID=1&LNGID=1&TMID=111&FID=624&PID=0&IID=737&TTL=Anti-Semitism_and_Jewish_Defense_at_the_ United_Nations_World_Summit_on_Sustainable_Development,_2002_Johannesburg,_South_Africa*

Manfred Gerstenfeld, "The United Nations: Leading Global Purveyor of Anti-Semitism," interview with Anne Bayefsky, Post-Holocaust and Anti-Semitism, No. 31, 1 April 2005. *http://www.jcpa.org/JCPA/ Templates/ShowPage.asp?DRIT=3&DBID=1&LNGID=1&TMID=111&FID=624&PID=0&IID=612&TTL=The_United_ Nations:_Leading_Global_Purveyor_of_Anti-Semitism*

19 Manfred Gerstenfeld, "Jews against Israel," *Post-Holocaust and Anti-Semitism*, No. 30, 1 March 2005. *http://www.jcpa.org/JCPA/Templates/ShowPage.asp?DRIT=3&DBID=1&LNGID=1&TMID=111&FID=624&PID=0&IID=614 &TTL=Jews_against_Israel*

they often serve to legitimize the actions of other antisemites. They are thus both originators and instruments.

(13) **High Schools:**[20] Biased teaching in high schools has two sources: biased text books and teachers. Regarding the former, studies are available in some countries. Only anecdotic information is available about the latter.

Instruments of antisemitism

(1) *Lawfare:*[21] In recent years the interpretation of international law in an anti-Israeli way has become a major tool in the battle against Israel.

(2) *Semantics:*[22] Extreme semantics have become a major tool against Israel. From the point of language anti-Zionism has evolved into an ideology. The master equation that dominates this discourse is that Zionism is Nazism. In recent years many of Israel's enemies have falsely accused it of being an apartheid state. This coordinated action was decided at the time of the Durban 2001 Conference.

(3) *Teaching:* Teaching at universities and high schools sometimes conveys antisemitic concepts. Some teachers at universities promote anti-Israeli ideology instead of the advancement of knowledge. At some universities Jewish students feel physically threatened. Conferences of an antisemitic character take place at several universities, for instance about Israel's right to exist. Similar discussions do not take place with respect to any other nation. This illustrates the highly discriminatory character of such gatherings.

(4) *Cartoons:* Cartoons are concentrated tools for transmitting antisemitic messages. Many originate from Arab and Muslim sources including countries

---

20 Manfred Gerstenfeld, "How American Textbooks Mislead on Jews and Israel," The Trouble with Textbooks: Distorting History and Religion, by Gary A. Tobin and Dennis R. Ybarra, Lanham, MD: Lexington Books, 209 pp. *Jewish Political Studies Review* 21:1-2, Spring 2009. http://www.jcpa.org/JCPA/Templates/ShowPage.asp?DRIT=4&DBID=1&LNGID=1&TMID=111&FID=625&PID=0&IID=3030&TTL=Manfred_Gerstenfeld_on_The_Trouble_with_Textbooks:_Distorting_History_and_Religion,_by_Gary_A._Tobin_and_Dennis_R._Ybarra

21 Abraham Bell, "International Law and Gaza: The Assault on Israel's Right to Self-Defense," *Jerusalem Issue Briefs*, Vol. 9, No. 29, 28 January 2008. http://www.jcpa.org/JCPA/Templates/ShowPage.asp?DRIT=1&DBID=1&LNGID=1&TMID=111&FID=378&PID=0&IID=2021&TTL=International_Law_and_Gaza:_The_Assault_on_Israel%E2%80%99s_Right_to_Self-Defense

Dore Gold, "Did Israel Use "Disproportionate Force" in Gaza?" *Jerusalem Issue Briefs*, Vol. 8, No. 16, 28 December 2008. http://www.jcpa.org/JCPA/Templates/ShowPage.asp?DRIT=1&DBID=1&LNGID=1&TMID=111&FID=378&PID=0&IID=2808&TTL=Did_Israel_Use_%E2%80%9CDisproportionate_Force%E2%80%9D_in_Gaza?

22 Manfred Gerstenfeld, "Deconstructing Apartheid Accusations Against Israel," interview with Gideon Shimoni, *Post-Holocaust and Anti-Semitism*, No. 60, 1 September 2007. http://www.jcpa.org/JCPA/Templates/ShowPage.asp?DRIT=3&DBID=1&LNGID=1&TMID=111&FID=624&PID=0&IID=1806&TTL=Deconstructing_Apartheid_Accusations_Against_Israel

Manfred Gerstenfeld, "Language as a Tool against Jews and Israel," interview with Georges-Elia Sarfati, *Post-Holocaust and Anti-Semitism*, No. 17, 1 February 2004. http://www.jcpa.org/JCPA/Templates/ShowPage.asp?DRIT=3&DBID=1&LNGID=1&TMID=111&FID=624&PID=0&IID=656&TTL=Language_as_a_Tool_against_Jews_and_Israel

which are at peace with Israel. They also appear in government journals. Many extreme antisemitic cartoons have been published in Europe also, mainly in Greece and Norway, but in other countries as well.

(5) **Internet:**[23] Antisemitism has adapted itself to the internet. Spreading antisemitism there is increasingly effective. It may well lead to a culture where antisemitism is socially acceptable.

(6) **The Battle for the Public Square:** During Operation Cast Lead a new phenomenon merited particular attention. Groups of often violent Muslims tried to conquer the public square and at the same time to remove Jewish and Israeli symbols from it. Sometimes the authorities assisted in this process, such as in some towns in Germany and Sweden. In various cities Muslims attacked pro-Israeli demonstrations as well as Jews in the streets. There were arson attempts against Jewish institutions. After some anti-Israeli demonstrations, Muslim prayer services were held in public places—in Europe and the United States. The roles of Muslim organizations in these activities have been not been sufficiently investigated. Attempts to remove Jewish and Israeli symbols from the public square have occurred in the past, mainly on an individual basis (such as attacking people carrying Israeli flags, or wearing kippot or Stars of David). In these cases the perpetrators were not necessarily mainly Muslims.

(7) **Abuses of Holocaust Memory:**[24] The main abuse of Holocaust memory has for a long time been Holocaust denial. Additional categories such as Holocaust justification, inversion and obliteration are however becoming important as well. These sometimes appear together with the

23 Andre Oboler, "Online Antisemitism 2.0. 'Social Antisemitism' on the 'Social Web'," *Post-Holocaust and Anti-Semitism*, No. 67, 1 April 2008. *http://www.jcpa.org/JCPA/Templates/ShowPage.asp?DRIT=3&DBID=1&LNGID=1&TMID=111&FID=624&PID=0&IID=2235&TTL=Online_Antisemitism_2.0._*

Michael Whine, "Cyberhate, Antisemitism, and Counterlegislation," *Post-Holocaust and Anti-Semitism*, No. 47, 1 August 2006. *http://www.jcpa.org/JCPA/Templates/ShowPage.asp?DRIT=3&DBID=1&LNGID=1&TMID=111&FID=624&PID=0&IID=566&TTL=Cyberhate,_Antisemitism,_and_Counterlegislation*

Manfred Gerstenfeld, "Anti-Semitism and Terrorism on the Internet: New Threats," interview with Rabbi Abraham Cooper, *Post-Holocaust and Anti-Semitism*, No. 20-A, 16 May 2004. *http://www.jcpa.org/JCPA/Templates/ShowPage.asp?DRIT=3&DBID=1&LNGID=1&TMID=111&FID=624&PID=0&IID=646&TTL=Anti-Semitism_and_Terrorism_on_the_Internet:_New_Threats*

24 Manfred Gerstenfeld, "Denial of the Holocaust and Immoral Equivalence," interview with Deborah Lipstadt, *Post-Holocaust and Anti-Semitism*, No. 11, 1 August 2003. *http://www.jcpa.org/JCPA/Templates/ShowPage.asp?DRIT=3&DBID=1&LNGID=1&TMID=111&FID=624&PID=0&IID=692&TTL=Denial_of_the_Holocaust_and_Immoral_Equivalence*

Manfred Gerstenfeld, "Holocaust Inversion: The Portraying of Israel and Jews as Nazis," *Post-Holocaust and Anti-Semitism*, No. 55, 1 April 2007. *http://www.jcpa.org/JCPA/Templates/ShowPage.asp?DRIT=0&DBID=1&LNGID=1&TMID=111&FID=624&PID=0&IID=1526&TTL=Holocaust_Inversion:_The_Portraying_of_Israel_and_Jews_as_Nazis*

Manfred Gerstenfeld, "The Multiple Distortions of Holocaust Memory," Jewish Political Studies Review 19:3-4, Fall 2007. *http://www.jcpa.org/JCPA/Templates/ShowPage.asp?DRIT=3&DBID=1&LNGID=1&TMID=111&FID=624&PID=0&IID=1903&TTL=The_Multiple_Distortions_of_Holocaust_Memory*

promotion of alleged Jewish conspiracy theories. A new book on the contemporary abuse of Holocaust memory is under preparation at the Jerusalem Center and will be published later this year.

The subjects of the media, the United Nations and Jewish antisemites, which are both originators and instruments of antisemitism have been discussed above in the section on originators.

Impacts of antisemitism

Global and national anti-Semitic incitement and aggression has already had a number of important impacts in various Western societies.

(1) Increased security measures had to be taken for Jewish and Israeli institutions. These often also concern locations other than places of worship and schools.

(2) Many Jewish communities try to adopt low profile attitudes.

(3) Threats have forced Jews in many places to disguise their identity in the public square. (Not wearing kippot or stars of David)

(4) Jewish communities attempt to avoid conflicts with authorities who take discriminatory positions.

(5) Attempts by anti-Israelis to change the content of Holocaust Memorial Day.

(6) Some Jews try to become acceptable to anti-Israeli elites by attacking Israel.

(7) Some Jews distance themselves as much as possible from the Jewish community, saying that identifying as Jews today has only negative consequences in the circles they frequent.

(8) A so far limited emigration of Jews from Europe has taken place, motivated by the reemergence of substantial anti-Semitism.

(9) The issue of the future of Jews in Europe has become again a matter of discussion in a number of European Jewish communities.

Recommendations

Many recommendations from the all-party Parliamentary inquiry into Antisemitism in Great Britain can probably be adapted for other countries.

The following specific recommendations are partly derived from the British report and partly from our experience in studying global antisemitism:

(1) Adoption of the EUMC Working Definition of antisemitism by the Government and law enforcement agencies.

(2) Consistent government and parliamentary condemnation of boycott attempts.

(3) The systematic monitoring and recording of antisemitic incidents by the competent authorities.

(4) Intensified policing of hatred on the Internet.

(5) The systematic monitoring of antisemitic incitement—including anti-Israeli incitement—and government financial support should be made available for such monitoring bodies.

(6) The establishment and support of academic centers for the study of antisemitism in Canada.

(7) The sponsoring of interdisciplinary study groups of case studies of antisemitism.

(8) In view of the global character of antisemitism and anti-Zionism a study group should be established to follow these phenomena.

Alain Goldschläger

Professor Alain Goldschläger is currently a professor at the University of Western University (London, Canada), with expertise in French language and literature of the Shoah. He is currently serving as Director of the Holocaust Literature Research Institute (HLRI), which he founded in 1996. The member of several prestigious research groups, Dr. Goldschläger was a founding member and president of the Canadian Semiotic Association (1981-1983), president of the Canadian Comparative Literature Association (1985-1987), a distinguished member of the Canadian Federation for the Humanities (1981-1988), and Director of the Canada-Israel Foundation for Academic Exchanges (1988-2003).

Since 2004, M. Goldschläger has been President of the League for Human Rights of B'nai B'rith—Ontario, helped create and taught at the *General Romeo Dallaire Summer Institute on the teaching of the Holocaust and Genocide,* member of the Canadian Commission of UNESCO sub-Committees on Culture and the Status of Women. Dr. Goldschläger was Chair of the National Task Force on Holocaust Education, Remembrance and Research (2009-2012), as well as the Canadian Delegate to the International Task Force on Holocaust Education, Remembrance and Research 2009 to present) and Canadian Delegate to the Holocaust Era Assets Conference (Prague 2009).

Professor Alain Goldschläger[*]

Director, Holocaust Literature Research Institute, University of Western Ontario; Ontario Chair, League for Human Rights of B'nai Brith Canada (London, ON)

Written Submission Prepared by Professor Alain Goldschläger for the Canadian Parliamentary Coalition to Combat Antisemitism prepared August 2009.

Antisemitism in Canada: Variations in Space and Time

Canadian antisemitism has constantly changed its shape to reflect the type of society, the times and the local situations. For many years, two kinds of antisemitism, corresponding to two different types of society, have been spreading in Canada.

In Anglophone settings, antisemitism has long taken the form of a social and linguistic encoding that tends to conceal prejudice while seemingly giving it a wide-open forum. Because it wants to keep its position of economic power, the English-speaking world rejects Jews since, while they are effective participants, their blood is the wrong colour. A number of laws, regulations, euphemisms and understatements serve to isolate the Jewish community while maintaining the appearance of polite acceptance.[1] Below polished exteriors, severe discrimination confines the Jewish community to occupational niches and specific locations whose presence reinforces hardened prejudices. This antisemitism avoids verbal outbursts and physical violence. It attempts to maintain social peace by imprisoning Jews in physical and social ghettos that keep them in a parallel life, in "apartheid." In the multicultural world of recent decades, the question of the Jews' status is seldom asked, because the children of Israel do not form part of the "visible communities." They therefore cannot claim the special protections reserved for social groups perceived as objects of discrimination. Jews find themselves in a kind of limbo. They are supposedly part of the national majority, but they are kept out of the decision-making centres and remain the object of prejudice that is as effective as it is discreet.

Traditionally, Quebec based its antisemitism on the doctrine of a religious idea. For that reason, it is less reluctant to proclaim its exclusionary attitudes toward those who are other, different. Through the constant defence of its national character, Quebec has little room for immigrant cultures. In a province

---

[*] Testimony of Dr. Goldschlager consist of a written submission presented to the Canadian Parliamentary Inquiry into Antisemitism, prepared in August 2009, outlining the evolution and nature of antisemitism within the Canadian context and the emergence of new forms of antisemitism.

1 Of interest in this connection is the description of "Noble and Wolf v. Alley" in *"Race" Rights and the Law in the Supreme Court of Canada*, by James W. St.G. Walker, 1997.

that is divided in two (Montréal and the rest of Quebec), the Jewish community has been virtually expelled from the regions and concentrated in the city. It forms a minority that is well established but takes little part in national governance. Marginalized because of its dual allegiance (to another faith and another language), it is regularly, sometimes virulently, attacked by the nationalists, yet receives no support from other political groups. Debate in Quebec's world is always marked by clearly defined positions. The strong emotions that are expressed frequently result in verbal excesses and sometimes in deplorable physical acts against minorities. The Jewish community is often singled out and used as the example of a group that remains outside the norms of social or moral acceptability and must therefore pay the price of its marginality.

The Jewish community's response to these attacks takes two contrasting paths. As soon as the community settled in Canada in the 19th century, its prominent members attempted to ease the worst effects of segregation through discreet manoeuvring and personal contacts with political leaders. They sought more often to downplay their presence than to obtain respect for their fundamental rights. Social peace became an end in itself: demands for full citizenship status were muted to avoid provoking a backlash by government leaders or local residents. That policy of appeasement at any cost undoubtedly had very serious repercussions when the Canadian government was particularly eager to close the door to refugees before and during the Second World War. We are all too familiar with Canada's dismal record in assisting European jewry. As a result, another voice, more vehement and more willing to resort to furious protests, is being heard today, offering the community two different spokespersons: one expresses himself in hushed tones with limited effect, while the other shouts out challenges that produce some visible successes and failures. Though their tactics differ, their goal is identical: to serve the community's basic needs and defend its rights.

Today we are coming to a critical point for the defence of Jews' fundamental rights. It is therefore time to raise our voices and take action on the public stage.

Canada happily entertains a self-image based on the art of conciliation. The perfect intermediary on the international scene, it seeks middle-of-the-road positions at the national social level, where accommodations of every kind are supposed to defuse conflict and, especially, prevent violence. From this perspective, Canada has been a haven for a wide range of attitudes and arguments, some of them extreme. Limits are placed on such stances only when the public peace is at risk. As a result, in the case of comments on the Middle East conflict, many incendiary words were uttered without much reaction by the authorities. For the sake of appeasement and conformism, Canada has long acquiesced to antisemitic statements and decisions adopted by the United Nations and other international organizations. e. That allegiance sent a clear message to the Jewish community: the government prefers to keep a low profile on the international scene, even if that policy involves victimizing a national minority. Even if this attitude has changed in the past decade, the consequence of the past attitude remains evident today with the worrisome resurgence of antisemitism. The Jewish community's physical and social well-being is in peril : synagogues, schools and community centers have to be placed under police protection. We are almost at the point where Canada, home to refugees from around the world, could become an exclusion zone for its Jewish community.

The close link between anti-Zionism at the international political level and antisemitism in the national social sphere is well known. A convenient pre-text for victimizing the Jews of the Diaspora, primary anti-Zionism, which has become the standard of the international left and many NGOs, is surging and melding with an ancient, viscerally racist antisemitism. Any Jew is being personally accused of blindly supporting every decision made by the Israeli gov-ernment, including its military decisions during hostilities. He thus becomes complicit in what is all too quickly labelled a crime against humanity as seen through the distorting prism of the anti-Zionists. The Canadian Jew is taking up the scapegoat's mantle that his ancestors wore for 20 centuries.

Canada's long silence on the Israeli-Palestinian question, its prevarica-tions regarding verbal excesses, its lack of political courage and its passivity on the international stage have incited a number of groups to use and abuse anti-Zionism to attack the Jewish community and give free rein to a sometimes violent but more often pernicious antisemitism, which poisons today's social discourse. The failure to denounce the excesses produced by various interna-tional organizations and to respond to the racist propagandists may have been perceived by many activist groups as an invitation to turn their resentment on the Jewish community. Today, respect for human rights seems to stop at the doors of the synagogues and the Jewish student clubs, community centres and cemeteries.

The Jewish community currently lives under heavy surveillance. The faithful have to pass by police officers on their way to pray, wracked by anxiety for their safety. Students have to conceal their ethnic identity in the classroom for fear of reprisals from various teachers who have no compunction about making openly racist speeches in front of their audiences, under the guise of discussing the inter-national situation. The Israeli flag, of which community members are proud, is conspicuously burned in the street, and the voices of representatives of Jewish associations are often drowned out by insults as soon as they try to speak. They are condemned even before they open their mouths. Gravestones are regularly desecrated, and some community buildings are "decorated" with Nazi graffiti. Anti-Apartheid week has become an antisemitic feast that university administrations refuse to recognize and open racist attitudes and words are tolerated.

We are seeing the emergence of a new form of antisemitism. The censure levelled at Israel and all of its actions, and the total lack of recognition for its accomplishments (and there are many) have become a breeding ground for the antisemitism that engulfs every Jew on the planet. Anti-Zionism is used to accuse and condemn every Jew of sordid, inhuman designs simply because he is Jewish. An accomplice in real or imaginary crimes against the Arab people, every Jew deserves to be excluded from Canadian society, because he supposedly brings to Canada the same mentality as the Israelis have.

The opposite attitude applies to the Arab world. Its representatives can deny or alter the facts about land with impunity; any comparison of the Arab community with the bellicose people of the region is immediately labelled as unacceptable Islamophobia. Arab propaganda is often accepted without much thought or questioning. Whereas the fate of the Palestinians who left their homes in 1948 is recalled a thousand times a day, the destiny of the more than 800,000 Jews driven from Arab lands and stripped of their property is never mentioned and remains an untouchable subject. The media never discuss it, nor do the politicians. Humanitarian discourse applies to only one group, and the Arab countries' successful ethnic cleansing is ignored. Those two ways of dealing with the same situation are in themselves an obvious form of racism.

In the antisemites' view, the Jew should be isolated and made to acknowledge his existential mistakes. Like the Church of the Middle Ages, which attempted to convert Jews and forced them to repent their nature and actions, the left and other groups demand that Jews buy social acceptance by condemning and pillorying Israel. Common in Europe, this new Judeophobia[2] is becoming more deeply rooted in Canada every day, and its ideas will probably lead to acts that violate basic human rights. We are on a slippery slope, and inaction by civil society and government could have dramatic consequences.

If Canada fails to respond vigorously today, it is opening the door to official discrimination and social exclusion of a particular group and effectively renouncing its own constitutional democratic principles. Such a situation would directly encourage Jews to uproot themselves, as they have done so many times in centuries past, and return to the path of exile.

---

2 See the major works of Pierre-André Taguieff, including *La Nouvelle Judéophobie* (2002)

With that alternative ever-present in our minds, we applaud the action undertaken by the CPCCA, and we remain more than ready to expand on the position taken in this brief.

Hon. David Kilgour, J.D

Oral presentation by The Honourable David Kilgour on November 09, 2008

Seventy years ago tonight, agents of Adolf Hitler murdered 92 Jewish Germans and arrested 25,000 others for deportation to concentration camps. More than 200 synagogues were destroyed and tens of thousands of Jewish homes and businesses were looted. It was the prelude to the Holocaust, committed against a religious community whose ancestry in Germany went back to Roman times.

It remains the solemn responsibility of each one of us to do all we can to ensure that the world understands and never forgets Kristallnacht and the Holocaust.

It must be said immediately that many in my own spiritual community—Christianity—stood by during the worst catastrophe in history inflicted on our sisters and brothers of Jewish faith. There were exceptions, but many Christians in Europe did too little to honour the second great commandment of Jesus—to love one's neighbour as oneself.

Canada's official role, or more accurately non-role, before entering the war is well set out in *None Is Too Many* by Irving Abella and Harold Troper.

Hitler

In Mein Kampf, Hitler provided much about his worldview. He was a confirmed antisemite as early as 1904 when he was only fifteen, partly because of the influence of antisemitic teachers at his schools. For him, Judaism was a race, not the religion it obviously is. His views were virtually indistinguishable from the antisemitism of the Middle Ages. He was a sado-masochist.

I quote the late Lucy Dawidowicz's excellent book *The War Against The Jews, 1933-1945*: "It has been my view-now widely shared-that hatred of the Jews was Hitler's central and most compelling belief and that it dominated his thoughts and his actions all his life ... It became his fixed idea, one to which he remained steadfast all his life ... The documents amply justify my conclusion that Hitler planned to murder the Jews in coordination with his plans to go to war for lebensraum (living space) and to establish the Thousand Year Reich."

5,933,900 Lives

The world must keep always in mind what Hitler had done by the time of his death in 1945. According to author Dawidowicz, the best estimated number of Jews Hitler and his followers murdered in Europe was 5,933, 900, or 67% of the continent's pre-Holocaust population, including three million Poles, or 90% of the Jewish population of Poland, 90% of the Jewish population of Germany, the Baltics and Austria, and high percentages in many other countries.

The percentages were much lower in Bulgaria, Denmark, Finland, France and Italy. Many in these countries strongly resisted Nazi efforts to get them to deport Jews to concentration camps. In occupied Denmark, for example, the king and large number of Danes wore yellow stars to show support for their Jewish neighbours. Danes risked their lives, smuggling a large number of Jewish Danes to neutral Sweden. Finland and Bulgaria simply refused Nazi demands to hand over their Jewish citizens.

Further away, a few other nations helped. The government of El Salvador, for example, issued more than 30,000 of its passports to Jewish Hungarians so that they could avoid the death camps. Raoul Wallenberg of Sweden disappeared in the Soviet gulag for doing the same thing.

Until World War Two, as David Matas has reminded us, non-Jews were mostly left untouched by history's antisemites. Hitler's regime sought to murder Jews everywhere, thereby launching, continuing and prolonging his war- even in Asia- and in the process inflicted immense losses of innocent lives.

The Jewish community lost about one third of its world population. The total estimated deaths during the war were sixty two million (37 million civilians and 25 million military). Thirty one million non-Jewish civilians died in what Davidowicz concludes was a war by Hitler designed to cover the planned murder of Jews everywhere. "Hatred of Jews dragged the whole world down," concludes Matas—and the world must still agree.

Many have asked since how a psychopath such as Hitler could have become Chancellor of Germany, whose people and culture rank highly among world civilizations. Did it have something to do with generations of German antisemitism? What responsibility should German and other Christians across the world bear for not having resisted Hitler more effectively? We needed many more Konrad Adenauers, Dietrich Bonnhoeffers and Raoul Wallenbergs.

In a questionable effort to keep Germany on side for the Cold War, the work of the Nuremberg Tribunal was stopped in 1948 with only half the cases finished and no doubt thousands of war criminals not yet even identified. Did the immunity in effect provided for Nazi war criminals after 1948 somehow help to provide a licence for ensuing genocides in Cambodia, Bosnia, Rwanda, Sudan and what has been happening to the Falun Gong community in China since mid-1999? 'Never again' became 'again and again.'

Three Lessons for Today

We continue to have much to learn from the Hitler years. Permit me to suggest three lessons for today:

(1) We need to stand united against hatred and indifference. The 20th century was undoubtedly the worst in history in terms of violence directed at believers of all faiths, mostly by totalitarian regimes like Hitler's. The major lesson for all faith communities is clear: had all of us stood shoulder-to-shoulder when anyone in our own or another religion was being persecuted anywhere, many innocent lives might have been saved.

There are encouraging signs of progress. For example, a number of years ago hundreds of Edmontonians of many faiths demonstrated at city hall, protesting the persecution of Muslims in Bosnia. Later, many of us did the same at the legislative assembly over the treatment of Christians in Pakistan; similar initiatives continue across Canada.

(2) We need to act early. Antisemitism tends to increase as certain kinds of nationalism grow. Consider the quote by Zlatko Disdarevic in Sarajevo: *A War Journal* (1993): "(Subverted nationalism exists) because somebody somewhere decided that the bestial concept of a herd, composed of only one colour, all speaking the same language, all thinking along similar lines, all believing in the same god, must wipe out everything else."

The desecration of Jewish synagogues and cemeteries has increased in recent years across the world; all faith communities and inter-faith councils should voice outrage about such incidents as soon as they occur. We should all speak out for a world that is multi-religious and multi-cultural. Civil society, community leaders, role models and governments at all levels must denounce anti-Semitism and hatred voiced against any other religion or culture while they are still in the shadows. More actions are needed.

Human dignity is ultimately indivisible; an attack on one faith community often becomes one against all as happened in Nazi Germany. People of good will can be silent too long and social toxins can overcome reason. Why, for example, were some of Hitler's schoolteachers allowed to voice antisemitism to impressionable students like him? "Bloody words," in David Matas' graphic phrase, can be as dangerous as shouting "fire" in a crowded theatre. We must be vigilant that this does not happen in Canada or anywhere else today.

Despite our strong preference for free expression, the criminalizing of wilful incitement to hatred of any identifiable religious, racial or cultural community by Canada's Parliament is sound public policy. We must ensure that such policy is enforced. (Several years ago, Edmonton police wanted to charge two diplomats from China for distributing pamphlets on the University of Alberta campus which in the investigators view violated in respect of the city's Falun Gong community the "willfully inciting hatred" of an identifiable group provisions of the Criminal Code of Canada. Details are available in Appendix 8 at *www.organharvestinvestigation.net.*)

It is important in every rule-of-law society to have in place institutions to protect every resident, popular or not, especially in times of social stress. Canada's entrenched Charter of Rights and Freedoms in place since 1982 is premised on the view that legal protection for the equal dignity of all Canadians must be beyond the reach of legislators. Our independent courts must be vigilant in their roles-always resisting pressure from the executive or inflamed public opinion. Lawyers must be encouraged to defend anyone charged vigorously and without harassment. The media must take seriously their important roles in building better open societies.

(3) The international community must condemn and deter aggression by totalitarian regimes against another country or religion. Nous devons protester et faire arrêter l'agression sur une nation ou religion.

In October 2005, Iran's President Mahmoud Ahmadinejad asserted that the Holocaust was a "myth that has been used for 60 years by Zionists to blackmail other countries and justify their crimes in occupied territories." He added that Israel should be wiped off the map ("Our dear Iman (Khomeini) ordered that the occupying regime in Al-Qods (Jerusalem) be wiped off the face of the earth. This was a very wise statement."). No one anywhere should take lightly such outrageous statements. As Rabbi Reuven Bulka says, "Holocaust deniers are not stupid; they are evil. The deniers would eagerly welcome another holocaust, which they and their ideological progeny would again deny ever happened."

The mere 36 votes Iran received in the UN General Assembly on its government's recent bid for election to the Security Council is hopefully an indication of mounting international concern about the nature of its regime. The Nobel Laureate Elie Wiesel, however, noting that Ahmadinejad was allowed again to speak at the UN General Assembly this fall, observed: "Ten years ago, and less, the ruler of a country that announced its aspiration for Israel to be wiped off the map would not have dared appear and speak on the UN's podium." This observation warrants serious attention.

On the subject of Iran, as an aside, many governments in my view still misunderstand both the long-suffering Iranian people and Ahmadinejad, mistakenly thinking that there are only two policy options available: (1) continued ineffective appeasement of the regime—often for commercial reasons—and suppression of Iranian opposition groups essentially as directed by the ayatollahs or (2) bombing strikes against Iran's nuclear facilities. An attack on Iran is the one thing that would unite Iranians behind their president and should be avoided at all costs. In my opinion, a third and peaceful option is to begin working with all Iranian opposition groups to bring the rule-of-law, peaceful intentions towards neighbours and the world and democracy to Iran.

Conclusion

I'll close with a true story about the Holocaust told by Dr. Truda Rosenberg of Ottawa, who lit a candle here tonight. Truda's entire family perished in the Holocaust. "Don't let anything destroy your Jewish soul" were her mother's last and parting words to Truda. Later as a 20-year-old, Truda survived only because she was small enough that others could push her out a small window in the wall of the train cattle car that was taking her and many others to the death camps. By 1951, Truda had managed to get to Britain, pretending she was a Catholic woman from Poland with an assumed name, and had become a nurse and mid-wife there. No one at the hospital where she worked knew about her background. One day, she was having tea with nurse colleagues, when one of them began to criticize Jews. "Why?" asked Truda. "Well", the other replied, "They are a lazy bunch. They are doctors and lawyers, but have you ever seen a Jewish nurse?" Truda was silent for a moment, but then replied, "You are look-ing at one." She and the others then went to her room, where she removed the name card from the door, wrote "Truda Osterman" on the back and put it on the door. After many years living under an assumed name, she became Truda again! Her soon-to-be published life story will be titled *Unmasked*. Today, in her 80s, Truda still goes to work daily in our city and Canada continues to benefit from her skills as a psychologist.

In two days, we observe Remembrance Day, when Canadians think of our family, friends and many others who perished in wars and con-flicts across the world. We must never forget any of the victims, including the children, women and men who were killed in the Holocaust only because of their religion. We must tell and retell their stories—we must never forget.

Ruth Klein

L. Ruth Klein is currently a Citizenship Judge. Prior to her appointment, she served as National Director of the League of Human Rights of B'nai Brith Canada, and its Institute of International Affairs. In these positions she spearheaded initiatives designed to combat antisemitism, racism and discrimination worldwide, as well as to advance Holocaust education and counter its denial. From 2009-2012, she also served as the Executive Director of Canada's National Task Force on Holocaust Education, Remembrance and Research (NTF), an initiative of B'nai Brith funded by the Canadian Government.

A graduate of the London School of Economics in History, with a Master's degree in Law from Osgoode Hall Law School, Ruth supervised B'nai Brith's many research, education and public policy initiatives, crafting its public education material, as well as its submissions to government and non-governmental bodies on a wide range of human rights issues. She is a Chartered Mediator who specializes in addressing cultural diversity within community and workplace conflict resolution paradigms.

Ruth Klein is the editor of *Nazi Germany, Canadian Responses: Confronting Antisemitism in the Shadow of War* (McGill-Queens University Press, 2012) and co-editor of *From Immigration to Integration: The Canadian Jewish Experience* (Millennium Bureau of Canada/Institute for International Affairs, 2000). For over a decade she was the Canadian co-contributor to the *World Survey of Anti-Semitism,* published by the Steven Roth Centre for the Study of Contemporary Anti-Semitism and Racism at the University of Tel Aviv.

Ruth Klein[*]
National Director, League for Human Rights of B'nai Brith Canada

Oral Testimony of Ruth Klein, National Director of the League for Human Rights of B'nai Brith Canada, delivered to the Canadian Parliamentary Coalition to Combat Antisemitism on 30 November 2009.

Good afternoon to the chair, the vice-chair, and all the members of the panel.

I am the national director of both the League for Human Rights of B'nai Brith Canada and its Institute for International Affairs, so I have had the opportunity to study antisemitism in Canada, not just in the purely Canadian context, but also in terms of the global scene. I am also executive director of Canada's new national task force on Holocaust Education, Remembrance, and Research. So both professionally and personally—I am the daughter of a Holocaust survivor— my goal is the preservation of historical truth, the countering of Holocaust denial, one of the many forms of antisemitism present in Canada today, and the fight against all forms of hate activity.

The League for Human Rights is the anti-defamation league here in Canada, documenting, analyzing, and responding to antisemitism. Similar functions are carried out by the Community Security Trust in the U.K. and by our other partners in the global forum on antisemitism. The league publishes an annual audit of antisemitic incidents, an audit that has tracked and reported antisemitism in Canada for the past twenty eight years in the context of using that data to check the pulse of racism in this country in general.

As other speakers have mentioned, when attacks against Jews are tolerated, attacks on other minority groups are never far behind. In that sense, the audit is often considered the barometer of prejudice in Canada. We share this information regularly, as well as strategies to counter hate, with all vulnerable groups, through many outreach activities, including a Community Alliance Forum held last year with the support of the Attorney General of Ontario. That brought together all groups in Ontario to look at this problem and see what can be done.

---

[*] The testimony of Ruth Klein is comprised of both an oral submission presented to the Canadian Parliamentary Inquiry into Antisemitism on 30 November 2009, and written submission presented in partnership to the Panel providing an overview and analysis of antisemitism in Canada and the role of B'nai Brith Canada. Full unabridged transcripts of Ms. Klein's testimony can be found at http://www.cpcca.ca/inquiry.htm.

Given the authoritative nature of this data, our audit figures have been cited by governmental and research bodies worldwide, such as the U.S. State Department, the Organization for Security and Cooperation in Europe, and the Steven Roth Institute for the Study of Contemporary Antisemitism and Racism at Tel Aviv University. The full list appears on the back of the audit, which you have.

But the audit is more than just facts and figures. It really is about people, about their fears, and about their anxieties. It is about community and governmental response or lack of it. It is also important to note that while the audit's consistency of definition and reporting methodology has allowed for long-term analysis of trends and trajectories, we can only report the tip of the iceberg in terms of the full dimensions of the problem.

For example, police experts and sociologists agree that usually only about 10% of victims ever come forward to report their victimization, and that's for any type of hate crime. We know that people who do come forward to call our 24/7 anti-hate hotline do so with trepidation. That is why this service has to be confidential.

Why this trepidation? Why should people be so nervous about coming forward to report incidents? Well, let's go first with age: elderly Holocaust survivors know from experience that things can only get worse. Again, as the daughter of a survivor, I know that I have imbibed some of those anxieties myself in terms of being very, very careful when you make a complaint and when you go to the authorities.

Those who have come more recently from countries with despotic governments or corrupt police forces fear any contact with the authorities. They, very unlikely, had to go to the police. That's why it is sometimes more comfortable for them to go to a community organization as a buffer.

The visibly orthodox Jewish population has a very philosophical approach. They seem to have accepted that if they look different, they will attract unwelcome attention, even in the multiculturalism of today's Canadian scene.

Also, there are certainly people who do not like to come forward because they think they'll be dismissed, that they won't be taken seriously and nothing will happen.

I tell you this, ladies and gentlemen, because I want you to fully understand just how much this initiative of yours, the All-party Coalition and the Inquiry, means to members of the community. They have received enormous comfort from the fact that this initiative even exists. Obviously, we hope there will be long-term ramifications and improvement, but you have taken the first step, and that means a tremendous amount to the people on the street.

I am very aware of the constraints under which you have been working and the open opposition you've faced in taking this step. And why? Because you are allowing the Jewish community the opportunity to describe its own experiences and to define its own victimization.

Really, that is where my presentation begins today, because I am wondering about these attempts by other groups here in Canada to deny the Jewish people that right, to try to co-opt it for themselves, and to minimize and dismiss what the Jewish community is saying. Really, in effect, that is the second layer of victimization: telling people that their perceptions and their feelings are invalid. For example, when a group of faculty and students of various backgrounds at York put together a statement claiming there is no antisemitism on campus, and there is not a visible Jew amongst them, we have to wonder. Who except a visible Jew, distinguished by external signs of religion, can tell you what it is like having to walk through a hostile environment and what it is like to be intimidated, ridiculed, and threatened? And who except a supporter of the Jewish state can tell you what it feels like in the classroom when their beliefs and their opinions are attacked, marginalized, or even dismissed, and they have a very strong fear that if they don't write the politically correct thing in their term papers, their academic standing might be affected?

Can you imagine this if you were having an inquiry on any other subject here today—on anti-black prejudice, or gay bashing, or what's called Islamophobia—and do you really feel that you would have this type of outpouring of opposition to what you were doing? I think this is very telling. It is only on the issue of antisemitism that we seem to have this rush to deny its existence. I call this type of activity "antisemitism denial."

Even putting that aside, there are many people today who will claim that vandalism at schools or synagogues is really just the work of kids, that it is just a few kids playing out, a few nutcases, and that it is really not that bad, unless, of course, there is open violence.

So in effect, we are really becoming more tolerant of antisemitism in Canada, not less, and part of it stems from this attempt to artificially separate the bonds between the Jewish people and their ancestral homeland and to deny the ancient national, religious, and cultural connections. The committee has already heard of the new antisemitism, which seeks to deny the Jewish people, as a collective entity, the same right to self-determination in their own homeland that all other people claim, and really, it is not that much different from attempts of traditional antisemitism to deny Jews, as individuals, the individual human rights that all people enjoy.

I would like to repeat this, even though other witnesses have said this. This has nothing to do with the legitimate criticism of the state of Israel of the kind that might be applied and should be applied to other states. This has everything to do with overt or covert calls for the destruction of the Jewish state. It has everything to do with using anti-Israel rhetoric as a mask, a cloak, for age-old anti-Jewish stereotypes and imagery.

Now, to bring this back to Canada, because we know that on the global scene these things happen, you are really being asked by people who are against the whole purpose of this inquiry to make an artificial separation between anti-Jew hatred and hatred of the Jewish state. But current realities make this task almost impossible. There is already an intertwining of these two threads, which cannot really be so easily separated.

For example, let us look back to 2002 and the firebombing of Quebec City's only synagogue. We met privately with a member of Parliament at that time who, while she regretted the incident and told us that she was sorry, said she would be unable to make a public statement condemning the firebombing because it might be looked at as being pro-Israel. In fact, that is what happened. She got up in the House subsequently. She did not make the statement. She spoke about the CBC. It was left to a colleague to condemn the firebombing.

So already these two themes are really mixed in people's minds. In Canada, these dual themes of antisemitism and anti-Zionism run parallel and are used interchangeably, as has been mentioned before. We see this in the sharing of rhetoric and images between the extreme left and the extreme right. The extreme left will borrow Holocaust imagery and age-old Jewish stereotypes to attack Israel, while the neo-Nazis use the Middle East conflict as a justification for furthering their anti-Jewish ideology. Years ago the talk was of Jewish control of the media and Jewish control of the government and the financial world. The terminology now has changed. It is Israeli control. It is Zionist control.

There are those who have caught on well to this stratagem. For example, the Canadian branch of Stormfront has advised its members to use the terminology "Zionists" or "Israel-firsters"— that's their little term—

because they get more mileage from that than saying "Jews" outright. The circle of hatred continues, from the old blood libels in which Jews were periodically accused of poisoning wells or murdering Jewish children to drink their blood for Passover rituals, to the modern-day allegations we hear today. Israel is poisoning wells, we hear, and there are cartoons showing Israelis preparing to drink the blood of Palestinians.

That's to say nothing about 9/11 conspiracy theories, which are really a mirror of the old accusations that Jews, just by their nature, were responsible for every natural or man-made disaster.

Here in Canada, just recently, there has been a wild claim, which originated here and is being disseminated on the Internet, that the Jews are responsible for the H1N1 virus.

An allegation remains on the website of a Canadian Islamic organization that Jews "institutionalized racism."

I know we have had a lot of talk today about the importance of groups working together to stamp out discrimination against all of us. That is not very helpful.

We even had a gratuitous dig in a media editorial just last week by a writer who probably did not even realize how he has internalized anti-Jewish prejudice. He wrote that for Jews, the term "never again" applies only to them, a real throwback to the old depiction of Jews as selfish, alien from their fellow citizens, with no human compassion for any other group.

It does not have to be as crass as the comment by a Vancouver man some years ago that Jews are the brothers of monkeys and pigs. It does not have to be the "Jews are dogs" slur that was chanted at a Montreal rally earlier this year, which, by the way, was attended by trade unionists and some politicians. Subtle can sometimes be more insidious since it raises fewer red flags. With fewer red flags, it's less likely to be noticed and it can be made to sound like a debating point.

To sum up, ladies and gentlemen, the facts from our studies are quite clear. Recent audit findings show an ongoing disproportionate targeting of the Jewish community compared to other minorities, and this is at a time when the Jewish population of Canada is declining. It is currently less than 1% of the total population.

A 2008 Statistics Canada study based on data on hate crimes from 2006 found that nearly two-thirds of hate crimes motivated by religion were directed at the Jewish faith. The Toronto Police, just to give one example, recorded 153 hate-related occurrences in 2008; 45 of them, a rather high proportion, were against Jews.

Where do we go from here? You have taken the first very important step, but what else can be done? You have several recommendations on file in my initial submission and also the submission from colleagues of mine in the League for Human Rights, but I would just like to really summarize them in terms of thematics: acknowledgment, terminology, and training.

In terms of acknowledgement, really, to move forward we are going to need a general acknowledgement that antisemitism is an issue, is a problem, is a challenge in Canada today, and that is a prerequisite for any type of change. If done formally by this inquiry, it will give a moral voice to efforts to counter it.

We know that the British report specifically recognizes the problem of antisemitism on campus. It is our hope that this inquiry will also focus on this area, because we have seen and I have heard previous testimony that university administrations seem very ready to dismiss this issue.

In terms of acknowledgement, we also note Senator Jerry Grafstein's long battle in the Senate to bring the issue of antisemitism to the attention of his Senate colleagues and to have them bring about a resolution that would mirror motions already adopted by the OSCE Parliamentary Assembly. We ask the inquiry to encourage the Senate to work together with this inquiry and to acknowledge the problem. Really, everyone has to work together on this.

In terms of terminology, we need one consistent definition to use here in Canada across the board. The working definition has been adopted by the EUMC and now the European Union Agency for Fundamental Rights. Units of the OSCE that work in combating racism already use this definition. The U.S. State Department uses this definition, and the London Declaration, to which Canada is a signatory, calls for expanded use of the definition to inform policy and training.

I agree in a certain sense that Natan Sharansky's definition hones in on specific points, but I think the benefit of the EUMC definition is that it gives very specific examples, and when we are dealing with fora—for example, universities—where apparently there is no definition, we are going to need one.

My final point is training. We need that training for hate crimes officers, crown prosecutors and judges, university administrations, as

I mentioned, and school administrations as well, since anti-Israeli coalitions are now going earlier and earlier into the educational system.

In fact, I would like to suggest that any public program that gets government money should have an anti-discrimination policy that includes, again, the same definition of antisemitism that we would all be using and that this inquiry I hope will support.

Thank you very much for your consideration.

Written Submission Prepared by Ruth Klein and the League for Human Rights of the B'nai Brith Canada for the Canadian Parliamentary Coalition to Combat Antisemitism on August 2009.

Antisemitism in Canada: An Overview
Introduction—B'nai Brith's Role

This submission is presented to the Canadian Parliamentary Coalition to Combat Antisemitism (CPCCA) by B'nai Brith Canada's League for Human Rights. B'nai Brith has been in operation in this country since 1875 as the Jewish community's senior advocacy and volunteer service organization. With its network of regional officers and cross-country membership, it is well-positioned to understand the specific concerns of the grassroots Jewish community and advocate on its behalf. Its League for Human Rights is dedicated to combating anti-Semitism and racism, undertaking major legal/legislative, educational and community outreach initiatives, and advocating for the rights of at-risk groups. A Special Advisory Committee, made up of representatives of many diverse minority communities, enhances the League's work in this area.

The League welcomes this opportunity to share its data and insights with the Coalition, putting them in the context of longer-term trends and influences, both domestic and international. The focus will be on moving the discussion beyond the purely philosophical aspects, to the realms of everyday reality. To this end, League experts are on hand to elaborate on these issues through oral evidence to the Inquiry.

The data and analysis presented here is based primarily on the League's *Audit of Anti-Semitic Incidents*, now in its 27th year, a study that has traditionally provided definitive data on bigotry and discrimination against the Jewish community. Given the authoritative nature of its data, the *Audit* has been cited by governmental and research bodies worldwide such as the US State Department, the Organization for Security and Cooperation in Europe, and the Stephen Roth Institute for the Study of Contemporary Antisemitism and Racism at Tel Aviv University.

The annual *Audit* is just one expression of the League's front-line assistance to victims of antisemitism. The incidents documented are reported to the League for Human Rights primarily via its 24/7 community Anti-Hate Hotline (1-800 892 BNAI [2624]) and its online reporting service (www.bnaibrith.ca). Working closely with police forces and the grassroots Jewish community, these incidents are corroborated, documented and analyzed, and victims receive culturally-sensitive assistance. This hands-on involvement with the victims allows the League to offer an assessment of the impact of antidemitism that goes well beyond the quantitative aspect alone.

The Data—Key Features

In 2008, 1,135 antisemitic incidents were reported to the League for Human Rights, an increase of 8.9% over the 2007 figures. Once again, this figure breaks through previous thresholds set since the League began recording incidents 27 years ago. The findings represent a more than fourfold increase over the last ten years. (See Appendix A for a more detailed summary.) This increase, therefore, is not an aberration, but the continuation of a growing trend of anti-Jewish prejudice and bigotry on the Canadian scene. After all, in the absence—untill the final days of the year—of the type of significant Middle East triggers that traditionally spark increases in antisemitic incidents, logic would suggest that numbers should, rather, be declining. We also have to remember that sociologists and police experts agree that only about 10% of victims ever come forward to report their victimization, so we are just seeing the tip of the iceberg through the available data.

To give just a few examples from the 2008 *Audit*, there were 50 incidents targeting Jewish places of worship and 17 against community centres. These venues continue to face heavy security costs, though there has been some relief in the form of the *Communities at Risk: Security Infrastructure Pilot (SIP) Program*. Such incidents should not be dismissed lightly; they include death threats against Rabbis and synagogue staff, as well as vandalism of Jewish communal institutions, and were perpetrated right across the country, including Moncton, Montreal, Toronto, Barrie, Winnipeg, Saskatoon, Edmonton, Vancouver and Kelowna.

Jews were targeted in their own homes in 105 incidents, including desecration of *mezuzahs*, (a *mezuzah* is a religious symbol that publicly identifies houses as Jewish). Such invasion of their private space makes Jews feels particularly vulnerable, as many victim impact statements on record with the League attest.

The explosion of hate on the internet was red-flagged by the League over a decade ago, as discussed in the three international symposia it has convened.

Reflecting the range of new technologies used to disseminate hate, there were 405 reports of web-based hate activity with a Canadian connection, over 30% more than the year before. Apart from ugly, graphic web site postings, we note that text messaging, Facebook and other social networking methods are being used to disseminate the range of harassment over cyberspace, from bullying to death threats. Targeted action is needed to hold back this newest frontier of hate, as suggested in the *Recommendations* section of this submission.

In 2008, the level of antisemitism continued to intensify on campus, where anti-Israel protesters have ratcheted up the tension, bringing in virulent anti-Israel propaganda. For example, in 2008, the Israel Apartheid Week signature poster depicted Israel raping "Palestine". In 2009, the poster depicted the Jewish State collectively in the role of child killer, with a gunship helicopter targeting a toddler holding a teddy bear. This is the epitome of the modern-day blood libel, and the fact that the target audience is impressionable Canadian students is red-flagged here for the Inquiry's attention.

The net result of this coordinated campus campaign has been an increase in openly antisemitic harassment, and even violence, against Jewish students. There were 76 reported cases of antisemitism on campuses in 2008 alone, more than double the 36 incidents just two years previously. The result is that many students report hiding their Jewish identity in order to avoid harassment and intimidation; some have told us they no longer participate in classroom discussions, for fear of possible academic reprisal. In spite of these factors, however, there is as yet no public acknowledgment of the dangers of this campaign of hate on Canadian campuses.

Analysis

While major, premeditated cases such as the fire bombings of Jewish schools in Montreal in 2004 and 2006, have the most potential to terrify a community, the random nature of other, less publicized incidents creates its own atmosphere of anxiety. This has led Jews to conceal visible signs of their religion, such as *kipas*, when traveling in certain areas, which is surely an unacceptable restriction on freedom of religion. And while Jews might have long felt vulnerable in certain urban venues, a newer trend the League noted recently is open expression of antisemitism in rural areas, such as the 2008 assault against a visibly Jewish tourist in the Laurentians, while bystanders watched.

The far-right-wing in Canada, a movement largely discredited and generally dismissed as of little significance, still warrants close scrutiny, given the rise of such extremism in Europe and the international connections between adherents of racist ideologies. Ongoing review of white supremacist sites and message boards indicates that such groups are active and located throughout Canada. One significant example is increased recruitment activity in Calgary. Swastikas and Nazi-related symbols also feature much more prominently in anti-Jewish incidents, while Holocaust deniers have emerged from the fringes in a bid for quasi-academic status, managing to secure guest speaking engagements in some university-based settings.

Over the past decades, there have been signs of increasing synergy between the far-right wing and its far-left counterpart in terms of anti-Jewish activity, with each side borrowing from the rhetoric of the other. Thus, right-wing extremists have evinced a sudden interest in the Israel-Palestinian conflict, adopting every possible slander about the State of Israel in order to denigrate Jews. In the same vein, left wingers have latched onto Holocaust imagery to fuel their allegation that the Jewish State is a Nazi-like regime.

Against this backdrop of animosity, in the last few years, antisemitic incidents have taken place in an increasingly diverse range of venues: at the workplace, on the transit system, in retails outlets, at fitness clubs, in physicians' offices, to name just a few. It is interesting, however, that some of the worst anti-Jewish outbursts take place in the midst of rallies against Israel, whether on campus or in the public domain. This should not be viewed as an aberration given the main themes of these activities—demonization and delegitimization of the Jewish State—which are included in the Working Definition of Antisemitism adopted by the European Monitoring Centre on Racism and Xenophobia (EUMC). The League suggests that the Inquiry adopt the EUMC definition in order to cover the full dimensions of this newest variant of antiemitism, which seeks to deny Jews as a collective entity—alone of all peoples in the world—the right to self determination in their own homeland, in much the same way as traditional anti-Semitism denied Jews as individuals human rights accorded to all others.

Continuing this theme, discriminatory moves against the Jewish State such as boycott campaigns need to be recognized for their antisemitic overtones. A precedent can be found at the European Court of Human Rights, which recently upheld a French court ruling that it is illegal and discriminatory to boycott Israeli goods. The Court further found that making it illegal to call for such a boycott did not violate any free speech rights. The ruling is now applicable to many European countries, and the League asks the Inquiry to take note of the opportunity this presents to address one of the most pernicious forms of anti-Jewish discrimination, commonly masquerading as anti-Zionism.

Implications

Recent *Audit* findings clearly show an ongoing, disproportionate targeting of the Jewish community compared to other minorities in Canada. This is especially significant at a time when the Jewish population is declining, making up less than 1% of the total population. By comparison, the Black and Muslim communities, which also report victimization, make up 2.5% and 2% respectively of the total Canadian population.

This finding is supported by other studies as well. For example, a 2008 Statistics Canada study, based on 2006 hate crime data, found that nearly two-thirds of hate crimes motivated by religion were directed at the Jewish faith. There were 63 incidents targeting the Jewish community, compared to the 21 cases against the next most targeted group, Muslims.

It is also significant that Toronto Police, which recorded 153 hate-related occurrences in 2008, documented 45 incidents against Jews who, as in past years, were the single most consistently targeted group. Other groups mentioned in the police report were Gays (34), Blacks (24), and Muslims (7). A similar trend was noted by the York Regional Police, which noted 81 incidents of hate, 26 against the Jewish community, with the next highest group being Blacks (19).

Attitudinal studies support such findings, speaking to prejudices both latent and overt about Jews having too much power, or being responsible for their own victimization. Such prejudices have been noted in Quebec in particular, the province with the second highest number of incidents reported to the League each year. In one study commissioned by the League, (*http://www.bnaibrith.ca/publications/audit2001/audit2001-01.html*), while 10% of Canadians outside Quebec perceived Jews as having too much power, the figure was 26% in Quebec. Such findings, since corroborated by additional studies, deserve further attention.

Conclusion

Each year, there are specific factors that influence the tide of antisemitism in Canada. In 2008, the fact that 547 incidents—close to half the total—took place in the last four months of 2008, can be linked to fall-out from the developing economic recession and the high-profile Bernard Madoff scandal. Historically, antisemitism has increased in this type of climate, as disgruntled citizens seek a scapegoat to blame for their personal difficulties. In some years, international events, particularly those linked to the Arab-Israeli conflict, appear to have been a significant factor. Since these themes—economic downturn and Mideast tensions—unfortunately appear to be, at least in the short-term, constant features affecting the Canadian scene, antisemitism cannot be expected to abate any time soon.

Overall, we are increasingly seeing manifestations of a new bigotry that often masquerades as anti-Zionism, that unholy hybrid of age-old and new-age bigotry, which purports to be merely legitimate criticism of Israel, but strays far beyond civil or legitimate discourse. As the anti-Israel rhetoric intensifies, new boundaries are being crossed in terms of the range of anti-Jewish canards that are being invoked once more.

There is also a move to deny the Jewish people the right to define their own victimization, a stratagem long used by the anti-Israel bloc at UN agency meetings. "We are Semites too," the argument runs, "therefore how can we be accused of antisemitism?" Those seeking to distance themselves from the politically incorrect taint of antisemitism, at the same time as they implicitly enable it, use this deliberate smokescreen. That is why the single-word descriptor "antisemitism"—already adopted by the CPCCA—is a more accurate description of the phenomenon than the easily-manipulated terminology "antisemitism".

It is clear that a holistic approach is necessary to eliminate antisemitism, one that includes legislative reform and implementation of existing international obligations, as well as training for police and prosecutors, and educational and community outreach. The League welcomes the opportunity to discuss these issues further with the Coalition. Meanwhile, seven key recommendations that arise from this submission—just a sampling of the League's arsenal of anti-hate measures—are tabled here for further discussion.

Summary of Recommendations

(a) Ongoing governmental support for the League's monitoring and documentation of antisemitism in Canada. The League already provides the data on antisemitism in Canada to international bodies such as the US State Department (Office of the Special Envoy to Monitor and Combat Antisemitism), and the Organization for Security and Cooperation in Europe (Office for Democratic Institutions and Human Rights). Its annual *Audit* forms the basis of the chapter on Canada in the *World Survey on Antisemitism* published by the Stephen Roth Centre for the Study of Contemporary Antisemitism and Racism at Tel Aviv University, and is cited in numerous other studies. In order to enable the League to enhance its current monitoring and reporting role, ongoing governmental support is requested. This will allow its functions to dovetail seamlessly with the work of the Canadian Parliamentary Coalition to Combat Antisemitism.

(b) Adoption of the Working Definition of Antisemitism set out by the European Union's Monitoring Centre on Racism and Xenophobia, in order to determine the Inquiry's terms of reference. The definition, reprinted in its entirety in Appendix B, would provide a useful framework for the Inquiry's study since it includes contemporary as well as historical manifestations of antisemitism, such as denying the Jewish people their right to self-determination, calling the State of Israel a "racist endeavour," or applying to it double standards not required of any other democratic nation. The Inquiry's scope would be too narrow if its terms of reference were limited to more traditional antisemitism alone.

(c) Public acknowledgement of growing antisemitism on campus under the guise of anti-Israel campaigning. The campaign of hate that is in danger of becoming entrenched in Canadian universities needs to be publicly acknowledged, as has already been done in Britain in the 2007 *Report of the British All-Party Parliamentary Inquiry into Antisemitism*. Such action would set a framework, setting down boundaries within which campus administrations can work with government and community partners to address this growing problem.

(d) Criminalization of boycotts against the Jewish State as discriminatory. A strong public stance is needed, with legislation to support it, to acknowledge that boycotts against Israel are discriminatory and thus illegal. This would follow the precedent set recently in the European Court of Human Rights. Such action would be well within the parameters of the EUMC's Working Definition on Antisemitism (see Appendix B), since the anti-Israel boycott campaign singles out Israel alone, applying standards and stratagems not used against any other country, in an overall bid to isolate the Jewish State and delegitimize its existence.

(e) A ban on racist groups in Canada. Since racist organizations are not presently prohibited in Canada, the growth of far-right-wing groups in Canada has been left unchecked. That failure puts Canada in violation of Article 4(b) of the relevant UN *Convention*. The Supreme Court of Canada, in the case of Suresh, held that the provision in the *Immigration Act*, which allows for deportation based on membership in a terrorist organization, is constitutional. The implication of the judgment is that a prohibition against racist groups would also be constitutional.

(f) A crack-down on online anti-Semitism. Attention needs to be focused both on Internet processes, and on its infrastructure—architecture, protocols and software—in order to understand the technical, as well as the strategic and policy issues involved in fighting online hate. Options need to be explored for adapting tracking systems currently in use to counter child exploitation, so as to be able to deal with online incidents of hate. As well, enhanced tools should be developed for tracing the online funding of hate groups, based on the possibility of utilizing existing fraud detection technology.

(g) Inclusion of Holocaust Denial as a hate crime offence. Since Holocaust denial is one of the most insidious forms of antisemitism, the *Criminal Code* needs an amendment—along the lines of the German legislation— to make it clear that the hate crime offence encompasses Holocaust denial. Such a provision could inhibit the dissemination of Holocaust denial, whether in a foreign language or in English. We note, however, that this amendment would need to be "much more finely tailored" than the former *Criminal Code* false news provision struck down by the Supreme Court of Canada as unconstitutional in the Zundel case.

Rt. Hon. Denis MacShane

The Rt. Hon. Dr. MacShane has been a Labour UK Member of Parliament for fifteen years. He is a former Minister of State for Europe at the Foreign and Commonwealth Office and currently sits as a UK delegate on the Parliamentary Assembly of the Council of Europe and NATO. His commentaries on international and European affairs are regularly seen in major UK and other European or American publications. He is the author of several books, including the recently published *Globalising Hatred: The New Antisemitism* (Weidenfeld and Nicolson), and was recently Chairman of the UK All-Party Parliamentary Inquiry into Antisemitism. He also chairs the European Institute for the Study of Contemporary Antisemitism, a British-based think-tank.

United Kingdom All Party Parliamentary Committee Against Antisemitism

The Parliamentary Committee Against Antisemitism harnesses the goodwill of parliamentarians from all sides, and both Houses, in the struggle against prejudice and discrimination. The Committee's purposes are to monitor and survey antisemitism wherever it arises; to exchange information amongst national Parliaments, non-governmental organisations and the public; to consider and take whatever action may be necessary to prevent further antisemitism; to promote inter-faith contact, dialogue and co-operation; to organise conferences, seminars, visits and other activities as may be desirable to achieve the Committee's purposes

The Committee provides parliamentarians, academics, journalists and members of the public with up-to-date information on antisemitism, antisemitic incidents and the efforts being made to combat them in the United Kingdom and abroad. The Committee commission researches, holds events, arranges briefings, publishes bulletins, and provides a forum for debate and discussion on the subject.

Rt. Hon. Denis MacShane[*]
Chair, All-Party Parliamentary Group Against Antisemitism Inquiry Panel, UK

Oral Testimony of Rt. Hon. Denis MacShane, Chair of the All-Party Parliamentary Group against Antisemitism Inquiry Panel, United Kingdom and Labour UK Member of Parliament. Delivered to the Canadian Parliamentary Coalition to Combat Antisemitism on 2 November 2009.

I am not exactly sure which language one should speak in this forum, but in England, we endeavour to speak from time to time in a civilized tongue. Therefore, I can continue in French, if that helps you at all.

Perhaps as I am a Brit, I will speak in English. Thank you very much for inviting me to be here. Who am I? I have been a member of the British Parliament since 1994. I was number two in the foreign office as Minister of State until 2005. When I stood down, my friend and colleague, John Mann, who is chairman of the All-party Parliamentary Group on Antisemitism, asked me if, on behalf of the House of Commons, I might be interested in forming and chairing a commission of inquiry into antisemitism. It is a subject I have long been involved in. The first political pamphlet I ever wrote was an attack on racism in the media. That was more than 30 years ago, but since then I have been tracking racism, and of course antisemitism is a component part of traditional and new racism. Both inside Britain and in my work as minister for Europe around the continent of Europe, I have certainly picked up quite a lot of anecdotal evidence on the resurgence of antisemitism organized politically from the hard right and sometimes from the hard left, sponsored by states. In particular, there was evidence that Jews in Britain were experiencing levels of discomfort in their full citizenship, which I considered unacceptable, but before making that assertion, I thought a committee of inquiry might help. So I asked other senior parliamentarians to join me—Iain Duncan Smith, the former leader of the Conservative Party; Mr. Chris Huhne, who was a very senior member of the Liberal Democratic Party; Khalid Mahmood, one of our Muslim members of Parliament; Lady Sylvia Hermon from the Ulster Unionist Party; as well as ex-ministers and privy councillors from the Conservative and Labour Parties. It so happened—it is just a matter worthy of note, and I did not really work it out this way—that none of us is Jewish, and I would say very few of us,

---

[*] The testimony of Right Honourable MacShane is comprised of an oral submission presented to the Canadian Parliamentary Inquiry into Antisemitism on 3 November 2009, a written submission detailing a summary and recommendations for the UK All-Party Panel Against Antisemitism (2008). Full unabridged transcripts of Rt. Hon. MacShane's testimony can be found at *http://www.cpcca.ca/inquiry.htm.*

myself included, have taken any active political interest in the Israeli-Palestinian debates that obviously are as lively in British politics as I am sure they are in Canadian politics. I went to Israel once in the early 1980s, and other than having a layman's knowledge of the problems there, and obviously supporting both the right of Israel to exist and the right of the Palestinian people to have their grievances met and dealt with, I have not been involved in their politics.

So we set up the Committee of Inquiry. It met in a very traditional way, almost harking back to 19th century committees of inquiry; that is to say, we have evidence sessions like this in the House of Commons. We invited people to send in their representations, and we received literally hundreds of different papers and witness statements that were sent in from both sides of the argument. We asked leaders of the Jewish community, the chief rabbi, the board of deputies of British Jews, which is the governing council of the Jewish community in Britain, and academic experts. But we also wanted to take this into the realm of government and public administration, so we asked the police to come and give evidence. We asked government ministers to come and give evidence. We did not want to narrow it down to looking at just what were considered to be antisemitic attacks—the daub on a synagogue wall, the desecration of a cemetery, the punch in the face of a rabbi, the jostling of a student—but to actually look at whether government departments and public administration in the United Kingdom were (a) recognizing it as a problem, (b) coming up with strategies to tackle it, and (c) educating and informing executives down to the level of vice-chancellors and police chiefs that this was a problem that had to be taken seriously.

Our committee met. I think we had fewer evidence sessions, sir, than you were planning. We also travelled outside of London to take evidence from students and school children in Manchester. We went to Paris as well to get a flavour of the European side of things. Actually, that did not feature in the report. Finally, after about a year's worth of work, we produced this report, which I am sure will be in your witness packs. If you look at it and read it, you will see that it is presented as a House of Commons white paper. It is actually printed by the stationery office, and it has a very traditional paragraph-by-paragraph set of points, arguments, and then conclusions.

I presented that, with some of the commission members, to Prime Minister Blair in September 2006. I do stress that this is a completely all-party thing. There is no difference between Labour, Conservatives, and Liberal Democrats on this issue. Mr. Blair promised to send it out to government departments for their reaction, and the government then collectively produced its response to this report in the spring, or perhaps a little later on, of 2007. Since then the government has produced an annual report on the problem of anti- Semitism every year. So that actually translates what was a parliamentary procedure into actual government practice.

For example, we were asking the Foreign Office to challenge the antisemitic behaviour and statements in some states where clearly the government itself could be seen to be sanctioning or approving antisemitism. Some of these states rightly make appeals to us if they feel that Muslim sensibilities have been offended, and states have a right to ask of other states that they take action in certain areas. One may not choose to follow those requests, but I think globally, from the democratically elected parliamentary states, we can also legitimately say to some other states—although I am not going to name them here, as that is for the Committee's work to do later on—that they have to accept responsibility for what is done in their state's name.

So that is pretty well it. It was punctuated by the Lebanon conflict in the summer of 2006, and then of course the Gaza conflict earlier this year, with very big spikes in anti-Semitic attacks and a decline of editorial standards, so you had the equation of Jews with Nazis, and Israel as an apartheid state. Having done a lot of work in the 1980s with the black trade union movement in South Africa, laying in ditches outside townships as the apartheid state rumbled around and tried to catch me, I think I know the difference between an apartheid state and undoubtedly the policy lines of Israel—which we have always insisted are perfectly open to criticism. To criticize Israel is not antisemitic, but equally, it is wrong to say that antisemitism is just an invention of people who want to defend Israel. It is real. It exists. It exists on campuses, and it exists in some politician's minds. As I have written in the National Post today, and I would almost like to read that article into the record, we are seeing now at the European Parliament overtly antisemitic politicians elected. We are seeing a banalization of antisemitism in European political discourse, which is very worrying.

To conclude, following on from that Commission of Inquiry's work, I welcome strongly that it was enlarged into an international coalition. The first conference is now being held in Germany and then in London, and I think it is coming to Canada next year. If parliaments themselves take this issue seriously, you can move away from the overexcited rhetoric of a speech or a person with a cause to plead, and you have to sift the evidence. This is an extraordinarily sober report. There are no dramatic adjectives here. This is not a report, in my judgment, that seeks to sensationalize or to find justification for any particular part of the arguments that swirl around the issue of new anti-Semitism, but in very much a Whitehall civil service way—if I can use that metaphor—it seeks to downplay.

However, because it downplays, because government departments have to come back and defend what their police services are doing, what the Foreign Office is doing, what the higher education departments are doing, they think, like any government, they are doing the right thing, and now they are under a bit more pressure to have to think through whether this is a problem or not and the extent of how they should handle it. So I think making it sober and turning it into an All-party Parliamentary Committee's work is a very concrete way of helping.

It is a way I can help as a parliamentarian. That is what I do. That is my profession. That is my business. I can write a book. I can make a speech. I can do articles. That is fine. But as parliamentarians, we do this work.

I really welcome the Canadian initiative. I wish this session every success in the future work of the committee.

David Matas

David Matas is a Winnipeg lawyer and senior counsel to B'nai Brith Canada.

When does Criticism of Israel amount to Antisemitism?
by David Matas[1]

Superficially, criticism of Israel and antisemitism seem distinct. Yet, sometimes they are connected. The illusion that the two are always distinct leads a minimization of the dimensions of antisemitism.

Criticism of Israel is often anti-Zionist, springing from a belief that the State of Israel should not exist. Not all criticism of Israel is anti-Zionist, but a lot of it is. We can see that this is so when there are gratuitous charges of criminality against Israel or Israelis, when there are highly selective criticisms of Israel or when criticism is completely unmoored from reality.

Though anti-Zionism can take many forms, the most common form in the international arena is accusation of criminality. Israel is accused of every international crime known to humanity.

According to the statute of the International Criminal Court[2] and the Geneva Conventions on the Laws of War,[3] only individuals can commit war crimes. States can be responsible for international crimes, but not criminally responsible.[4] Accusing Israel as a whole of war crimes is an imposition of collective guilt.

---

1 This text is adapted and condensed from a presentation to a Stephen Roth Institute of Tel Aviv University seminar on antisemitism, held at Budapest, Hungary, November 7, 2006.
2 Article 25(1).
3 Article 146, Fourth Convention.
4 See *Bosnia v. Serbia*, I.C.J. paragraphs 155 to 179.

The reason anti-Zionists target Israel rather than individual perpetrators is their desire to delegitimize the State of Israel. Through delegitimization, they hope to achieve the result of destruction of the Jewish state.

Collective guilt leads to collective punishment. That indeed is what anti-Zionist accusers have in mind. Anti-Zionists accuse Israel of killing innocents, because they want to deny to the Jewish community the right to their own state.

There may indeed be some individual Jews who have been complicit in war crimes or crimes against humanity, just as there may have been over two thousand years ago some individual Jews complicit in the death of Christ. But to blame the Jewish state for those crimes, like blaming the Jewish people for the death of Christ, is straight bigotry.

The problem, though, is not just the misplacement of the target. These so-called crimes never happened. They are anti-Zionist inventions. Accusing the Israeli leadership rather than the State of Israel for grave crimes, which is also quite common, is also mostly just anti-Zionism. Israelis are accused of crimes which have not been committed by anyone.

Systematic charges against either Israel or Israelis of genocide, colonialism, terrorism, war crimes, crimes against humanity, apartheid, ethnic cleansing, racism, illegal occupation, illegality of settlements, disproportionate response to terrorist attacks and breaching a Palestinian right of return, are wrong in either fact or law, and often both.[5]

These never-ending charges of criminality against the Jewish leadership have much the same intent as the charges of criminality against the Jewish state. They are not levied to improve the behaviour of the leadership. The last thing anti-Zionists want is a better Jewish state. They are levied to discredit and delegitimize the Jewish state.

While accusing a state of international criminality is legally inappropriate, it is certainly proper to criticise a state for human rights violations. However, when Israel, virtually alone, is the target of criticism, the targeting becomes political rather than principled. Selective criticism directed to Israel, when the real offender countries and non-governmental entities are ignored, is obviously about something else than promoting respect for human rights. That something else is demonization and, ultimately, destruction of the State of Israel.

Zionism is the expression of the right to self determination of the Jewish people. The self determination of peoples is a fundamental human right. Anti-Zionism is the expression of the view that the Jews, alone amongst the peoples of the world, should be denied this right.

5 David Matas *Aftershock: Anti-Zionism and Antisemitism*, Dundurn Press, 2005.

Antisemitism is a denial of a broad range of human rights to the Jewish people. Anti-Zionism is the denial of one particular human right, the right to self determination of peoples.

Charging anyone or any group with a criminal offence is a libel unless it is grounded in reality. The myriad of international criminal charges which are levied against Israelis are just that—libels, without any foundation in reality.

If you accuse individual Israelis of crimes against humanity and Israelis have committed crimes against humanity, then it is a legitimate criticism. If you accuse Israelis of crimes against humanity and Israelis have committed no such crimes, then it is defamation.

These accusations are slurs because they are not real. If there really were a Jewish conspiracy for world domination, then it would be legitimate to criticise such a conspiracy. But to fantasize such a conspiracy in order to criticise Jews is antisemitism.

The same can be said of Israeli human rights violations. If there really were the massive violations which anti-Zionists fantasize, it would be legitimate to criticise them. But it is just antisemitism in another form to fantasize these violations in order to justify an anti-Zionist diatribe.

The consequence of all the phoney criminal charges against Israel is the painting of the Jewish community world wide as a criminal population for its actual or perceived support for the Jewish state. Yesterday, Jews were considered to be a criminal population for their complicity in the death of Christ. Today, Jews are considered to be a criminal population for their complicity in the killing of innocent Palestinians or Lebanese.

The current accusation is as false as the old accusation was. And the results are much the same—hatred, discrimination, and violence against an innocent Jewish population and its institutions worldwide.

The motivation behind many incidents is cumulative. For many antisemitic attacks today, anti-Zionism is reinforcement, joining with traditional antisemitism to form a poisonous cocktail. Unless we keep firmly in mind the linkage between anti-Zionism and antisemitism, the chance of identifying incidents with Jewish victims as antisemitic is significantly reduced.

We can see the impact of anti-Zionism on antisemitism by looking at the identified perpetrator population. There has been a huge increase world wide in attacks against Jews perpetrated by Arab Moslems.

The purveyors of anti-Zionist propaganda attempt to cultivate an Arab Moslem constituency. A lot of anti-Zionism is in the Arabic language and couched in Islamic religious terms. Many of the leading fomenters of anti-Zionism are Arabic-speaking

Moslem clerics. When we see that it is Arab Moslems who are attacking Jews, that tells us that the antisemitism which is anti-Zionism is at work.

Here is an example to show that there is no meaningful distinction between anti-Zionism and antisemitism. A suicide bomber drove a car bomb in the Israeli embassy in Buenos Aires Argentina in March 1992. The attack killed 29 people and injured 100. Ibrahim Hussein Berro, a second suicide car bomb terrorist, attacked the Jewish community centre, the Israeli-Argentine Mutual Association, in Buenos Aires in July 1994, killing 85 and wounding over 200.

The Argentinean intelligence service investigated this second attack and concluded, in a detailed report, that the attack was planned and organized by the Government of Iran. The decision to mount the attack was taken in August 1993 by Iran's National Security Council. Participating in the decision were the then and current leader Ayatollah Khamenei, as well as the then president Hashemi Rafsanjani. Iran used Hezbollah to perpetrate the attack. [6]

Given the proximity in time and parallel in techniques, the two attacks likely had the same source, Iran. Both attacks were both anti-Zionist and antisemitic. Pretending there is a difference between them ignores the perspective of the perpetrators. Once the perpetrators equate the two, we befuddle our own defences against these sorts of attacks if we pretend they are different.

We can see spikes of attacks against Jewish communities worldwide whenever anti-Zionist propaganda gets particularly intense, for instance, at the time of the fabrications of a massacre at Jenin in April 2002. An escalation in the conflict between Israel and its neighbours leads to greater prominence for anti-Zionist propaganda. It is the demonization of Israeli efforts of self defence which generate the antisemitic incidents, rather than the conflict itself.

Distinguishing between criticism of Israel and antisemitism racist becomes an excuse for inaction in response to racist attacks against Jews. Locating in the Middle East the cause of attacks against Jews worldwide suggests that the solution is in the Middle East rather than at home.

There are people who will say that they support the existence of the State of Israel but then endorse the wildest, most outrageous accusations made against Israel. Are these people antisemitic? By intent, I would say no. But, by impact, I would say yes. Racism can occur either by intent or impact. An abstinence from antisemitic rhetoric, even an abstinence from antisemitic beliefs, does not absolve a person or an organization from a charge of antisemitism.

---

6 Anti-Defamation League "Investigation finds Iranian, Hezbollah and Syrian involvement in 1994 bombing of Argentine Jewish Community Centre" October 2003, at www.adl.org.

The failure to see the link between many criticisms of Israel and anti-Zionism and between anti-Zionism and antisemitism has harmful effects on the struggle against antisemitism. Given the sorry state of human rights in the world, advocates of respect for human rights must prioritize. When we take anti-Zionism out of the antisemitic mix, both the number and severity of antisemitic incidents decrease. That leads to a lower priority for these abuses.

A Canadian example of the link between criticism of Israel and antisemitism is to be found in the January 5, 2009 statement of CUPE Ontario "supporting a ban on Israeli academics doing speaking, teaching or research work at Ontario universities as a protest against the December 29 bombing of the Islamic University in Gaza." This statement in a nutshell shows the linkage between false charges against Israel and discrimination.

Hamas engaged in terrorist attacks against Israel, firing rockets at civilian populations—between December 27, 2008 and December 29, 2008, more than 110 rockets. Israeli Defence Forces responded on December 29 by attacking buildings which stored the rockets and other explosives, research and development centres used for the development of explosives and meeting places for senior Hamas officials. The buildings were located at the Islamic University.

There were three noteworthy aspects of this exchange of fire. One was that the Hamas attacks had no military significance and targeted civilians only. The second was that the Israeli response was an act of self defence with a military objective. The third is that Hamas failed to respect the principle of distinction,[7] failing to distinguish between military and civilian structures.

CUPE Ontario then criticised Israel, but not Hamas, decontextualizing the Israel self defence from the terrorist attack which generated it. In this exchange, Israel did nothing wrong and Hamas was entirely to blame. Yet, CUPE blamed Israel and not Hamas.

A CUPE Ontario statement of January 14, 2010 labelled the Israeli response to Hamas rocket attacks on Israel disproportionate and called for an end the occupation. But that correcting statement was not much better.

There is no requirement of proportionate response in international humanitarian law.[8]

Switzerland, to United Nations, Palais des Nations, panel discussion on "Proportionality Under International Armed Conflict".

---

7 Article 48 Protocol 1 to the Geneva Conventions on the Laws of War

8 See David Matas *The charge of disproportionality against Israel*, remarks prepared for delivery 20 March 2009 Geneva

Israel was respectful of international law in reaction to the Hamas rocket attacks, trying as best it could, in an attempt to defend itself against terrorist attacks, to distinguish civilian from military structures despite the Hamas effort to blend the two. As well, Israel had withdrawn from Gaza long before Hamas launched its rocket attacks.

Whether CUPE Ontario was motivated by a desire to see the destruction of the State of Israel or just plain ignorance hardly matters in terms of the result, a straightforward call to bigotry—a ban on Israeli academics.

It is this sort of logic the Jewish community sees again and again. The starting point is unfounded criticism of Israel. The end point is discrimination and violence against Jews. If we are going to be effective in combating antisemitism, we cannot ignore what is all too often the place from which it comes—baseless criticism of Israel

Dr. Gregg Rickman

Gregg Rickman is the former United States State Department Special Envoy to Monitor and Combat Anti-Semitism. Mr. Rickman has directed the United States Senate Banking Committee investigation, into the disposition of assets of Holocaust victims held by Swiss banks since World War II, ending with a $1.25 billion settlement on behalf of the survivors. He has served as the Director of Congressional Affairs at the Republican Jewish Coalition. He has also served on the staff of the United States House of Representatives International Relations Committee where he served first on the Subcommittee on the Middle East and Central Asia and handled numerous issues including anti-Semitism and Holocaust restitution. He was a Senior Fellow at the Institute for Religion and Public Policy in Washington, D.C., and a Visiting Fellow at The Yale Initiative for the Interdisciplinary Study of Antisemitism (YIISA) at Yale University and a Research Scholar at the Initiative on Antisemitism and Anti-Israelism of the Institute for Jewish & Community Research in San Francisco. He has authored three books, *Swiss Banks and Jewish Souls* (1999) and *Conquest and Redemption, A History of Jewish Assets from the Holocaust,* (2006) and *Hating the Jews: The Rise of Antisemitism in the 21st Century* (2012). He received his Bachelor's and Master's degrees from John Carroll University and his Ph.D. in International Relations from the University of Miami.

Dr. Gregg Rickman[*]
Former Special Envoy to Monitor and Combat Antisemitism for the U.S. State Department,
As an Individual

As a matter of background, I served in the United States Department of State as the first U.S. special envoy to monitor and combat antisemitism, serving from 2006 to 2009. During that time, I travelled around the world to twenty-eight countries, including many countries with significant Muslim populations, some of whom espoused a mindset and collection of historical and political biases that were very disturbing.

Specifically to this point, I will address the subject of relations between Jewish communities and ethnic and Muslim minorities in Europe and how these relations have impacted the fate of Jewish communities on that continent. I will finish with a few recommendations.

In my travels, I found that in many of these Muslim countries, or in countries with large Muslim populations, the relationship between the two communities is tense at best. On the one hand, Muslim community leaders tell me they respect the role Jews have made for themselves, admiring the access Jewish leaders have and the influence and relative wealth the community has come to accumulate. On the other hand, there is jealousy. One Muslim leader in southern France told me he wanted to catch up with Jewish groups organizationally. This leader spoke to me about a "competition of memories" with Jews, pointedly expressing a problem. This goes to the point of Professor Weisskirchen earlier today.[1] His concerns centred on Muslims' perception of their comparative disadvantage in Europe vis-à-vis the Jews. He told me about real societal discrimination against Muslims in employment, religious observance, and in general daily life, not at all the responsibility of the Jewish community. Yet despite the perception of their status, they offer up the support of the Jews in southern France and how they exhibit that support towards Israel as the real reasons for the present situation.

He complained that Jews came as colonialists, with other Europeans, to North Africa, received French citizenship, and then moved to France. Muslims, on the other hand, lived in French-speaking North Africa and also immigrated to France, but were denied the same level of acceptance. These same Jews, he said, now unfairly appropriate the history of the Holocaust, and he intimated

---

[*] The testimony of Dr. Rickman is comprised of both an oral and written submission presented to the Canadian Parliamentary Inquiry into Antisemitism on 3 November 2009. Full unabridged transcripts of Rabbi Baker's testimony can be found at http://www.cpcca.ca/inquiry.htm.

1 Please see above

that it was not their history to claim. "Now we Algerians," he told me, "suffer from it."

Many Muslims believe their suffering locks Muslim communities and individuals in a second-class position. Yet this view, according to the director of one Dutch NGO in Amsterdam, is not necessarily the correct one. According to him, the community itself is not without blame in this regard. Young Muslims' own cultural and religious reluctance to integrate does not help matters. Their diminished prospects for employment are tied to their reluctance to seek proper schooling or even higher levels of education.

I have been told of this problem in Germany as well. The effects on Muslim teenagers of not staying in school were explained to me in great detail. Dropping out of school places them at a clear disadvantage economically and socially. The fact has been reinforced by a study published by the Open Society Institute EU Monitoring and Advocacy Program, which found in 2007 that foreign-born German children were three times as likely as children born in Germany to stop at secondary school, failing to move on. Furthermore, in 1998, according to the report, about one-third of foreigners aged 20 to 29 remained without a professional qualification, compared to only 8% of Germans of the same age group. It has not gotten much better a decade later. Think, though, of the effects now on that age group self-deprived of an education.

In Dutch schools, as the Dutch NGO director and former Dutch parliamentarian Aayan Hirsi Ali explained to me, Muslim schoolchildren are disruptive in class, and teachers are reluctant to counter their obstreperous practices. Worse, according to another version of the Open Society study, in 2007 in the Netherlands, less than ten percent of the Turkish and Moroccan students there finished higher education or university education.

As second-generation Muslims, these youth are caught in a netherworld. They do not feel fully European, and with inadequate Arabic language fluency, they do not feel fully Arab. Add a lack of education to this mix of circumstances and the sense of despair is only worse. These concerns have been expressed to me across Europe.

Confused European Muslim youth go back home, as it were, to the countries of their parents and grandparents, yearning to acquire that identity, but are rejected there as not wholly Moroccan, Algerian or Turkish. Rejected in both homes, they return to Europe confused, looking for meaning and of course someone to blame, and that is how they fall prey to charismatic imams, imported from abroad ... into mosques financed from abroad and under whose influence these people fall.

This need to blame, as well as the learned hatred, is passed on to younger Muslim kids, who harass Jews in west Amsterdam, for example, in the *banlieue* near Paris, and in other European cities. I have talked with a number of people in Amsterdam—rabbis, Jewish teenagers, and even elected officials—who told me stories of young Muslims who yell "Kill the Jews" and routinely throw rocks at Jews leaving synagogues or those daring to walk through Muslim neighbourhoods. As one Jewish leader in Europe told me, "Jews are the only ones who go to synagogue or school under police protection." This has become a normal existence for Jews in Europe. I have seen it first-hand. Due to this ongoing pattern of Muslim harassment of Jews in Europe, it has come to the point that an intentional segregation is taking place. Jewish families are moving out of mixed Muslim-Jewish neighbourhoods. Because of the frequency and intensity of anti-Jewish harassment, it is simply no longer worth living in these areas.

Moreover, according to Catholic Church officials and Jewish leaders in France, in 2007 nearly sixty percent of Jewish students attended private schools in France, Jewish or Catholic, with their parents fearing their security in the public schools. As in the Netherlands, teachers are unable to guarantee the safety of Jewish students. I was told stories, fascinating stories but depressing ones, of ongoing efforts at interfaith work talking with Muslims in the *banlieue* outside of Paris. The efforts produced frightening results. I was told of declarations from Muslims warning those attempting this work that Jews were a "damned and rejected people". I was told that one Muslim man declared, "Every day I pray for you to become a Muslim so I wouldn't be obligated to kill you."

It must be clear that the discrimination Muslims face is not a myth, yet Muslim communities suggest a greater role for the problem and weave it into the story of their victimhood, taking on strong notes of succeeding the Jews as the newest victims of discrimination, all the while blaming them for their ills. "In broader terms," I was told, "Arabs are Semites, and therefore, 'Islamaphobia' is a new kind of anti-Semitism." I was told this repeatedly across Europe. This sentiment was echoed to me by another source, who casually suggested that Islamaphobia in Europe is "ten times" that of anti-Semitism. I heard this comparison from Saudis, Emiratis, Egyptians, Lebanese, and people all over the world. Yet just as Muslims accuse Jews of appropriating a history that they claim is not theirs, so too are they appropriating one themselves. We need to be clear about this point: anti-Semitism means discrimination or violence against Jews, not Muslims. Relations between Muslim and Jewish communities are overwhelmed by the extension of the Middle East conflict to European shores. The hatreds, jealousies, and historic disputes are now being played out in new lands.

The conclusions of the European monitoring centre's *Summary overview of the situation in the European Union 2001-2005* only reinforce this conclusion:

There has been some evidence to support the view that there is some link between the number of reported anti-Semitic incidents and the political situation in the Middle East.... Moreover, some of the data indicate that there have been changes in the profile of the perpetrators. It is no longer the extreme right which is seen as solely responsible for hostility towards Jewish individuals or property.... Instead, victims identified "young Muslims," "people of North African origin," or "immigrants" as perpetrators.

The EUMC concluded that in Europe:

> Antisemitic activity after 2000 is increasingly attributed to a "new antisemitism," characterized primarily by the vilification of Israel as the "Jewish collective" and perpetrated primarily by members of Europe's Muslim population. Throughout the Middle East and in many Muslim communities in western Europe and beyond, anti-Zionist rhetoric finds frequent and powerful expression, especially in Arab-language newspapers and magazines, on the radio, on television, via the Internet, and in sermons delivered in mosques. Antisemitism emanating from Muslim communities throughout Europe provides a corrosive atmosphere for Jews there and provides for an expanding hotbed of anti-Jewish feelings, attitudes, and actions.

In an area so historically and tragically associated with antisemitism, for this virus to return in yet another guise is both infuriating and extremely worrying. History, as well as common decency, dictates that European authorities as well as individual Europeans have a distinct responsibility to curb this evil before it is allowed to again overwhelm the Jewish people, and worse, spread to other lands. We must not veer our eyes as Jews elsewhere suffer from anti-Semitism, ignoring the problem since it fails to rise to such a threatening level around us. Before I close, I wish to provide a few recommendations toward this end.

First, I recommend that this committee pursue the creation of a post of special envoy to monitor and combat anti-Semitism, similar to the post I held. When I held this position in the United States, I had very few international compatriots with whom to speak, and it would benefit this country greatly.

Second, require your foreign ministry to publish an annual report on antisemitism, assembled by your embassies overseas. They are on the ground. They are talking with people every day, and they are in the best place of all to see what's happening in these countries.

And third, require the government to assemble annual reports on acts of antisemitism occurring in this country. In this way you will have a base of data from which to work. Otherwise you can't define the problem if you don't know the statistics behind it.

In conclusion, ignoring this problem is an abandonment of the Jews there, in Europe, and another scar upon the history of Jews and of freedom and goodwill itself. As Edmund Burke has said to have declared, "All that is necessary for the triumph of evil is that good men do nothing." It is certainly time to do something.

Dr. Charles Small

Dr. Charles Small, is the Director and Founder of the Yale Initiative for the Interdisciplinary Study of Antisemitism (YIISA). He received his Bachelor of Arts in Political Science, McGill University, Montreal; a M.Sc. in Urban Development Planning in Economics, Development Planning Unit (DPU), University College London; and a Doctorate of Philosophy (D.Phil), St. Antony›s College, Oxford University. Dr. Charles Small completed post-doctorate research at the Groupement de recherche ethnicité et société, Université de Montréal. He was the VATAT Research Fellow at Ben Gurion University, Beersheva, and taught in departments of sociology and geography at Goldsmith College, University of London, Tel Aviv University, Tel Aviv and the Institute of Urban Studies, Hebrew University, Jerusalem. He was also an Associate Professor and the Director of Urban Studies at SCSU, Connecticut. He worked as a consultant and policy advisor in North America, Europe, Southern Africa and the Middle East; and lectured internationally. Dr. Small specializes in social and cultural theory, globalization and national identity, socio-cultural policy, racism(s)—including Antisemitism. He is also the President and Founder of the Institute for the Study of Global Antisemitism and Policy.

Yale Initiative for the Interdisciplinary Study of Antisemitism (YIISA)

Yale Initiative for the Interdisciplinary Study of Antisemitism (YIISA) is the first comprehensive interdisciplinary research initiative dedicated to the study of Antisemitism based a North American university. This approach to the examination of Antisemitism promotes interdisciplinary analysis at the historical, sociological, political, philosophical, psychological and economic levels. In the contemporary context of globalised relations it appears that Antisemitism has taken on new complex and changing forms that need to be decoded, mapped and critiqued.

Dr. Charles Small[*]

Director, Yale Initiative for the Interdisciplinary Study of Antisemitism (YIISA), Yale University

Oral Testimony of Dr. Charles Small, Director of the Yale Initiative for the Study of Antisemitism, Yale University. Delivered to the Canadian Parliamentary Coalition to Combat Antisemitism on 2 November 2009.

It is a great honour to be here with you. I want to say for the record that when I was at the London conference in February, I was very proud, as a person who is from Montreal, to be at the conference and to see there the all-party partic- ipation of the Canadian members of Parliament. I was very proud to see this participation. So I would like to commend the MPs here for participating in this conference and for really being leaders in the global community on this issue and taking up this inquiry.

I would like to start with a story. In the last academic year, Elie Wiesel came to Yale Law School to give a talk when he was being honoured. It was a packed room, with standing room only. They had an overflow room with a video hookup because so many students and faculty came to the lecture. There were about seven hundred people there, including some of the finest students— the future leaders of the United States—and law faculty in the country.

Elie Wiesel spoke about the possibility of another genocide against the Jewish people in talking about the destruction of the State of Israel. Elie Wiesel had family in Montreal. I would see him speak at synagogues regularly as I was growing up and coming of age, and to see Elie Wiesel, who is not only a symbol of the Shoah, but also, I think, a symbol of somebody who has fought for human rights from South Africa to Cambodia to Darfur to Sarajevo—the list goes on— to see him in his lifetime, this symbol of that generation, speak about the possibility of another genocide against the Jewish people, I thought was one of the most pathetic things I've ever seen in my life. Elie Wiesel spoke about this. What was even more devastating was that he went on to say that the thing that really disturbs him, as if this wasn't enough, is the fact that there's a silence. He asked where are the students and the student leaders, where are the fac- ulty, and where are the leaders of the Jewish community and the leaders of the free world in the face of this clearly articulated, clearly stated, very open, very honest—and I'm using my words carefully—genocidal anti- Semitic movement

---

[*] The testimony of Professor Small is comprised of an oral submission presented to the Canadian Parliamentary Inquiry into Antisemitism on 2 November 2009. Full unabridged transcripts of Dr. Small's testimony can be found at *http://www.cpcca.ca/inquiry.htm.*

that is sweeping parts of the world and that is infiltrating organizations and institutions even in the western world? We're met, by and large, with a silence. So I hope this committee and inquiry will become a beacon of light and stop the silence that is still prevalent mainly in the western world.

I would like to start by saying, just very briefly, that there are several stages of antisemitism historically. There was a sort of religious and theological form of antisemitism. When people viewed the world through the lens of religion, when religion was dominant, the Jews were the wrong religion. When religion was replaced by notions of race, ethnicity, and national identity, the Jews were the wrong race, ethnicity, and nationality; they actually became foreigners in lands they had inhabited for many generations. Now we are entering a new phase. If I could make one strong point to the committee, I think it is very important to realize that the world has changed and antisemitism has changed. We are no longer fighting the antisemitism of the brownshirts, Nazis, and fascism of 60 or 70 years ago. We have to now focus on a new and emerging type of antisemitism.

This new type of antisemitism, I would argue, is a globalized form of antisemitism. On the one hand, we have the dispossessed in parts of the Middle East who are being sucked into a sort of vacuum of radical Islamicists. I am not speaking about Islam and I am not speaking about Muslims; I want to make this point very clear. I am speaking about political Islam. The doctrine of political Islam has at its core a form of genocidal antisemitism that the social movement is using almost in the classic sense, blaming the Jews for all sorts of ills, which Professor Cotler mentioned earlier, while they subjugate and take away basic human rights from their own populations. As Professor Cotler said, antisemitism begins with Jews, but it never ends with Jews.

If you look at Iranian society, it is a clear case in point. While they blame the Jews for every imaginable ill in the world that you can think of, they are taking away women's basic human rights; women are worth literally 50% of a man under law and under the judicial system in Iran. As well, gay people are being executed, and the Baha'i community is being totally stripped of its basic human rights while they focus attention on Israel and the Jews.

It is an amalgamation of this. You have a reactionary, radical, and political Islam on the one hand, and in Europe and North America to an extent, but mostly in Western Europe, as Gregg Rickman was saying, you have almost an acquiescence. You have Europe emerging out of the Second World War with the destruction that was rampant throughout Europe, which was blamed, rightfully so I think, for the excesses of nationalism that Europeans suffered from, and now the intellectual world has entered into this phase of postmodernism. It is postmodernism combined with a liberalism, I think. They are very weary of national identities. They speak of notions of hybridity, of European identity more than specifically, say, English, Scottish, or French identity.

I think once again that Israel, with a strong national identity, and the Jewish people in Europe and North America, with a strong attachment to this State of Israel for cultural, religious, political, and historical reasons—and the list goes on—sort of fly in the face of the emerging postmodern European model of integration and multiculturalism, which I think is quite different from the Canadian model.

So you have in a sense, I would argue, an acquiescence to a social movement that is diametrically opposed to the basic human rights and human values that are embedded in democracy. If you think of notions of citizenship, under western democratic principles in Canada, for example, everybody ought to be equal under one legal system. In radical Islamic notions of caliphates and what they want to replace democratic states with, you have different levels of citizenship. So Jews, in a sense, would not have the right to self-determination in the Middle East. Women would be second-class citizens. Gay people would be essentially eliminated. So the notion of citizenship is replaced with another type of citizenship. I think this is very important.

When we look at Iran, it is, as we know, intent on building a nuclear weapon. I was recently at a conference organized by Pugwash, which actually has its roots in Canada. There were scholars, physicists, and security people from Russia, China, all over the European Union, Canada, the United States, and Israel. Everybody at the table agreed that Iran is trying to build a nuclear weapon. There was no debate. The only debate was about how long it would take and whether, if Iran had the weapon, it would use it. But everybody agreed that Iran was trying to build a bomb. I think it's very important to realize that Iran has consistently and openly and in an upfront way spoken about destroying the State of Israel. They are clear about it. If you read the writings of Ayatollah Khomeini and those of the present regime and the present supreme leader, they are clear and consistent about their wish to destroy the State of Israel. I think what's very important from a radical Islamic perspective is that the Jewish people are the only others to have self-determination on what is perceived as Islamic land and that would become part of this Islamic caliphate. This is why, I would argue, there is such a determined focus on Israel. According to radical Islamic thought, you cannot have the other with self-determination, with governance over land; they have to be subjected to second-class citizenship.

If you look at Shiite Islam, there were *fatwas* passed mainly in the 1600s and 1700s. Two very well-known scholars, David Menashri and Daniel Tsadik, look at how Shiite Islam had *fatwas* in which Jews were considered untouchable or impure. To this day, Jews cannot go out in Iran in the rain because they are impure. *Fatwas* have been set that say if a Jew is out in the rain and their clothes become permeated with water and the water drips onto the pavement—and this is a religious ruling—you have to dig up the pavement and dispose of it because it's contaminated by the impurity of the Jew.

So you have a fusion, if you will, of the old pernicious forms of Shiite Persian anti-Semitism or Judeophobia combined with the geopolitical discourse of the social movement of radical Islam and the demonization of Israel. The demonization of Israel is at the core of the new antisemitism.

In the Hamas charter, the Hamas charter supported by Iran, it is not the rantings and ravings of a few extremists within the Hamas party or the military extreme wing of the party. This is the covenant. This is the covenant, the constitution, the raison d'être of Hamas. Literally, they call not only for the killing of Jews, in black and white, in their covenant, in their constitution, but they also fuse ... If it were not so serious, it would almost be as comical as a Monty Python skit on some level. Here is a radical Islamic organization that is trying to recreate some sort of fictitious golden age and replace Israel and Crusader Christian and Jewish influence on the region, to rid it of these outside influences, and recreate a purely Muslim Islamic reality, recreating the golden age. They actually use the "Protocols of the Elders of Zion", the pernicious form of European antisemitism, and fuse it throughout its constitution. The theme that runs through the covenant of Hamas, which is right here, is the "Protocols of the Elders of Zion". It is unbelievable. Here, as we heard from Professor Cotler, the "Protocols of the Elders of Zion" is becoming rampant once again. I would argue—I can show you details during the questions and answers—that the Iranian revolutionary regime, Hamas, Hezbollah, and other radical Islamists are using the "Protocols of the Elders of Zion" to spread not only the dehumanization of the State of Israel but also classical forms of antisemitism.

When the deputy foreign minister of South Africa stood up about a year ago in Soweto and gave a speech about how the Jews were controlling the economy of the United States, 18,000 people, probably most of whom had had no direct contact with Jews in their lives, gave her a long-standing ovation. A young woman in Connecticut was shot dead at point-blank range in a café several months ago by a man who was stalking her who had a copy of the "Protocols of the Elders of Zion" in his knapsack.

I was at the Durban II conference when President Ahmadinejad spoke in Geneva. You can see that the themes of his language, of his whole speech, regarding Jews and the State of Israel were based on the "Protocols of the Elders of Zion". On the one hand, while they are trying to build weapons of mass destruction, and the west by and large continues to deal with them in terms of business as usual, European Union, German, and other countries' trade actually continues to increase with the regime. Despite its genocidal anti- Semitism, its sexism, its homophobia, and now the stealing of an election and persecuting its own citizens, this continues. The exporting of the "Protocols of the Elders of Zion" is even more dangerous, probably, than their nuclear weapons program. We know that the Holocaust, the crematoriums, the bricks and mortars that built the crematoriums, began with ideas, began with words. The "Protocols of the Elders of Zion" paved the way to the crematoriums. It was created as a forgery in the late 1800s in France, or perhaps in Russia. These words and these concepts actually paved the way for the genocidal antisemitism that swept Europe.

As we know from the European experience, yes, six million Jews were liquidated in a horrific fashion. But look at the death and destruction that other people in Europe suffered too: tens of millions of other people died. Economies were totally destroyed.

So the disease of antisemitism, which is being unleashed openly and overtly in the Middle East, and is now, as we have heard from the other testimony, seeping into western European political discourse, intellectual discourse, and human rights discourse, is extraordinarily dangerous, I think, not just to the Jews and Israel but to the very basic notions of democratic principles that I am sure everybody here, regardless of our political views, agrees on.

Bernard J. Shapiro

Barnard Shapiro became the Principal and Vice-Chancellor of McGill University on 1 July 1994 and Principal and Vice-Chancellor and Professor Emeritus in January, 2003.

Dr. Shapiro earned his undergraduate degree at McGill University and his Doctorate in Education from Harvard University. After graduating from Harvard in 1967, he joined the faculty of Boston University where he later became Associate Dean of the School of Education. He returned to Canada in 1976 to become Dean of the Faculty of Education at the University of Western Ontario, where two years later he was appointed Vice President (Academic) and Provost.

In 1980, he assumed the position of Director of the Ontario Institute for Studies in Education (OISE) until 1986 when he was appointed Deputy Minister of Education for the Province of Ontario. Since that time he has also served as Deputy Minister of Skills Development, Deputy Secretary of Cabinet, Deputy Minister and Secretary of Management Board and Deputy Minister of Colleges and Universities. In 1992, following his retirement from the Ontario Public Service, Dr. Shapiro joined the University of Toronto as a Professor of Education and Public Policy..

He is the past president of the Canadian Society for the Study of Education, the Social Science Federation of Canada, and the Canadian Bureau for International Education (CBIE). He has also served on the executive committee of the International Association for the Evaluation of Educational Achievement (IEA) and as Chairman of the governing board of the Centre for Educational Research and Innovation in Paris. In May 2004, he was appointed the first Ethics Commissioner of Canada, a position he held until 2007.

Currently, Dr. Shapiro is the Chair of the Board of Directors of the Canadian Bureau for International Educations (CBIE), Chairman of the Board of Governors of the Royal Military College, Co-Chair of the Societe du Havre in Montreal, Chair of the International Review Committee of the Leading Edge Foundation in British Columbia, and Vice-President of the CJA Federation in Montreal. Currently, he is on the Board of the Institute for Research in Public Policy, the Royal College of Physicians and Surgeons and Quest University. In September 1999 Dr. Shapiro was appointed Officer of the Order of Canada and in 2002, he was appointed as Grand Officier de l'Ordre National de Quebec

Bernard Shapiro[*]
Former Principal and Vice-Chancellor of McGill University

Written Submission prepared by Bernard Shapiro to the Canadian Parliamentary Inquiry into Antisemitism.

CPCCA Members:

Thank you for having asked me to participate in today's meeting. I am most appreciative of the opportunity that you have provided.

I was originally approached to come to this meeting by the Honorable Irwin Cotler. I agreed to come, and some few days later I was approached by the Principal of McGill University to ask if I could, in some informal sense at least, represent the University at this hearing. I agreed to do so, but I do not want to represent myself to the Parliamentary Commission is a formal representative of the University.

Although it is clear that the Commission's focus of interest in on combating anti-Semitism, I want to begin by outlining what I understand as McGill's position with regard to freedom of speech. In this context, I would like to quote from—partly because I agree with it—a recent essay by McGill's Assistant Provost, Morton Mendelson. "Freedom to express a wide range of ideas ... is essential in a modern university. Sharing ideas is indispensable to the quest for knowledge which drives the intellectually curious who makeup a university. It shapes our research and our attempts to discover what we do not yet know. It enriches our understanding, allowing us to add dimension and nuance to what we thing we know and what we may take to be accepted truths. And it helps us to understand that, in fact, there is so much yet to learn.

Therefore, a university must provide a very wide berth to the ides that can be expressed within its community, and it must act to defend the right to free expression when someone attempts to undermine it.

There are, however, limits to what may be said an disseminated on campus. Our legal system prohibits hate speech, defamation (libel or slander) and obscenity—prohibitions that apply, course, to the University as well. On the campus, there are also limits imposed on the placement of disturbing images meant to support positions or on handouts to people who have not willingly agreed to accept such materials."

---

[*] Testimony entails the written submission by Bernard Shapiro to the Inquiry Panel of the Canadian Parliamentary Coalition to Combat Antisemitism on the state of freedom of expression and Canadian universities.

There is another limit. Accepting and protecting another's right to express a point of view does not preclude our right to express our own opposing opinion. But there is a crucial difference between expressing disagreement and preventing others from presenting their views in the first place. Keeping others from speaking, or otherwise stifling debate or exploration, violates the concept of free speech that is "fundamental to a university and, thereby, attacks the very core of the academy ... stifling others' speech goes too far and undermines a basic tenet of the university."

I must also add that there is a difference between " disagreement" and "disagreeable" just as there is, in this immediate context, a difference between legally defined hate speech and speech that some may find hateful. Hate speech is not permitted, but hateful speech can be even if some are very disturbed by it. Our tolerance will, of course, be tested, but as long as the audience is present by choice and not by accident or requirement, even objectionable speech can have its place. A University must have an open dialogue both inside and outside the classroom , often on topics about which people hold deeply felt, divergent points of view at least as long as this discourse " remains civil" and does not violate the law or the University's codes on conduct and discipline.

Of course, the University must take all possible steps—often in advance of any particular difficulty—to avoid "the creation of a hostile environment for any of the members of its diverse community; to uphold civil discourse and to refrain from imposing our view on others."

It would, of course, be easier to have more rigid rules. One could say all speech is allowed at all times. Alternatively, one could imagine a regime in which on certain topics, no opinion whatever is allowed to be expressed. Since neither of these approaches seems acceptable—at least to me—the universities will constantly find themselves in an awkward middle where judgement is necessary and ambiguity and, probably, controversy is bound to emerge. We will, therefore, have to continue to struggle, and sometimes, hopefully rarely, matters will get out of hand.

The specific concern about antisemitism arises now—both in Canada and elsewhere—in a context not only of the existence of the State of Israel and political events in the Middle East but also of a marked increase in cultural nationalism and in the growth of religious fundamentalism—i.e., a context not conducive to accommodating the problematic or the complex but one in which the demonization or the dehumanization of the "other" seems to emerge seemingly, but only seemingly, without effort and conscious planning.

My personal experience of life in Canadian universities in London, in Toronto and in Montreal—and here I speak entirely on my own behalf—has not led me to perceive a generalized atmosphere of antisemitism on at least these university campuses. It is clear to me, however, that incidents of antisemitism occur more frequently now than was previously the case.

That anti-Israel points of view are increasingly present on university campuses both here and elsewhere is obvious. Equally obvious is the ease with which many people slip either from opposition to the State of Israel to opposition to Jews and Jewish people more generally, or , for that matter, from anti-Semitism to opposition to the State of Israel as a more "acceptable" or "politically correct" form of generally prior religious prejudices.

I think that the responsibility of Canadian universities going forward has three dimensions:

- First to hold fast to the importance of freedom of speech—at least as I have described it above.
- Second, to move from statements of internal policy as regards free speech and those who threaten it, policies directed primarily to the university community to more specific and more public statements in this area.
- Third, and most importantly, to react, and, where necessary, to discipline more quickly and more publicly any departures from policy, indeed, any actions that create at the institution an atmosphere of harassment on virtually any grounds. I recognize that "zero tolerance" policies have their own challenges, but my experience is than minor harassments inexorably build and become major ones that often could have been avoided if prior attention had actually been paid.

None of us can afford any departure from the pressing and continuous need for what has been referred to as a real "reciprocity of respect."

Gil Troy

Gil Troy is Professor of History at McGill University in Montreal. The author of eight books, and editor of two others, his latest book, *Moynihan's Moment: America's Fight Against Zionism is Racism*, published by Oxford University Press, examined the ideological underpinning—and Soviet Communist roots—to today's "New Antisemitism" and anti-Zionism. His book *Leading from the Center: Why Moderates Make the Best Presidents* was published in 2008 by Basic Books. He has also written books about Hillary Rodham Clinton, the Reagan Revolution and the 1980s, Presidential Couples from the Trumans to the Clintons, and a history of presidential campaigning. In 2012, Troy edited the revised and updated edition of the classic multi-volume work by Arthur M. Schlesinger, Jr., and Fred Israel, *History of American Presidential Elections*.

Dr. Troy is also the author of *Why I Am a Zionist: Israel, Jewish Identity and the Challenges of Today*. The book has been hailed as a "must read," and the most persuasive presentation of the Zionist case "in decades." It has been released in a third expanded and updated edition, having sold nearly 30,000 copies.

Troy is a native of Queens, New York. He received his bachelor's, master's and doctoral degrees from Harvard University. After receiving his PhD in History in 1988, he taught History and Literature at Harvard for two years. In September 1990, Troy became an assistant professor of history at McGill University. In 1995, Troy was promoted to Associate Professor and granted tenure. From 1997 to 1998 he served as chairman of McGill's history department. In March, 1999 he was promoted to Full Professor. *Maclean's* magazine has repeatedly labelled him one of McGill's "Popular Profs" and the History News Network designated him one of its first 12 "Top Young Historians."

Formerly a contributing writer to *Policy Options*, Canada's premier public policy magazine, he is a regular contributor to *The Jerusalem Post* and the *Canadian Jewish News*, Troy has also commented on American politics and the presidency on television, radio, and in various publications, with dozens of articles and book reviews published in *The Globe and Mail*, *The Wall Street Journal*, *The Montreal Gazette*, *The New York Times*, *The New York Post*, *The Washington Post*, *The National Post*, *The Jerusalem Report*, *The Wilson Quarterly*, the *Raleigh News & Observer*, and *USA Weekend*.

Troy has attended the Israel Foreign Ministry's Global Forum against Antisemitism in Jerusalem and participated at the Experts Forum at the Inter-Parliamentary Forum against Antisemitism in London (2008). He chairs the Birthright Israel International Education Committee and co-chaired the task force on "Delegitimization of Israel: 'Boycotts, Divestment and Sanctions,'" at the Global Forum against Antisemitism in December 2009.

Oral Testimony of Dr. Gil Troy, Professor of History, McGill University. Delivered to the Canadian Parliamentary Coalition to Combat Antisemitism on 7 December 2009.

I hate this issue. I take no joy in noting the ugly outbreak of antisemitism in the world today. I hate that the problem is so serious as to merit this kind of inquiry. It violates the post-Auschwitz covenant between the world and the Jewish people—and into which I was born in 1961.

This was supposed to be a relic of Europe, of the Old World. And here and now, today, in the New World, too many—not all, but too many—Jews on campus don›t feel comfortable expressing their Jewishness, being pro-Israel.

Today, here and now, in the new world, since 2001, my kids and other kids have had to pass through security systems and security guards to go to Jewish day schools, in Westmount, in Côte Saint- Luc, otherwise among the world's safest neighbourhoods. Today, here and now, in the new world, synagogues have been vandalized. People have been harassed for the sole crime of being Jewish. This is unacceptable.

I thank you for taking the time to look into this issue. I wish you not just Godspeed—good luck—but real speed. Finish this issue, solve the problem, and become irrelevant.

I know it won't be easy. Already this commission has been falsely accused of squelching genuine criticism of Israel by invoking the pejorative "Antisemitism". Your critics claim it is hard to distinguish between criticism of Israel and antisemitism. But that is true only because they camouflage ugly bigotry behind the noble fight for human rights. In fact, underlying the new Antisemitism is the continuing Arab rejection of Israel's right to exist, often expressed in the Arab world in the harshest, most traditionally antisemitic terms, but in the West, as you've heard this morning, often perfumed by human rights rhetoric.

I echo Professor Eltis: Israel and Zionism do not deserve special treatment; they deserve equal treatment. Many anti-Zionists show their true colours expressing traditional anti-Jew hatred. They throw pennies at Jewish students at demonstrations in Concordia. They firebomb Jewish schools. They target synagogues while supposedly only criticizing Israel.

So no, it is not antisemitic to criticize Israel, to question Zionism.

However, it is not "just" criticism of Israel —but it reeks of antisemitism when the criticism is so disproportionate. It continues the West's historic obsession with the Jew.

It is not "just" criticism of Israel—but it degenerates into antisemitism when Israel is demonized with traditional anti-Jewish tropes, tics really, exaggerating the "Jewish lobby's" secretive power, making the Jewish state the one pariah nation, transforming the old big lie, "Christ killer", into the new big lie, "apartheid state, Nazi state."

It is not "just" criticism of Israel—but resonates with historic antisemitism when Israel is the only nation singled out and delegitimized, and Zionism, which means Jewish nationalism, is the only form of nationalism deemed racist, even while nationalism remains the world's central vehicle for organizing large political entities. We have 192 nation-states in the United Nations.

And it is not "just" criticism of Israel—but becomes the new antisemitism when the BDS, the boycott, divestment, and sanction movement, which is actually the blacklist, demonize, and slander movement, targets Israel alone among nations. The burden of proof is on the blacklisters. They must explain why we'd exile democratic Israel from the family of nations and not dictatorships like Libya, Iran, China, the Sudan.

Underlying all this is an essentialism familiar to scholars of antisemitism and of all forms of prejudice. People poisoned by hatred denounce the actor, not the act. Why leap from what might be justifiable criticism of an Israeli action into negating Zionism, into talking about the "apartheid nature of the Israeli state"? I'm quoting from a union resolution.

Here is the double-double standard. Israel is held to artificially high standards and denounced disproportionately. Then key groups violate core ideals themselves to denounce Israel. Gays overlook Muslim homophobia. Feminists ignore Arab sexism. Liberals forget Israeli libertarianism. Academics override their professional obligation to acknowledge the complexity of the world, and reduce everything instead to a simple black and white story with Israel as the evil perpetrator.

When some—not all—gay activists, feminists, liberals, academics, and others violate who they truly are and their own group interest in order to malign Israel, they are doing what bigots do. But I do not want to wallow in a he-said-she-said debate about what constitutes Antisemitism. I learn from my feminist friends, my gay friends, and my civil rights friends: the burden of proof is on the oppressors, not the victims.

I invite Israel's honest critics: confuse us. Prove you are not antisemitic. Denounce the ugly anti-Jewish caricatures in the Arab press, the rank antisemitism polluting Islamism, the Hamas Charter, much Palestinian media, and so many anti-Israel protests. If anti-Israel protestors stood up to Jew hatred and said "no, take down that sign, don't publish that cartoon, and change your charter," we would not need parliamentary inquiries like yours, and you would not need the courage you're displaying, knowing that you're going to get criticized for undertaking this important work. So let us focus on some strategies.

First, name and shame. The Harper government showed at Durban II in Geneva and has shown repeatedly at the UN General Assembly how governments can recoil and should recoil from Mahmoud Ahmadinejad and his ilk. The Honourable Irwin Cotler proposes to try Ahmadinejad for inciting genocide. Let us apply that principle consistently. Let us try the Saudis, Egyptians, the Palestinian Authority, and others whose leaders may be more subtle, but whose institutions and elites broadcast venomous antisemitism. And let us train and instruct our diplomats to object to antisemitism and all forms of oppression— to take it personally.

Second, let us defend human rights as part of the Canadian patrimony by confronting the human rights community on its role as the "useful idiots" of Arab antisemitism. We should be so proud of Canada's role in drafting the early declarations on human rights. We should teach legislators and diplomats that when the language of human rights is hijacked by dictators or demeaned by hypocrites, it is a Canadian issue, because Canada has a historical, ideological stake in the human rights infrastructure.

Let us monitor the monitors. Let us create a working group of parliamentarians of Canada—or perhaps beyond—issuing yearly report cards. Let us assess the UN, its Human Rights Council, and maybe human rights NGOs, demanding they maintain the high standards of universality, consistency, uniformity, and fairness embedded in the Universal Declaration of Human Rights.

Third, let us avoid fights about rights. The government's bully pulpit can change the dynamics on campus, the media, and the Internet. When Israel's critics cross the line from opposing Israel's policies to fomenting antisemitism, they hide behind rights talk. Professors yell "academic freedom"; journalists cry "freedom of the press."

Let me be clear. I support academic freedom; I oppose educational malpractice. A professor should be free to criticize Israel in the classroom, but that professor commits educational malpractice if students feel harassed for disagreeing. Unfortunately, that often happens when professors turn their lecterns into political soapboxes. Similarly, if reporters print lies about Israel they should be censured by fellow professionals, not censored.

The government can help universities protect students, first by raising awareness about the problem of educational malpractice. Let us change the language; professors who bully students politically are not doing their jobs.

Second, universities can protect students by establishing procedures for students to document abuses when they occur and to get a fair hearing.

Fourth, let us have leadership, not censorship. When violence erupts, universities have failed. I ask, "Where are the grown-ups?" If any students feel threatened, we as professors have failed, and we must take it as our professional responsibility to defend those students.

Our students watch us. When we professors, who are the moral authorities on campus, cower, don›t stand up, don›t turn the violence at York University into a teachable moment, and instead leave it to administrators who have much less contact with students while we simply go home or stay in our offices, we have failed. Government should not dictate what to do, but it can encourage and teach professors to lead by developing protocols for asserting leadership when things sour on campus.

Finally, let us stop playing defence. Let us turn this ugliness into something beautiful. As an educator, I say more is more: the more Canadians learn about Jews and Judaism and the Jewish state, the harder it will be to demonize Jews, Judaism, and the Jewish state. But more important than that, let's take this ugliness and turn it into an opportunity to teach about civility and democracy and liberty.

Let us deputize the next generation of Internet users to fight hate through a "citizenship 2.0" program in schools. I am a parent. Everyone frets about the blogosphere, about the kids spending too much time on the Internet. If we knew that our kids were educated on how to be good citizens on the Internet, how to fight hate, we would feel a lot better about it, and you would have taken, in a jui-jitsu move, the ugliness and turned it into something positive.

Ultimately, this is a struggle for the soul of the West and the Canadian patrimony. Canada's commitment to universal human rights must be applied fairly, consistently across the board. I congratulate you for being on the right side of history and for just saying no to Antisemitism, no to hatred, and no to bigotry but also saying yes to higher ideals of democracy, civility, and liberty.

Thank you.

Written Submission presented to the Canadian Parliamentary Inquiry into Antisemitism by Dr. Gil Troy, Professor of History, McGill University.

Crossing the Line While Obscuring the Line: The Deceitful, Destructive Dance Between Anti-Zionism and Antisemitism

A strange thing happened at the Gay Pride parade in Toronto in June, repeated at Montreal's Pride parade in August. Some participants marched under the banner "Queers Against Israeli Apartheid (QuAIA)." The dirty little secret QuAIA must suppress is that Israel is the safest refuge in the Middle East for persecuted homosexuals, including Palestinians. These antics take anti-Zionism to an absurd extreme, defying logic, perverting history and distorting priorities. "Queers Against Israeli Apartheid" reflects such hatred against the Jewish State that maligning Zionism overrides all other causes, including gay liberation; it eclipses all identities including sexual identity—on a day celebrating sexual identity.

Unfortunately, Jews have long experience with such self-defeating behaviour. In the twentieth century, Communism's commitment to the brotherhood of man somehow failed to include Jews. Similarly, Nazi Germany's appreciation for military heroes from the Great War included all German war veterans but the Jews. We can recognize those glaring inconsistencies from the past as motivated by anti-Semitism. Yet we often hesitate to label the modern manifestations of this ancient plague, even when they are only slightly less subtle.

Defining and defeating the new antisemitism in Canada is difficult because some of the noblest impulses in Canadian society and the West are used to obscure some of the ugliest impulses in the world today. The unholy alliance uniting Arab anti-Zionism with Western anti-racism and anti-imperialism allows many of new antisemites to claim: "I am not antisemitic, I am only anti-Zionist." Even as this posture places Israel's defenders on the defensive, it fails to convince, given the intensity of the hatred and the unreason of the attacks. All oppressed people understand that a clear sign of prejudice is a willingness to override self-interest or other interests to vilify a targeted group.

Israel and Zionism do not deserve special treatment—but they deserve equal treatment. The singling out of Israel, the demonizing of Zionism, have all too frequently descended from the realm of the political to the pathological. It is hard to explain without taking antisemitism into account. Moreover, anti-Zionists are honest if not consistent. Again and again they show their true colors, expressing rank antisemitism while attacking Israel. During the Concordia riot of 2002 when violent pro-Palestinian protestors prevented Benjamin Netanyahu from speaking on Concordia University's downtown Montreal campus, some protestors threw pennies and coins[1] at Jewish students and attacked students with yarmulkes. In April, 2004, at least one Lebanese-born Montrealer (probably more) expressed anger at Israel by firebombing the library of a Jewish elementary school. And, most recently, during the Lebanon War of 2006 and the Gaza operation of 2008-2009, after controversial Israeli actions traditional antisemitic crimes spikes, targeting synagogues, Jewish schools and individual Jews, in Canada and throughout the world. Thus, again and again, anti-Zionists have actively crossed the line despite their rhetorical attempts at delineating the line between anti-Zionism and antisemitism.

These violent outbursts represent the milder Canadian offshoots of a systematic, vitriolic antisemitic campaign that has coursed through the Arab world—and much of the Muslim world—for decades. It is rooted in the Palestinian leader Haj Amin el Husseini ugly alliance with Adolf Hitler in the 1930s and early 1940s, as well as most Arabs' utter rejection of Israel's right to exist. The antisemitic language in the Hamas charter, the antisemitic imagery even in the Jordanian and Egyptian media despite peace treaties with Israel, are but a few examples of a vicious Jew hatred, representing Jews in traditional antisemitic tropes as hooked-nosed, all-powerful, greedy, deceitful, and bloodthirsty.

At the same time, the demonization of Israel and the romanticization of Palestinians come from Canadians' and progressive Westerners' salutary commitment to human rights, to fighting imperialism, to ending racism. The dominant Middle East narrative on campus, in many unions, even in much of the media, misleadingly treats Jews as white, imperialist interlopers who dispossessed the Palestinian natives and now oppress them. This one-sided, inaccurate storyline plays to the best impulses cultivated in the last half-century, thanks to, among other phenomena, the anti-imperialist revolts in the developing world after World War II, American and Canadian leadership in developing the UN and human rights law, the Civil Rights revolution in the American south, and the defeat of South African apartheid. In the mid-1970s, Soviet and Arab propagandists figured out how to use these noble impulses to bash Western democracies, especially Israel, and give Third World dictatorships a free pass on many civil rights abuses. Tragically, this New Big Lie outlasted the Soviet Union and thrives in the twenty-first century.

---

1 *http://www.aish.com/jw/s/48884942.html*

Do not be misled. It is easy to criticize Israel without degenerating into anti-Zionism or antisemitism. Despite the caricature of the monolithic, omnipotent Jewish lobby (a traditional antisemitic motif), there is a vigorous debate in the Jewish world, both in Israel and beyond, about Israeli actions. Israelis and other Jews have shown there are many ways to criticize Israel robustly, aggressively, without crossing any lines, just as it is easy to criticize many Canadian actions without demonizing Canada or to criticize the United States without questioning its right to exist. But given modern antisemites' lethal vitriol, considering Jew-hatred's tragic history, East and West, the burden of proof is on Israel's sincere critics to distance themselves from the antisemitism that characterizes most modern anti-Zionism.

Instead, here are the most persistent ways Israel's critics repeatedly cross the line, raising the stakes from justifiable criticism to a justification for genocide—eliminating Israel:

- *Disproportionality:* The sheer volume of complaints and protests is suspicious. Why little Israel commands so much attention is a mystery, unless one considers antisemitism as an explanation. When Hamas terrorists killed their fellow Palestinians in Gaza, York University was quiet. When Mahmoud Ahmadinejad stole an election in Iran and cracked down on his own people, calm reigned on Canadian streets. Yet many much milder Israeli actions, even in self-defense, trigger intense opprobrium, on the streets, at campuses, and in the press.

- *Exaggeration:* To justify this singular focus, Israeli actions are repeatedly blown up into war crimes as Palestinian suffering is exaggerated. Yes, Palestinians have experienced anguish since the 1948 war and since the 1967 war. But the comparisons du jour to Jewish suffering under Nazism are simply absurd. During these decades, the Palestinian population has mushroomed, as have rates of Palestinian education, sanitation, life expectancy. More recently, Mahmoud Abbas, the President of the Palestinian Authority himself, insisted that life was good in the West Bank, and the leading towns there are enjoying economic booms. Exaggerating the Palestinian-Israeli conflict into Israel's Nazi-like, "genocidal" occupation reflects a deep bias against the alleged oppressor, the Israelis, as does the inversion whereby the Jews are depicted as turning into their worst, most deadly, most evil enemies, the Nazis.

- *Demonization:* Exaggerating Palestinian suffering and Israeli iniquity inevitably demonizes Israel. The most popular expression of this phenomenon in Canada is the growing linkage of Israel with the old South

Africa's reprehensible, racist Apartheid regime. Israel Apartheid week—the two words should not even be linked together—began in Toronto and has spread worldwide. Treating the national conflict between Palestinians and Israelis as a racial conflict is an act of bad faith; comparing the security barriers and byroads Israel felt compelled to construct in the wake of Palestinian terror to the systematic color-based racism of South African apartheid turns history on its head. At the heart of the South African regime was a series of laws linking civil status to color; such an approach does not work in the Middle East with dark-skinned Israelis like the Ethiopians and light-skinned Palestinians. More important, such an approach would violate core Israeli and Zionist ideals, epitomized in the Israeli Proclamation of Independence, which offered equal rights to all citizens, regardless of religion or race. The evil, inaccurate equation between Israel and Apartheid updates the United Nations' General Assembly's wrongheaded resolution in 1975 equating Zionism with racism. That resolution, repealed in 1991 and denounced eloquently by Canada's Ambassador to the UN in 1975, Saul Rae, among others, represented an ugly marriage of Nazi-style race propaganda, Soviet Cold War strategy and Arab antisemitism.

• *Delegitimization:* Delegitimization, questioning Israel's right to exist, follows naturally from demonization. A regime as reprehensible as South Africa's—or Nazi Germany's—deserves a similar fate. It is not coincidental that Israel has been compared to the two most hated regimes of the twentieth century, neither of which survived. Underlying all this is an essentialism familiar to scholars of antisemitism and other forms of prejudice. People poisoned by hatred denounce the actor not the act, the essence of a phenomenon rather than a manifestation of it. To criticize Israeli actions regarding the Palestinians can be reasonable, justified; to leap from criticizing actions to repudiating Zionism and Israel's right to exist frequently leaps from political debate to the realm of the irrational.

Zionism is Jewish nationalism, the idea that the Jews are a people, a nation, not just a religion, tied to one historic homeland Israel, even while being spread out and serving as loyal citizens in countries around the world. That in a world where nationalism remains the major vehicle for organizing nation-states, one form of nationalism—Jewish nationalism—is singled out and questioned further suggests a deep-seated bias distorting the debate. Why should Israel, of all countries, be on probation six decades into its existence? We know European imperial cartographers haphazardly drew borders for countries like Iraq. We know that Pakistan is an artificial creation, carved out of the crumbling British raj around the same time that Israel was established in the Jews' traditional, Biblical homeland. Why is it that we do not hear questions about Iraq's or Pakistan's existence, even when Saddam Hussein invaded Kuwait or Pakistan spread nuclear weapons and terrorism throughout the world?

- *Ostracism:* As a result, the calls by union leaders, by academics, to boycott Israel are, at their best, anti-Semitic in effect if not in intent, as the former Harvard President Larry Summers put it. The burden of proof is on boycott proponents. They have to explain: why ostracize democratic Israel and not dictatorships like Libya, Iran, China, the Sudan? They have to justify their and too much of the Human Rights community's particular zeal for bashing Israel. They have to distance themselves from the rank antisemitism of their own allies.

- *The Double-Double Standard:* There is a twofold inconsistency at work. First, Israel is held to an artificially high standard and denounced disproportionately. Even more disturbing, key groups then violate core ideals in their zeal to denounce Israel. We see some gays defining their activism and identity through the prism of fighting Israel despite Israel's progressive stance on gay rights. We see some feminists overlooking Muslim and Arab sexism, as well as Israeli egalitarianism, in their zeal to bash Israel. We see some academics overriding their primary professional obligation to tell the truth and acknowledge the world's complexity in their rush to caricature Israel. When gay activists, feminists, academics, and others violate their core identities and defining values to malign Israel, they only indict themselves and suggest that we are dealing with bias against Jews and their state, not just criticism of the Jewish state.

Sacrificing integrity and credibility to demonize a democracy is an irrational act of bad faith. Naming and shaming the perpetrators, amid a broader educational campaign about Zionism, antisemitism, and the need for a Jewish state, are important first steps in the march toward a solution. Canada needs to take the lead in denouncing Arab antisemitism in Iran and elsewhere—backed up by sanctions—and confronting the human rights community on its role as the "useful idiots" of Arab anti-Semitism. At home, more vigilance against the casual antisemitism of the politically correct anti-Israel community would do wonders.

Inquiries like this one and groups like the Parliamentary Coalition against Antisemitism are essential in raising awareness. You cannot legislate hate away. But you can make people more sensitive to the ways they are perpetuating an ancient scourge, sometimes even unintentionally.

Professor Gert Weisskirchen[*]
Personal Representative of the OSCE Chair-in-Office on Combating Antisemitism

Oral Testimony of Professor Gert Wisskirchen, Personal Representative, OSCE Chairman-in-Office on Combating Antisemitism and Member of the German Parliament, Spokesman on Foreign Affairs of the SPD-Group. Delivered to the Canadian Parliamentary Coalition to Combat Antisemitism on 2 November 2009.

First I would like to thank you for inviting me, chères collegues, to come here and give a short report about what I have been doing and what I did. I would like to first recommend what Denis mentioned at the end. My proposal would be that you should follow along the line or the kind of proposal that the Parliament in London has been doing, and deliver it. In my understanding, my observation, and analysis, that kind of inquiry is the best that parliamentarians can do in order, first, to look at the things going on, on the ground, and second, to draw conclusions out of this on at least three levels. First is on the local level, how to improve the exchange of what can be done on the ground with people and local authorities. Second is to ask the government to improve their instruments. Third, and this is crucial, in my opinion, could best be linked to the first level, to encourage civil society and non-governmental organizations.

If you look into the problem, you will find out. That's my observation, and I've done it since 2002—to observe what is going on in the different 54 member

* The testimony of Professor Weisskirchen is comprised of both an oral submission presented to the Canadian Parliamentary Inquiry into Antisemitism on 2 November 2009, and written submission presented to the Panel outlining the current state of affairs in combating antisemitism in OSCE member states and the role of parliamentary democracy and education in combating new forms of antisemitism. Full unabridged transcripts of Professor Wesiskirchen's testimony can be found at *http://www.cpcca.ca/inquiry.htm.*

217

states of the OSCE. Canada is a member of it, as you know. My observation is that there is no doubt that the political elite, especially the governments, are clear-cut in fighting against antisemitism. Sometimes there is some uncertainty found indifferent governments—not in Canada, Great Britain, Germany, or France. The point is, and this is worrying, if you go down to the society, on the local level, you find problems. There is at least a discourse on a very formal level. Again, it is clear-cut. But there are narratives coming from different angles of the given societies. Take a look at, say, Hungary. The last political developments there show that antisemitism in on the rise in a very brutal way.

So this is the picture I have discovered. It is clear-cut on the level of formal politics, but if you go down into the circles of societies, you can observe problems arising. I recommend again what Denis touched on.

Parliaments should take the lead in this regard. I served 33 years in the German Parliament, and last Monday, one week ago, I left Parliament in Germany. We know that as parliamentarians we are a kind of seismograph of what is going on in the constituencies, how people are thinking, and we observe what is going on. If you were to ask Jewish communities on the ground, you would find out that they are now finding out that they are in trouble, and sometimes they are in danger. They feel they are in danger. That means the climate is gradually changing. Personally, I think that we as parliamentarians have the responsibility to figure out what is going on in the local area.

If you then ask what is really going on, you will find at least two different patterns. The first is the old anti-Judaism, which is historically clear-cut. Then there are the new forms of antisemitism, the last of which relates to criticism of Israel. There is awhile variety of things you can find in the public discourse. In my case, in Germany, in addition to this is a third discourse going on. It is a narrative that is changing, because as the witnesses, not only to the Holocaust but also to the Second World War, are disappearing one by one, there arises the psychological problem of what kind of history they are telling their great-grand-children. As you know, as we all know, sometimes when we are looking back into our memory of what has happened, we are trying to save our identity. In some regard, these great-grandparents are telling their great-grandchildren a different story, not what really happened. They are giving them a picture of what they would like to be understood.

Now, you can imagine that when this kind of personal narrative is changed, we are going to be in trouble. So not only historians but we as parliamentarians are responsible and share the obligation for the kind of new cultural memory that is now being shown to the public.

It is our responsibility to try to figure out what new world the younger generation is going into. In this regard, education is key.

Who is responsible for education? At first, we as parliamentarians are responsible for laying out principles not only regarding content, but especially regarding forms of education and how teachers should be introduced and taught, and how they should be teaching in light of this problem, this crucial paradigm shift we are in, constructing a new picture of what has happened in the past. This is cultural memory, not personal remembrance. Right now, we are faced with constructing this picture. So I hope some of the findings of your inquiry will help you be productive as parliamentarians.

This is my last point. Next week, OSCE's 2008 report on hate crime will be published. ODIHR, an institution within OSCE, produced this report, which included one paragraph on anti-Semitic events. It is a comprehensive study, a comprehensive report, and there is one part dealing with antisemitism. You have the possibility of getting that report. If necessary, you can ask me; I am going to send it to members of the House here.

First, there is limited official information available on antisemitic hate crimes in the OSCE region. Why? The problem is that you have a clear-cut data base, but the member states are not ready to deliver that clear-cut data base, so that is one problem we are facing in the OSCE area.

Second, while 19 participating states reported that they collect such data— Austria, Belgium, Canada, Croatia, the Czech Republic, France, Germany, Italy, Liechtenstein , Moldova, the Netherlands, Poland, the Russian Federation, Serbia, Spain, Sweden, Switzerland, the United Kingdom, and the United States—that number means that two-thirds of the member states are not delivering. They are not actively participating in what they have decided on.

Third, only eight submitted figures for 2008 to ODIHR, and Canada is lacking in this regard. I have two points in addition. Austria and the Czech Republic reported an increase in incidents compared to 2007. Germany, Italy, and the United Kingdom reported a decrease. The other three countries did not report comparable figures from 2007.

Last, there are non-governmental sources for data on antisemitic crimes in 2008 in many OSCE participating states, and this is the only reliable source the OSCE really can depend on. But as you know, NGOs are sometimes alarmist, and in some way you can be sure this alarmist signal is not serious enough to take into account.

What I was talking about and what I would like to ask you to do as parliamentarians is to use the lever of the OSCE in your national parliament in order to strengthen the idea that all the participating states should follow their obligations and the decisions they made.

Thank you so much.

Written submission of Professor Gert Wisskirchen, for the Canadian Parliamentary Coalition for Combating Antisemitism prepared January 2008.

Some Views

Since 2005, I have been appointed by the respective Chairman-Office to the position of Personal Representative on Combating Antisemitism. Now in my third year of this mandate, it is time to take stock of the current situation, point to successes and positive trends, make critical assessments, and then look ahead to the future.

OSCE Conference in Bucharest

The mandates of the Personal Representative of the Chairman-in-Office were created as a consequence of OSCE antisemitism conferences held in Vienna, Berlin, Paris, Brussels and Cordoba. A further OSCE conference was held in Bucharest from 7 to 8 June 2007: the High-Level Conference on Combating Discrimination and Promoting Mutual Respect and Understanding. It was preceded by a NGO meeting.

The Bucharest Declaration contains the following passage:

> Recognizing its unique and historic character, [the participating States] condemn antisemitism without reservation, whether expressed in a traditional manner or through new forms and manifestations. [They] Reiterate previous OSCE declarations that international developments, or political issues, including in Israel or anywhere else, can never justify antisemitism.

Prior to that the NGOs formulated nine recommendations and made reference in the context to the special role of education and parliaments. I strong support all of these recommendations and in particular the appeal issued by the NGOs to take action against expressions of racial hatred and antisemitism discourse on the Internet. I have listed these recommendations for you at the end of this part.

As of June 2007, a total of 48 separate commitments had been made by OSCE participating States in reference to the fight against antisemitism. These commitments are necessary. There is a need now to strengthen the political will to implement these commitments in all OSCE countries. Many countries have been quite exemplary in this area. Unfortunately, there are other countries whose efforts have not been sufficient.

Current state of affairs

Despite the considerable effort that have been undertaken in many participating States and the numerous conferences that have been held, there have been recurrent manifestations of antisemitism in many countries of the OSCE region. This includes countries whose governments and public institutions have had an excellent record in the fight against antisemitism. In Germany, for instance, a rabbi from the Jewish congregation in Frankfurt was injured in a knife attack. In addition to egregious acts of violence like this one, there are often other, much more subtle forms of antisemitic attitudes predominant in public discourses.

One of my objectives is to create an awareness of different forms of antisemitic discourse. I can give two examples from this from my work.

In May 2007, the British University and College Union (UCU) called for an anti-Israel boycott. Other unions followed this example with similar action. I issued a press release immediately condemning this call for a boycott. I travelled to London in July to talk with the unions in a further attempt to raise public awareness of this matter.

There was a disquieting development in Croatia. The popular singer Marko Perkovic, alias "Thompson", stated showing various symbols from the Ustasha era at concerts. During a country visit to Croatia in 2007 I was able to talk to a number of government representatives as well as representatives of the Jewish communities. The objective here was to reach a consensus with my Croatian interlocutors that nationalistic tendencies of any kind need to be nipped in the bud.

I wrote a letter to all the heads of government of the OSCE participating States in which I proposed that an inquiry similar to the British All-Party Parliamentary Inquiry be carried out. This was also recommended by the NGOs in Bucharest. I enclosed the Magenta Foundation report on the 1st International Conference on Academic Antisemitism and the ODIHR-FRA Working Definition of Antisemitism. In the meantime I have received answers from some of the governments. Most of them use the working definitions of antisemitism that was jointly formulated by ODIHR and the Fundamental Rights Agency. Unfortunately none of the reply letter has made any concrete statements to the effect that plans are being made to use an instrument similar to the All-Party Parliamentary Inquiry.

CiO Personal Representative mandates

The role of the CiO Personal Representatives encompasses three areas:

(1) They implement the decisions taken by the participating states at OSCE Conferences.

(2) They draw attention to both progress and setbacks in the implementation process.

(3) They encourage efforts by civil society groups and promote national and transnational cooperation between social, parliamentary, and governmental actors.

It will hardly be possible to carry out these tasks in a satisfactory manner with the current mandate structure. The Personal Representatives mandates need to be equipped with further instruments if they are to be able to do justice to these functions. At the moment there is a considerable gap between what would actually be required and what exists in reality and this gap needs to be closed.

It would be nice if there were more support from the OSCE participating States. This year only one country visit has been agreed thus far, i.e. to Croatia. Unfortunately there have been no further invitations from other countries. Contacts and meetings with NGOs and representatives of the Jewish communities in the various countries is very important in terms of doing justice to the CiO Personal Representative mandates.

Prior to the appointment of the Personal Representatives the following six areas were declared to be in particular need of attention:

(1) Data collection
(2) Legislation
(3) Law enforcement
(4) Education
(5) Media
(6) Parliaments

Progress has been made over the past few years in most of these areas.

In November 2006 OSCE ODIHAR held a Tolerance Implementation Meeting in Vienna on the subject of Data Collection, NGOs formulated various recommendations which I have listed in my written statement. I want to focus here on one of the most important recommendation the NGOs formulated:

> We remind participating States of their commitment
> to provide hate crime statistics on a regular basis and to
> respond to violent manifestations of intolerance;

Various tools provided by OSCE ODIHR have proven to be very helpful. The OSCE ODIHR Law Enforcement Officer Programme has already been implemented in some countries and is in either the planning or preparatory stages in others. ODIHR is also working on a training programme for public prosecutors.

Teaching materials on the subject of antisemitism have been developed for a number of counties are now in use there.

A code should be developed together with authors, journalists, and publicists that would constitute a voluntary moral and autonomous agreement to show tolerance and recognize the rights of minorities. A project of this kind has already been discussed with the OSCE Representative on Freedom of the Media.

The OSCE PA can be used as a laboratory for testing new legislative approaches. National parliaments should be encouraged to strengthen their ability to monitor the results of decisions in the OSCE. An instrument comparable to the All-Party Parliamentary Inquiry could be employed in other countries as well. It would be a good thing if OSCE PA national delegations were to promote an initiative of this kind in their parliaments.

Outlook

Many parliaments have been exemplary in their efforts to fight antisemitism and recognize the scale of the problem. Nonetheless, there has been growing acceptance of antisemitic statements and stereotypes in some countries, as was observed in the autumn of 2006.

As such, it is of crucial importance that civil society be included in the fight against antisemitism. We cannot afford to lose those who are in the middle of the political spectrum. It must be guaranteed that social initiatives and projects will receive the support they need to be able to do their work successfully. It is a task for the national parliaments to see to it that there is sufficient funding for civil society projects of this kind.

We need to work towards an exchange of informative on promising methods of fighting antisemitism. We are currently able to say that there are a number of particularly successful projects that could be implemented in other countries.

In Sweden, for instance, there is an exit programme for radical neo-Nazis. Over a period of many years caseworkers have succeeded in getting numerous individuals out of the right-wing extremist scene. No one is given up for lost.

In France official data on antisemitic violence and other manifestations of antisemitism is compared with data received from NGOs. Since NGOs do not use the same strict criteria for data collection, a more precise picture emerges as to the scale of antisemitic crimes.

The appointment of special envoys responsible for dealing with the subject of antisemitism and relations with Jewish communities results in the problem being seen more clearly on the part of executive government as well. There are special envoys of this kind in the United States, France, Poland, Spain and Germany.

The following countries stand out for their efforts to fight antisemitism through education by taking part in the ODIHR Anne Frank House Project and developing relevant teaching materials: Germany, Croatia, Denmark, Spain, Lithuania, the Netherlands, Poland, the Russian Federation, Slovakia, and Ukraine. I have actively supported this ODIHR programme from the outset and I am pleased by the success it has had in many countries.

As has already been mentioned, the CiO Personal Representative mandates need to expanded so that they can be carried out in a satisfactory manner. The provision of physical and human resources would be helpful in making our work more effective.

I am certain that we will continue to have strong support for carrying on the fight against antisemitism.

Part III: Conclusion

A Call for Action in Canada

As has become evident from an examination of the growing phenomenon of antisemitism in Canada and around the globe, serious discussions are being taken upon by decision-makers, civic leaders, enforcement agencies, and individual members of our communities about strategies and approaches in dealing with this criminal and malicious form of hate. With the concluding section of this book, we take an in-depth look at the multiple forums and methods of addressing this issue. From the many stakeholders and experts present in the preceding section of this book, several approaches are advocated and recommendations of how to properly deal with the rise of antisemitism in Canada.

Legal Approaches

One of the contentious issues in addressing the issue of antisemitism is the role of criminal and human rights codes in dealing with hate speech in general and antisemitism in particular. This matter forms part of a larger discussion on the extent to which hateful speech can or should be criminalized As such, the *Criminal Code* can serve as an useful tool in dealing with extreme manifestations of antisemitism.

Some proponents have argued in favoured of a more aggressive prosecution of incitement to hatred violations, in particular when advocated from behind the curtain of the internet. For example, Allan Adel of B'nai Brith has argued that "Canadian legislation should be strengthened to increase effectiveness in countering hate of the internet and to close potential loopholes that could jeopardize successful prosecutions."[1] More broadly, the Canadian Jewish Congress has recommended that the "existing statutory 'fence of protection' both in the

---

1 Submissions of Allan Adel, League for Human Rights of B'nai Brith Canada.

Criminal Code and in human rights legislation [needs to] be reaffirmed and where appropriate, strengthened."[2]

Yet, on the contrary and reflective of the delicate issue surrounding human rights and hate crimes legislation, some have opposed hate speech law altogether on civil libertarian grounds. As Professor Kenneth Marcus of the College of the City University of New York has argued:

> Even biased and hateful statements contain elements
> that need to be protected But ... there are many things
> that can be done to rebut biased, hateful or simply
> wrongheaded and illegitimate approach that have no
> ramifications for the suppression of speech. The first is
> to speak out against it ...[3]

As has been seen, a fine line is constructed between the rights of the majority and the values of greater society versus the rights and protection of those marginalized.

Within this in mind, as explained by the Honourable Andrew Swan, Minister of Justice and Attorney General of Manitoba, there are two provisions within the *Criminal Code* that require the authorization of the Attorney General prior to the laying of charges—s.318, the advocating of genocide, and s.319(2), willfully promoting hatred against an identifiable group. In addition, there are other provision requiring the Attorney General to authorize a request for a warrant to seize hate propaganda.[4] With limitations in place, it is difficult for the Crown to prove that an accused was motivated by hate; a condition necessary to secure conviction.[5] There has generally been greater success in dealing with incidents as regular criminal offence and pursuing enhanced penalties under s.718 of the *Code* which includes sentencing enhancements for crimes motivated by hate.[6] As noted by several law enforcement officials tasked with enforcing hate crime legislation, the establishment of procedures, which demand prior approvals to purse hate crime classifications, impedes officers from using "on-the-spot" judgement.[7]

---

2 Submissions of the Canada Jewish Congress
3 Testimony of Professor Kenneth Marcus, November 16, 2009, 12
4 Tesimony of Hon. Andrew Swan, February 8, 2010, p3.
5 Testimony of Detective Sergeant Monica Christian, December 8, 2009, p11
6 Ibid, p. 9
7 Ibid, p. 11

What is required is for police to be 'liberated' from the requirement of seeking prior approval to prosecute a hate crime case.[8] However, at the same time, officers are routinely trusted to lay charges for serious crimes without prior approval, including for murder and egregious crimes, there is still good policy reasons for requiring prior approval. The stigma associated with being charged with a hate crime and the relatively high profile nature of such cases represents one of many considerations in this event. As such the evidence in respecting the difficulty in prosecuting hate crimes is of great concern and must warrant further study and consideration.

From the other perspective of human rights laws in Canada, federal and provincial human rights commissions, allow recourse to those who believe themselves to be victims of non-criminal forms of behaviour that is antisemitic of discriminatory in nature. Such prohibited behaviour includes discrimination in employment or housing and is guaranteed under s. 13 of the *Canadian Human Rights Act*.

Currently the debate over whether to strengthen, roll back, or even abolish section of the *Human Rights Act* and other aspect of Canada's hate speech laws is not primarily a debate about antisemitism. Rather, it is an aspect of the ongoing debate as to what degree, in the service of reducing hate speech, it is desirable to restrict free speech, or the extent to which it remains constitutionally permissible to do so under the *Charter of Rights*.

Along these lines, hate speech has displayed an uncanny ability to propagate using the Internet and social networking sites to spread hatred. As Professor Robert S. Wistrich noted, the relationship between the emerging globalization of antisemitism and the use of these technologies within Canada:

> In certain respects, [Canada] has a greater access to millions of people because of the nature of contemporary technologies, and particularly of the internet. At a click of a button, you can enter a website more or less free and be exposed to text that in the past were extremely difficult to obtain, such as the *Protocols of the Learned Elders of Zion*, and there it is downloaded, easily accessible and passed on to others.[9]

These conditions are alarming as antisemitism has adapted itself to the Internet and has become increasingly effective. The potential exists that this current

---

8 Testimony of Julian Fantino, December 8, 2009, p17-18
9 Testimony of Professor Robert S. Wistrich

use of technology to promote hate unabashed may well lead to a culture where antisemitism is socially acceptable.

The proliferation of hate on the Internet has come to represent one of most concerning and difficult challenges to the fight against antisemitism. While this issue has been discussed elsewhere in this book, there is much needed recognition that there is an important need for inter-jurisdictional cooperation in order to address Internet through legal means.

As with adapting to changes in technology and to help alleviate the problems of anti-Semitism, there is aneed to engage more thoroughly enforcement through the establishment of hate crime units and training of police officers. As noted by Superintendent Mike Burns of the Halifax Regional Police: "hate crime and specific antisemitic behaviour are difficult crimes for police to identify, investigate, and prosecute." Indeed, hate or bias crimes often go unrecognized. What is needed is more emphasis on the importance of better educating and equipping front-line officers with the expertise to identify hate crimes.[10] Facing forecasts of significant personnel turnover in the next decade due to retirement of the baby boomer generation reinforces the need for appropriate training programs. As stated by Superintendent Burns:

> Education in relation to the dynamics of hate-based crime and the human impact of antisemitism is an essential police skill set if we as a police community are to competently identify, investigate and prosecute such criminal behaviour. A police officer properly informed on the relevant issues will be better equipped to engage the public in community-based solutions to decrease community fear and tension.[11]

Along this line, there is precedence. The Saskatoon, Vancouver and York Region Police Services send officers to the "Tools for Tolerance" program run by the Simon Wiesenthal Centre in Los Angeles.[12] Such programs represent valuable tools in training offices in responding to hate crimes.

In addition, in where police enforcement have been able to effectively deal with hate crime incidents are with police services that have employed hate crime units,

---

10 Testimony of Detective Sergeant Monica Christian, December 8, 2009, p. 11; Testimony of Commissioner Julian Fantino, December 8, 2009, p11

11 Testimony of Superintendent Mike Burns, February 8, 2010, p. 33

12 Testimony of Chief Clive Wighill, February 8, 2010, p.32; Testimony of Inspector John de Haas, February 8, 2010 p.21; Testimony of Chief Armand La Barge, February 8, 2010, p.30

or individuals specifically responsible for responding to hate crimes did a better job of correctly and consistently identifying and categorizing hate crimes than those who did not. Currently, municipalities and provinces that include hate crimes units or officers includes: The British Columbia Hate Crime Team, Vancouver's Diversity and Aboriginal Policing Section, Alberta's Hate and Bias Coordinator, the Calgary Police, the Hamilton Police Hate Crime Officer, York Regional Hate Crime Unit, Toronto Police Hate Crime Unit, Ottawa Police Hate Crimes Unit, and the Ontario Municipal Hate Crimes Team. The Saskatoon Police, do to its relative size, does not have a hate crimes unit of officer, but charges one officer with the portfolio of responding to hate crimes when they occur. As Deputy Chief Ken Leenderste of the Hamilton Police Service noted the important role of the hate, crime unit is in supporting the victims of crime and in liaising with communities to "curb the escalation of social tension that can destroy communities."[13] Hate crime units can work with community organizations to encourage the reporting of hate and bias incidents, which are recorded whether they constitute a crime. Working with community groups, such as the Calgary Police Force's "Hate—Don't Buy In" program which targets junior and senior high school students helps gives individuals within the greater community the knowledge they need to address hate/ biased-related incidents and to protect themselves from becoming targets.[14]

Not only limited to domestic enforces, inter-governmental relations and partnerships across different levels of government agencies provide a useful tool in tackling antisemitism. Further actions and the use of customs and immigration remedies can be helpful in preventing the importation of antisemitism into Canada. Currently, customs and immigration statues and regulations have reflected to a satisfactory fashion in stopping the spread of antisemitism in Canada. The *Immigration and Refugee Protection Act*, SC 2001, c. 27, provides that a foreign national is inadmissible on grounds of criminality if he or she is found to have committed an act or offence outside of Canada, or upon entry, that would constitute an indictable offence in Canada.[15] Under the *Criminal Code*, wilfully

---

13 Testimony of Deputy Chief Ken Leenderste, February 8, 2010, p. 22
14 Testimony of Deputy Chief Murray Stooke, December 8, 2009, p.14
15 2) A foreign national is inadmissible on grounds of criminality for

(*a*) having been convicted in Canada of an offence under an Act of Parliament punishable by way of indictment, or of two offences under any Act of Parliament not arising out of a single occurrence;

(*b*) having been convicted outside Canada of an offence that, if committed in Canada, would constitute an indictable offence under an Act of Parliament, or of two offences not arising out of a single occurrence that, if committed in Canada, would constitute offences under an Act of Parliament;

(*c*) committing an act outside Canada that is an offence in the place where it was committed and that, if committed in Canada, would constitute an indictable offence under an Act of Parliament; or

promoting hatred against an identifiable group is an indictable offence.[16] From this, the facts that constitute immigration inadmissibility under this provision include facts for which there are reasonable grounds to believe that they have occurred or may occur.[17]

On this basis, an individual may be denied entry to Canada because there are reasonable grounds to believe that the person may engage in antisemitic activity. A person may be deported from Canada on the basis that there are reasonable grounds to believe that the person has engaged in antisemitic activity. The security certificate provisions of the *Immigration and Refugee Protection Act* are also available. A person may be denied entry or removed on the basis that the person poses a danger to the security of Canada;[18] although such a person can nonetheless enter or stay in Canada if the person satisfies the Minister that his or her presence in Canada would not be detrimental to the national interest.[19]

In this fashion, customs law has similar standards. The *Customs Tariff*, SC 1997, c. 36, and Consolidation prohibit the importation of:

> Books, printed papers, drawings, paintings, prints, photographs or representations of any kind that ... constitute hate propaganda within the meaning of subsection 320(8) of the *Criminal Code*.[20]

Challenging the denial of entry of items that allegedly constitutes hate propaganda is subject to a special provision within the *Customs Tariff*. Determinations are to be the relevant provincial or territorial superior court instead of the Canadian International Trade Tribunal.[21]

(*d*) committing, on entering Canada, an offence under an Act of Parliament prescribed by regulations.

16 *Criminal Code* Section 319. (1) Every one who, by communicating statements in any public place, incites hatred against any identifiable group where such incitement is likely to lead to a breach of the peace is guilty of

    (*a*) an indictable offence and is liable to imprisonment for a term not exceeding two years; or

    (*b*) an offence punishable on summary conviction.

17 Section **33.** The facts that constitute inadmissibility under sections 34 to 37 include facts arising from omissions and, unless otherwise provided, include facts for which there are reasonable grounds to believe that they have occurred, are occurring or may occur

18 **34.** (1) A permanent resident or a foreign national is inadmissible on security grounds for (*d*) being a danger to the sec,urity of Canada;

19 34.(2) The matters referred to in subsection (1) do not constitute inadmissibility in respect of a permanent resident or a foreign national who satisfies the Minister that their presence in Canada would not be detrimental to the national interest.

20 *Act* section 136(1) and Tariff Item, 9899.00.0

21 *Act section 71,1*

From the immigration side, Canada's Immigration laws have a role to play in providing refuge to those who are fleeing antisemitism in other countries. As Shelley Faituch, the Community Relations Director of the Jewish Federation of Winnipeg articulated her belief that "Canada will be facing an increasing number of immigration claims because of the rise in antisemitism, particularly in European and countries like Venezuela."[22] Based on nature of rising antisemitism international, especially when compared to Canada, these predictions are troubling. For this purpose, the Canadian Minister of Citizenship and Immigration, the Honourable Jason Kenney, explained that Canada's *Immigration and Refugee Protection Act* has a special designation of "source country" which allows the government to "recognize certain people ... as refugees for resettlement purposes." As such, we could have a review of the list of countries that could be added to the list of source countries.

Within this framework, legislation and law enforcement approaches are important and necessary components of the fight against antisemitism. Yet there is a limit as to how far these strategies may go in addressing the problem of antisemitism. Some of these limits arise for the manner in which the laws are enforced. Rabbi Andrew Baker, the Personal Representative, OSCE Chairman-in-office on combating antisemitism and Director of International Jewish Affairs of the American Jewish Committee argues that legislation to punish hate speech can be ineffective or even harmful:

> Legislation often does not work. It may exist but it is not uniformly or frequently imposed. In some cases where court examinations have been brought, the length of time between bringing a case and reaching some settlement can often be months or even years. Penalties, when penalties are applied, may be so limited as to not be a deterrent. In some countries, the mere fact that you have a legal process has allowed political leaders to be quiet, whether by choice or whether by law, to be able to say this is now a matter for the prosecutor, a matter for the courts, and they won't speak. More is needed to determine the best ways of dealing with this hate speech.[23]

---

22 Testimony of Shelly Faintuch, November 30, 2009, p14.
23 Testimony of Rabbi Andrew Baker, November 23, 2009, p, 20

In light of these limitations, Rabbi Baker noted that "most of us recognize a critical element is for political and civic leadership to speak clearly, loudly and swiftly to make such expressions taboo".[24]

More fundamentally, it is recognizable that law has a limited ability to address the roots of this form of prejudice. In the words of Rabbi Reuven Bulka:

> The law can address an evil, but it cannot change the fiber of society. I hope the general approach ... [must] be to develop a strategy that will minimize the likelihood of antisemitism rearing its ugly head, not because the law says you cannot but because people will not want to. They will not want to because it will be unacceptable; people will appreciate each other, and this will not be part of their conversation. Laws in this area are necessary, obviously, for the same reasons other laws are. ... We are not going to get that far with [a purely legal] approach we will just basically address the hate-mongers who are out in the open and who are apprehended. Nevertheless, we will not really get to the question of what we are doing to build the Canada of tomorrow that our children and grandchildren will be happy to live in.[25]

With this in mind, it is important that non-legal strategies, such as those including education and inter-cultural dialogue, as discussed below, are crucial and equally applied as important strategies to fighting antisemitism.

Security Initiatives

Despite the efforts of law enforcement officials, Jewish communities in Canada often have to implement extra security measures in order to protect themselves from external threats. The heightened threats to Canadian Jewish institutions have paralleled world events and the rising tide of global antisemitism. As explained by Rabbit Reuven Bulka:

> All that changed in 1991, around the time of the Gulf War. It was a watershed. We started getting threat-

---

24 Ibid.
25 Testimony of Rabbi Reuven Bulka, November 30, 2009, 10

ening calls. I myself had my life threatened, and we had to start doing what many other synagogues across Canada had to do, which was basically to lock our doors and put in a system that required you to identify yourself before you entered. We have security in place that is costing us, who can ill afford thousands of dollars a year just to protect our membership [to practice their religion].[26]

In 2005, Doron Horowitz was hired as the Director of Community Security for the United Jewish Appeal Federation of Greater Toronto. Such positions have become common and their sole job is protecting Jewish communities from violent crime.[27] Such options in hiring a security expert is not a viable option for smaller communities in Canada, even though they still face threats of violence. Many synagogues, community centres, and Jewish day schools employ security guards to act as a deterrent against physical violence.[28]

In 2007, the Department of Public Safety implemented the Security Infrastructure Pilot Program in response to a number of minority communities expressing concern about their vulnerability to hate crime. The program assists vulnerable communities to finance security assessments and improvements to their facilities. The Security Infrastructure Pilot Program has helped targeted minorities to implement the necessary precautions to protect themselves.[29] The success of the program has received the strong support and endorsement of national organizations such as the Canadian Jewish Congress. The implementation of this program as a permanent feature with sustained funding for the Jewish and other at-risk communities to upgrade security at community institutions in the face of the contemporary threats of violence.

Campus Reform

Of the many incidents of antisemitic behaviour across Canada, perhaps none is as threatening in creating a culture of acceptance and tolerance of hate and bigotry as the activity of antisemitism on university campuses. Universities have a responsibility to uphold the rights to free and critical academic inquiry and

---

26 Tesimony of Rabbi Reuven Bulka, November 30, 2009, p.5

27 Testimony of Doron Horowitz, December 8, 2009, p2-3

28 Submissions of Calgary Jewish Community Council and submissions of Canadian Jewish Congress, Ontario Region.

29 Testimony of Hon. Jason Kenney, February 8, 2010, p.12

to free political expression that have so long been a feature of the university experience. In recognizing that by doing so, universities serve the broader polity through the introduction of new ideas and theories concerning the world around us, these rights must be balanced with the responsibility of ensuring academic rigour in both research and teaching. What is important is the creation of provision of a learning environment in which all students feel safe, accepted, and able to focus on their studies.

Therefore, in approaching this issue, university administrators and professors must take a series of steps in combating antisemitism on Canadian university campuses First and foremost, they must protect the safety of students by implementing and enforcing strict student codes of conduct, which among other things, prohibit and enforce academic (or legal) penalties for harassment of other students. University administrators must ensure that proper security and police are allowed to monitor events that have potential to turn violent. In promoting this environment there should be a designation of certain "student spaces" on campus which should be reserved as a sanctuary from advocacy for various causes.

Tied to these are the fundamental protection of the equal right to freedom of speech for all students. This can be achieved by applying the same standards to both pro- and anti-Israel events and promoting academic discourse on campus. The right to exercise their own rights of free speech, and their responsibilities as academics by condemning discourse, events and speakers which are untrue, harmful, or not in the interest of academic discourse, including Israeli Apartheid Week should become a hallmark of Canadian university professionals. In addition, student unions and governing bodies must operate in the interest of the broad campus community in promoting a culture of tolerance and respect. At same time, students must be granted the right to opt-out of university funding and fees that take on openly political and partisan positions.

Within this perspective, the Federal Government can consider offering assistance sponsoring conferences and other similar initiatives, or the issuance of statements of principle to help combat hate on campus. Working with the provinces can be effective to help administrators develop suitable tools and structures to deal with this burgeoning problem in an effective and principled manner by support programs aimed at elevating the academic discourse surrounding contentious issues and fostering programs aimed at achieving real dialogue and holding professors accountable for the academic rigour of their curricula.

Research & Education

In addressing research and education on the issue of antisemitism in Canada, much progress needs to be done. Across the globe initiatives and research programs are thriving in tackling the issues in stemming the rise of antisemitism around across countries. Within the United States, however, the Yale Initiative for the Interdisciplinary Study of Antisemitism (YIISA) is the first and only North American university research centre examining the phenomenon of antisemitism. As Dr. Charles Small has noted, there is a serious "void" in this area of research more generally.[30]

In addition, this position has been advanced by Dr. Manfred Gerstenfeld, of the Post-Holocaust & Antisemitism Program with the Jerusalem Center for Public Affairs. As such, Canada can play an important role in undertaking research into antisemitism and could become an international leader in the field. This would not require an extra-ordinary adaption. Canada is currently an international leader in the field of national Jewish studies with government-funded chairs in Canadian Jewish studies at both Concordia University and York University.[31] These institutions are ideally situated to house research centres specializing in the study of antisemitism. This would not require a stretch as initial investment in Canadian research centre would work in advancing the role of academic research in addressing not only antisemitism, but issues of hate and racism in a Canadian and international context.

Closely tied to the role of research is the importance of education as a tool in combating antisemitism. The importance of early exposures to education in schools provides a strong safeguard in preventing the spread of such vile and racist thought in the minds of the next generation in creating a culture of understanding and tolerance. As Rabbi Reuven Bulka express:

> How do we counter antisemitism? To me, the very simple is teach, teach, teach…. We need to create foot soldiers, and those foot soldiers are the children of the next generation. We owe it to them. We owe it to the legacy of our founding fathers and mothers that children going through any elementary or high school system will have been so inoculated against hate by the they get to university that when they see it, they will reject it.[32]

---

30 Testimony of Dr. Charles Small, November 2, 2009, p20
31 Testimony of Dr. Manfred Gerstenfeld, November 16, 2009, p2
32 Testimony of Rabbi Reuven Bulka, November 30, 2009, p.5

Such programs, illustrate the importance of incorporating Holocaust education into school curricula.[33] Currently, Canada has taken an active role in such programs through its participation alongside twenty-six other countries on the International Task Force for Holocaust Education, Remembrance, and Research. In addition, the contribution of programs such as the Asper human rights Holocaust program[34] and Fighting Antisemitism Together (FAST) which has developed, in conjunction with the Canadian Jewish Congress, educational materials on antisemitism for children in grades six to eight. The success of the FAST program has reached more than half a million children from across Canada.[35]

In addition to the children of the future, attention should be paid in addressing the improvement of media literacy education as an important and effective method to prevent the spread of hate dialogue and youth recruitment by hate groups through the Internet.[36] In working through schools and educational institutes across Canada to develop and implement media intervention programs to help youth develop the critical thinking skills to be able to identify, reject and report hate media when experienced. Tied to this, the importance of newcomer education, especially in light of the fact that some immigrants may come from counties where old prejudices about Jewish people are commonplace. Along with above education and immigration reform, the addition of human rights should form a part of newcomer education in which combined with language training programs seeks to distill the development of a stronger and more inclusive Canadian identity.[37]

Inter-Faith and Inter-Community Initiatives

As important is the role that inter-community dialogue has as an important role in building relationships and trust among Canada's various religious communities. As Mark Freiman, President of the Canadian Jewish Congress points out:

> All the indications of racial prejudice and hatred seem
> to demonstrate ... that the more you know [about] the
> object of prejudice, the less likely you yourself will be
> prejudiced. Prejudice and hatred are highest in com-

---

33 See example. Testimony of Mr. Navid Khavari, November 23, 2009 p5; Testimony of Yehuda Bauer, November 16, 2009. P.8

34 Testimony of Shelly Faintuch, November 30, 2009, p 14

35 http://www.parl.gc.ca/HousePublications/Publication.aspx?DocId=5926120&Language=E&Mode=2&Parl=41&Ses=1

36 Testimony of Matthew Johnson, December 1, 2009, p3

37 Testimony of Reverend Majed el-Shafie, November 30, 2009 p11; Testimony of Mr. Fo Niemi, December 1 2009, p10

munities and among individuals who know the least
about the target community.[38]

Along this line, commendable work and progress has been the result of local
faith-based initiatives, such as those organized by Father John Walsh of St. John
Brebeuf of Montreal, where Holocaust survivors are invited to speak at the
parish church and evening prayers are held with participants form many faiths,
including Jews, Christians, Muslims, Hindus, Sikhs, and Buddhist.[39]

This sentiment has been supported by the Canadian Ethnocultural Council
(CEC) as "one of the most important means in combating hate, in general, and
antisemitism, in particular, is by providing opportunities for diverse ethnocultural communities to meet regularly, build relationships, learn and understand
from each other, discuss issues of mutual concern, and support one another."[40]
Such organizations such as the CEC serve as a forum for dialogue fo diverse
ethnocultural populations in Canada, where member organizations collabo-
rate and share ideas and concerns affecting their communities.[41] Through their
work, organizations such as the CEC play an important role in the fight against
antisemitism and intolerance.

Inter-faith and inter-community dialogue is particularly important between the
Jewish and Muslim communities. The government has a role to play in creating
institutional structures to bring together political and community leaders from
across this country, including representatives from the Jewish and Muslim communities. For example, as impressed upon by Minister Jason Kenny, such programs
serve to bring together impressionable individuals. Regarding the Somali-Jewish
Mentorship Project: "It brings together young Canadians of Somali origin—many
of [who] grew up in refugee families and have faced social exclusion and had very
limited opportunities—typically with professions and businesses owned by Jewish
Canadians, many of whose grandparents or parents arrived here as refugees with
nothing and faced discrimination and persecution as well."[42]

Similar innovative projects such as "Peace it Together" initiative in British
Columbia seek to create inter-communal connections. A Jewish Canadian
woman from Montreal and a Palestinian Canadian man from Vancouver started
the group. The organization recruits senior Israeli, Palestinian and Canadian

---

38 Testimony of Mark Freiman, December 7, 2009, p11; Testimony of Father John Walsh,
  November 30, 2009, p. 4.
39 Testimony of Father John Walsh, November 30, 2009, p. 7
40 Testimony of Peter Ferreira, November 30, 2009, p7
41 Testimony of Dominic Campione, November 30, 2009, p.6
42 Testimony of Minister Jason Kenney, February 8, 2010, p. 12

high school students to participate in a "peace camp" in Vancouver, for peace studies, making films addressing issues relating to the Middle East and the Peace Process.[43] The support of creative youth-focused initiatives through the belief that such initiatives have lasting influence in developing cross-cultural understanding between community and interfaith groups is vital. The promotion of dialogue and community cohesion is crucial in combating anti-Semitism. As such there is a role for the federal government in creating a formal structure to facilitate and promote joint leadership among Muslim and Jewish youth.

United Nations

While domestically, antisemitism within Canada is a sordid experience, it often does not pale to the nature and resurgence of antisemitism in countries around the world. As such, much work needs to be done in combating this phenomenon globally. Of particular concern is the role of the United Nations. This is exemplified by the 1975 UN General Assembly resolution equating Zionism with racism. Though the resolution was repealed, Zionism is still frequently equated with racism now, both in domestic and international forums, as was the notable case at the World Conference against Racism at Durban in 2001, and its NGO Forum. Yet the problem persists—singling out of the Jewish and the Jewish State on the international stage through other international forums such as the UN Human Rights Council. In the five years of its existence, the Council has adopted 35 condemnatory resolutions on Israel, and little over a dozen for the rest of the world combined. That translated into roughly seventy percent of the Council's moral outrage being deployed to demonize and delegitimize the only democracy in the Middle East. All of these resolutions on Israel have been one-sided condemnations that refuse to condemn terrorist organization such as Hamas and Hezbollah and their state sponsors, the Islamic Republic of Iran.[44]

The Government of Canada has recently taken the stance of distancing itself from the one-sided condemnations of Israel at the United Nations and the affirmation that standing out against a consensus is preferable to joining one. In addressing this issue, the Committee of Foreign Affairs of the House of Commons should study the equity of the United Nations Human Rights Council regarding its over-emphasis of alleged human rights abuses by Israel while ignoring flagrant human rights abuses of other member states.

Such initiatives are recommended by the Government of Canada would stress the need to reform the International Human Rights regime. The cen-

---

43 Testimony of Hon. Stephen Own, January 25, 2010, p, 12-13
44 Testimony of Hillel Neuer, Executive Director of UN Watch, January 25, 2011

trepiece of such reformations would entail the move to ratify and enact the various international instruments dealing with antisemitism. These instruments include international commitments to combat antisemitism and Holocaust denial, enshrined in the Berlin Declaration on Organization for Security and Cooperation in Europe (OSCE) and similar UN resolutions. Canada, as a political and diplomatic leader in the international sphere, is positioned to take on the special obligation to challenge such expressions of antisemitism and threats to genocide in the international arena. Rejection of statements by foreign leaders, foreign diplomats and representatives at international forums such as the UN and through internationals conventions and protocols represents not a choice but a moral obligation in staying the plague of antisemitism.

With this in mind, the creation of a permanent, and publicly accessible 'ambassadorial' position under the auspices of an appropriate Department, such as Foreign Affairs, Justice or Multiculturalism, to develop and implement policies, projects and research on combating antisemitism furthers these aims is urgently required. This Office should used to monitor implementation of priority recommendations and ensure compliance and accountability through annual reporting of each federal Department and tabled in annual Report to Parliament on progress and challenges in combating antisemitism in Canada.

We are please that on February 19, 2013, the Government of Canada officially opened its Office of Religious Freedom, within Foreign Affairs with the mandate to:

- protect, and advocate on behalf of, religious minorities under threat;
- oppose religious hatred and intolerance; and
- promote Canadian values of pluralism and tolerance abroad.

Through the Office of Religious Freedom, Canada will continue to work with like-minded partners to speak out against egregious violations of freedom of religion, denounce violence against human-rights defenders and condemn attacks on worshippers and places of worship around the world. Such efforts could enhance protections afforded to vulnerable religious minorities across the globe, including Jewish victims of antisemitism.

Apendices

Appendix I: OTTAWA PROTOCOL

Preamble

We, Representatives of our respective Parliaments from across the world, convening in Ottawa for the second Conference and Summit of the Inter-parliamentary Coalition for Combating Antisemitism, note and reaffirm the London Declaration on Combating Antisemitism as a template document for the fight against antisemitism.

We are concerned that, since the London Conference in February 2009, there continues to be a dramatic increase in recorded antisemitic hate crimes and attacks targeting Jewish persons and property, and Jewish religious, educational and communal institutions.

We remain alarmed by ongoing state-sanctioned genocidal antisemitism and related extremist ideologies. If antisemitism is the most enduring of hatreds, and genocide is the most horrific of crimes, then the convergence of the genocidal intent embodied in antisemitic ideology is the most toxic of combinations.

We are appalled by the resurgence of the classic anti-Jewish libels, including:

- The Blood Libel (that Jews use the blood of children for ritual sacrifice)
- The Jews as "Poisoners of the Wells"—responsible for all evils in the world
- The myth of the "new Protocols of the Elders of Zion"—the tsarist forgery that proclaimed an international Jewish conspiracy bent on world domination—and accuses the Jews of controlling government, the economy, media and public institutions.
- The *double entendre* of denying the Holocaust—accusing the Jews of fabricating the Holocaust as a hoax—and the nazification of the Jew and the Jewish people.

We are alarmed by the explosion of antisemitism and hate on the Internet, a medium crucial for the promotion and protection of freedom of expression, freedom of information, and the participation of civil society.

We are concerned over the failure of most OSCE participating states to fully implement provisions of the 2004 Berlin Declaration, including the commitment to:

> Collect and maintain reliable information and statistics about antisemitic crimes, and other hate crimes, committed within their territory, report such information periodically to the OSCE Office for Democratic Institutions and Human Rights (ODIHR), and make this information available to the public.

We are concerned by the reported incidents of antisemitism on campuses, such as acts of violence, verbal abuse, rank intolerance, and assaults on those committed to free inquiry, while undermining fundamental academic values.

We renew our call for national Governments, Parliaments, international institutions, political and civic leaders, NGOs, and civil society to affirm democratic and human values, build societies based on respect and citizenship and combat any manifestations of antisemitism and all forms of discrimination.

We reaffirm the EUMC—now Fundamental Rights Agency (FRA)—working definition of antisemitism, which sets forth that:

Contemporary examples of antisemitism in public life, the media, schools, the workplace, and in the religious sphere could, taking into account the overall context, include, but are not limited to:

- Calling for, aiding, or justifying the killing or harming of Jews in the name of radical ideology or an extremist view of religion.
- Making mendacious, dehumanizing, demonizing, or stereotypical allegations about Jews as such or the power of Jews as collective—such as, especially but not exclusively—the myth about a world Jewish conspiracy, or of Jews controlling the media, economy, government or other societal institutions.
- Accusing Jews as a people of being responsible for real or imagined wrongdoing committed by a single Jewish person or group, or even for acts committed by non-Jews.
- Denying the fact, scope, mechanisms (e.g. gas chambers) or intentionality of the genocide of the Jewish people at the hands of National Socialist

Germany and its supporters and accomplices during World War II (the Holocaust).

- Accusing the Jews as a people, or Israel as a state, of inventing or exaggerating the Holocaust.
- Accusing Jewish citizens of being more loyal to Israel, or to the alleged priorities of Jews worldwide, than to the interests of their own nations.
- Examples of the ways in which antisemitism manifests itself with regard to the State of Israel taking into account the overall context could include:
- Denying the Jewish people their right to self-determination, e.g., by claiming that the existence of a State of Israel is a racist endeavour.
- Applying double standards by requiring of it behaviour not expected or demanded of any other democratic nation.
- Using the symbols and images associated with classic antisemitism (e.g. claims of Jews killing Jesus or blood libel) to characterize Israel or Israelis.
- Drawing comparisons of contemporary Israeli policy to that of the Nazis.
- Holding Jews collectively responsible for actions of the State of Israel.

However, criticism of Israel similar to that levelled against any other country cannot be regarded as antisemitic.

Let it be clear: Criticism of Israel is not antisemitic, and saying so is wrong. But singling Israel out for selective condemnation and opprobrium—let alone denying its right to exist or seeking its destruction—is discriminatory and hateful, and not saying so is dishonest.

Members of Parliament meeting in Ottawa commit to:

(1) Calling on our Governments to uphold international commitments on combating antisemitism—such as the OSCE Berlin Principles—and to engage with the United Nations for that purpose. In the words of former U.N. Secretary-General Kofi Annan, "It is [...] rightly said that the United Nations emerged from the ashes of the Holocaust. And a Human Rights agenda that fails to address antisemitism denies its own history";

(2) Calling on Parliaments and Governments to adopt the EUMC Working Definition of Antisemitism and anchor its enforcement in existing law;

(3) Encouraging countries throughout the world to establish mechanisms for reporting and monitoring on domestic and international antisemitism, along the lines of the "Combating Antisemitism Act of 2010" recently introduced in the United States Congress;

(4) Encouraging the leaders of all religious faiths—represented also at this Conference—to use all means possible to combat antisemitism and all forms of hatred and discrimination;

(5) Calling on the Parliamentary Forum of the Community of Democracies to make the combating of hatred and antisemitism a priority in their work;

(6) Calling on Governments and Parliamentarians to reaffirm and implement the Genocide Convention, recognising that where there is incitement to genocide, State parties have an obligation to act;

(7) Working with universities to encourage them to combat antisemitism with the same seriousness with which they confront other forms of hate. Specifically, universities should be invited to define antisemitism clearly, provide specific examples, and enforce conduct codes firmly, while ensuring compliance with freedom of speech and the principle of academic freedom. Universities should use the EUMC Working Definition of Antisemitism as a basis for education, training and orientation. Indeed, there should be zero tolerance for discrimination of any kind against anyone in the university community on the basis of race, gender, religion, ethnic origin, sexual orientation or political position;

(8) We encourage the European Union to promote civic education and open society in its European Neighbourhood Policy (ENP) and to link funding to democratic development and respect for Human Rights in ENP partner countries;

(9) Establishing an International Task Force of Internet specialists comprised of parliamentarians and experts to create common indicators to identify and monitor antisemitism and other manifestations of hate online and to develop policy recommendations for Governments and international frameworks to address these problems;

(10) Building on the African representation at this Conference, to develop increased working relationships with parliamentarians in Africa for the combating of racism and antisemitism;

(11) We urge the incoming OSCE Chair, Lithuania, to make implementation of these commitments a priority during 2011 and call for the reappointment of the Special Representatives to assist in this work.

Appendix II: RECOMMENDATIONS OF THE INQUIRY PANEL

Recommendation: 1
The CPCCA supports and adopts the EUMC Working Definition of Antisemitism for the purpose of this report and recommends that the Definition be adopted and promoted by the Government of Canada and law enforcement agencies.

Recommendation: 2
The Inquiry Panel is concerned about the effects of Islamist ideology in propagating antisemitism in Canada.

We recommend that the Government of Canada and Canadian legislators uphold freedom of speech principles, so that all those who oppose and seek to combat this radical ideology have a protected voice with which to advocate against it.

We recommend that the Government of Canada continue to include in its list of terrorist organizations, groups such as Hamas and Hezbollah, who seek the destruction of the Jewish people, and that it restrict or prohibit Canadians from funding them.

Recognizing the vulnerability of immigrant communities, we recommend that funding guidelines should be strengthened to withhold any form of government funding or other support for NGOs that preach hatred or antisemitism—particularly those involved in integration and settlement of new Canadians where they may influence understanding of the responsibilities and obligations of Canadian citizenship.

We recommend that political leaders stress the need for civil discourse, based on Canadian values, among groups in Canada, especially when dealing with contentious political issues.

Recommendation: 3

Therefore, the Inquiry Panel agrees with the recommendations put forth by many law enforcement professionals,236 specifically those of then Commissioner Julian Fantino of the Ontario Provincial Police, who recommended that Canada should establish "national standards for police services across the country so that we have a common understanding of what constitutes an antisemitic crime, together with consistent across-the-board mechanisms for data reporting and statistical analysis."

We recommend that police services across Canada begin to report hate crimes broken down by targeted community.

We recommend that the resulting data be compiled and released in the annual Uniform Crime Reporting Survey.

Recommendation: 4

Therefore, the Inquiry Panel recommends that the Canadian Centre for Justice Statistics adopt and promote a standardized definition of "non-criminal antisemitic incident." This definition should be formulated with reference to the EUMC definition of antisemitism.

Recommendation: 5

Therefore, in order to ensure the most comprehensive understanding of the level and nature of non-criminal antisemitic incidents in Canada, the Inquiry Panel recommends that all bodies, including police, human rights commissions, and not-for profit agencies, work to coordinate and pool information about antisemitic incidents in Canada.

Recommendation: 6

The Inquiry Panel adopts the recommendation of Mr. Niemi, executive director of the Center for Research-Action on Race Relations (CRARR), that the fight against antisemitism must take place "effectively and equally in French and in English. It needs to take into account the special dynamics of the French-speaking collectivity in Canada ..."

Recommendation: 7

The Inquiry Panel adopts the recommendation of Mr. Niemi, executive director of the Center for Research-Action on Race Relations (CRARR), that the fight against antisemitism must take place "effectively and equally in French and in English. It needs to take into account the special dynamics of the French-speaking collectivity in Canada ..."

Recommendation: 8

The Inquiry Panel therefore recommends that Canadian universities work together to develop protocols and procedures for the reporting and pooling of information relating to antisemitic incidents on campus, as defined with reference to the EUMC Working Definition of Antisemitism. All university staff and students should be encouraged to document and report antisemitic incidents whenever they occur.

Recommendation: 9

The Inquiry Panel agrees with the conclusion of the UK Inquiry that "calls to boycott contact with academics working in Israel are an assault on academic freedom and intellectual exchange."

Recommendation: 10

We encourage universities to adopt clear and consistent guidelines aimed at protecting the security of speakers on campus

Recommendation: 11

We recognize the complexity surrounding the issues in the Middle East, and the desire of many Canadians, especially on campus, to debate and propose solutions to those issues. We suggest that the best resolutions and recommendations for complex problems can only be developed through serious and rigorous debate, free of intimidation and threats.

The Inquiry Panel finds that the concept of Israeli Apartheid Week, like the comparison of Israel to an apartheid state in general, is aimed at delegitimizing the State of Israel, and demonizing those who support it. Because of its sheer size and nature, we are concerned about the intimidating effect this experience has on Jewish students.

We commend the Legislative Assembly of Ontario for passing a motion condemning Israeli Apartheid Week, and recommend that Canadian politicians openly condemn Israeli Apartheid Week on campus and the intimidation that it creates.

Because of our commitment to free speech, and to the maintenance of open discourse on university campuses, the Inquiry Panel does not think, despite the vulgarity of Israeli Apartheid Week, that it would be appropriate for university administrators to refuse to allow the event to take place. However, the Inquiry Panel does have a number of recommendations to protect the safety of Jewish and pro-Israeli students, which are listed at the end of this section.

Recommendation: 12

We assert that on a limited number of university campuses, antisemitism is a serious problem of which, taking the most charitable view, some university administrators are unaware. At the other extreme, the Inquiry Panel is concerned that some administrators are, in fact, aware of the extent to which antisemitism exists on their campuses, but are unwilling to admit this fact or to take the steps needed to eliminate it.

Furthermore, the Inquiry Panel commends the work of Dr. Sheldon Levy, President of Ryerson University, who has taken bold steps to combat antisemitism and all forms of racism at his University.

Recommendation: 13

Therefore, we recommend that university administrators and professors:

- First and foremost protect the safety of students by implementing and enforcing strict student codes of conduct, which among other things, prohibit and enforce academic (or legal) penalties for harassment of other students. They must also ensure that proper security and police are allowed to monitor events that have potential to turn violent;
- Designate certain "student spaces" on campus which should be reserved as a sanctuary from advocacy for various causes;
- Protect the equal right to freedom of speech for all students, by applying the same standards to both pro- and anti-Israel events and promoting academic discourse on campus;
- Exercise their own rights of free speech, and their responsibilities as academics by condemning discourse, events and speakers which are untrue, harmful, or not in the interest of academic discourse, including Israeli Apartheid Week;
- We recommend that student unions operate in the interest of the broad campus community;
- We recommend that the Federal Government and/or the Inquiry consider offering assistance sponsoring conferences and other similar initiatives, or the issuance of statements of principle to help combat hate on campus;
- We recommend that the Federal Government and/or the Inquiry work with the provinces to help administrators develop suitable tools and structures to deal with this burgeoning problem in an effective and principled manner;
- We recommend that students be permitted to opt-out of non-union organizations that take positions on partisan issues;

- We further recommend that when student fees are automatically directed to campus organizations, that students be able to opt-out of such fees online and prior to paying them, rather than in person and by way of refund;
- We recommend that university administrations support programs aimed at elevating the academic discourse surrounding contentious issues and fostering programs aimed at achieving real dialogue; and
- We recommend that professors be held accountable for academic rigour of their curricula.

Recommendation: 14

The Panel supports the continued use of the Criminal Code to combat manifestations of hate- and bias-motivated crime.

The Inquiry Panel finds that evidence respecting the difficulty in prosecuting hate crimes is of concern and merits further study.

Recommendation: 15

The Inquiry Panel notes that the constitutionality of Section 13 will be decided by the Federal Court of Canada in Lemire v. Warman. Because of this fact, and because opinion was so profoundly split in the testimony presented to us, the Inquiry Panel declines to make any specific policy recommendations on this issue.

Recommendation: 16

The Inquiry Panel recommends that police forces across Canada send their officers to the "Tools for Tolerance" program at the Simon Wiesenthal Center for hate crimes training.

Recommendation: 17

We recommend that the Department of Citizenship, Immigration and Multiculturalism review, and take into consideration rising international antisemitism when designating source countries and targeting specific countries/people for resettlement.

Recommendation: 18

The Inquiry Panel believes that non-legal strategies, such as those including education and inter-cultural dialogue discussed below, are crucial and equally important strategies to fighting antisemitism.

Recommendation: 19

We recommend that the Security Infrastructure Pilot Project be made permanent with sustainable funding for the Jewish and other at-risk communities to upgrade security at community institutions in the face of the contemporary threats of violence.

Recommendation: 20

We recommend that the government provide seed money to establish a Canadian academic research centre for the study of antisemitism, to be housed within a Canadian university.

Recommendation: 21

The Panel recommends that schools across Canada develop and implement media intervention programs to help youth develop the critical thinking skills to be able to identify, reject and report hate media on the Internet.

Recommendation: 22

The Inquiry Panel agrees with the recommendations of Reverend Majed El Shafie and Mr. Fo Niemi that human rights should form a part of newcomer education, which could be combined with language training programs.

Recommendation: 23

The Inquiry Panel concludes that the promotion of dialogue and community cohesion is crucial to combating antisemitism and that the federal government has a role to play in the creation of formal structures to facilitate and promote this dialogue among community leaders.

We also adopt the recommendation of the UK Inquiry Panel that "the Jewish and Muslim communities and interfaith groups promote joint leadership programs for young Muslims and Jews."

Recommendation: 24

The Inquiry Panel recognizes that the work of the United Nations in relation to Israel is beyond the purview of this report, and therefore recommends that the Committee of Foreign Affairs of the House of Commons undertake a study of the equity of the United Nations Human Rights Council, particularly regarding its over-emphasis of alleged human rights abuses by Israel, while ignoring flagrant human rights abuses of other member states.

We recommend that the Government of Canada spearhead initiatives to reform the International Human Rights regime.

We recommend that the government move quickly to ratify and/or enact the various international instruments dealing with antisemitism (including international commitments to combat antisemitism and Holocaust denial, including but not limited to, the Berlin Declaration on the Organization for Security and Cooperation in Europe (OSCE) and similar UN resolutions) and prepare constructive suggestions and resolutions befitting its role as host for the 2011 conference.

We recommend that political and diplomatic leaders take up their special obligation to challenge expressions of antisemitism and threats of genocide in the international arena, including the rejection of such statements by foreign leaders, foreign diplomats and representatives at international forums such as the UN and through international conventions and protocols to which Canada is a signatory.

We recommend the creation of a permanent, publicly accessible "ambassadorial" position under the auspices of the most appropriate Department (Foreign Affairs, Justice, Multiculturalism) to develop and implement policies, projects and research on combating antisemitism, including the provision of funds to NGOs to further these aims. This office should also monitor implementation of priority recommendations and ensure compliance and accountability (including annual reporting by each Department on the implementation of Inquiry recommendations and other action items within their jurisdictions). An annual Report to Parliament should be also be tabled on progress made and challenges outstanding in combating antisemitism in Canada, triggering a government response.

We commend the Government of Canada's proposed initiative to open an office dedicated to Religious Freedom within the Department of Foreign Affairs. The efforts of this proposed office could enhance protections afforded to vulnerable religious minorities across the globe, including Jews at risk of being the victims of antisemitism.

Supplication Submission to the Parliamentary Inquiry into Antisemitism

OKAY, SO WHAT CAN WE DO ABOUT IT?

After submitting "Crossing the Line While Blurring the Line," I begged the committee's indulgence for time to supplement my description of the problem with some prescriptions for confronting it. Herewith are some suggestions, respectfully submitted:

- Deputize the Next Generation of Internet Users to Fight Hate through a Citizenship 2.0 Program in Schools: regarding hate on the Internet in particular, defensive strategies are insufficient. Everyone seems to worry about the blogosphere's deleterious effect on civil society, on children, on Western culture. Part of the fight against anti-Semitism should entail enlisting educators and community leaders to envision Citizenship 2.0, teaching students to avoid polluting on line-discourse themselves, to combat on-line hate, to assess on-line information critically, and to use the net's grassroots power to defend democratic values against the haters. The Internet works democratically, let's mobilize and deputize Canadian youth to fight hate wherever they see it (and, of course, never indulge in it)

- Name and shame—publicly and privately, the government must make it clear that Canada does not associate with anti-Semitic governments or governments that wink at anti-Semitism in the media, on the streets, etc. The Harper government has shown in the battle of Durban II, and recently, at the UN General Assembly meetings in New York how governments can lead in recoiling from Mahmoud Ahmadinejad and his ilk (and history will judge these courageous moves generously). The next step is widening the perspective, chiding the Saudis, Egyptians, and others whose leaders are more subtle but whose institutions and elites perpetuate the problem. Connected to this, my colleague, Dr. Gregg Rickman notes, is accepting the EUMC working definition of anti-Semitism and collecting information worldwide via embassies and within Canada documenting anti-Semitic incidents—noting that we must name, before we can shame.

- Pursue the Perpetrators—The government should embrace the Hon. Irwin Cotler's initiative to prosecute Mahmoud Ahmadinejad for incitement to genocide. Such a strategy puts the offenders on the defensive, and in this case would also help neutralize a major strategic threat to the world.

- Continue Defending Human Rights as Part of the Canadian Patrimony: emphasizing Canada's critical role in drafting the early declarations on human rights, then in implementing them, should help raise awareness among legislators and diplomats when the language of human rights is hijacked by dictators, or demeaned by hypocrites, it's a Canadian issue because Canada has an important historical and ideological stake in the human rights infrastructure.

- Spearhead Initiatives to Reform the Human Rights Community: in 1975 US Ambassador to the UN Daniel Patrick Moynihan warning that using the language of human rights to single out Israel threatened the entire post-war mechanism of human rights. A working group of parliamentarians in Canada and beyond should issue a report card, assessing the UN in general, its Human Rights Council, maybe human rights NGOs as well, seeing if they perceive a bias, where they find a bias, and making suggestions of how to improve it.

- Take Anti-Semitism Personally: fighting anti-Semitism should be considered part of a diplomat's mission. If a French newspaper published an anti-Quebecois screed, presumably a Canadian diplomat would object. If that same French newspaper published an anti-Semitic screed, would the Canadian diplomat "get involved?" The diplomat should take offense, both because Canadian Jews are hurt by the hatred and because a country with ideals should uphold them for all, whether or not their citizens are directly involved. Now, what if it wasn't a newspaper but the Venezuelan government—first harassing Canadians, then harassing Jews? What responsibility should Canada take for fighting that? This is a stretch, but we need to evaluate Canada's responsibilities for fighting anti-Semitism and other evils in general, asking what training and direction diplomats receive regarding these issues, training diplomats to look at anti-Semitism not as an "internal matter" but an assault on us all.

- Encourage More Grassroots Organizations: The FAST model (Fighting Antisemitism Together) pioneered by the civic leaders Tony and Elizabeth Comper should be supported and expanded.

- Fund and Expand Community Policing Models and Information Gathering: fund and encourage specific initiatives like the ones in Ottawa that fight anti-Semitic hooliganism on a grassroots level; part of that is tracking anti-Semitic outbreaks systematically.

- Encourage A Community Self-Policing Model—with more accurate and honest tracking, those communities where anti-Semitism festers can be identified and pushed to take more responsibility for policing themselves.

- Avoid Fights About Rights: The government's bully pulpit can be used to change the dynamics on the various battlefields (campus, media, internet) etc. When Israel's critics cross the line from opposing Israel's policies to fomenting anti-Semitism, they hide behind "rights talk." Professors yell "academic freedom"; journalists cry "freedom of the press." I support academic freedom—I oppose *educational malpractice*. A professors should be free to criticize Israel in the classroom, but that professor commits educational malpractice if students feel bullied, squelched, harassed for disagreeing—and all too often, that is what happens when professors turn their classroom lecterns into political soapboxes. Similarly, we should talk about constructive criticism and professional responsibility not free speech. I did not question the freedom of the Swedish press to print the recent article with those inaccurate claims that Israel harvested Palestinian body parts. However, I did not think that Israel's constructive criticism violated the reporters' freedom of speech or freedom of the press—and if the Swedish government had criticized the article, that too would have been an example of constructive criticism not a violation of freedom. Moreover, the question that needs to be raised is one of the reporter's and editors' professional responsibility (and in this case competence)—rather than their freedom to spread these lies.

Appendix III

From the forthcoming ODIHR publication, "Hate Crimes in the OSCE Region: Incidents and Responses—Annual Report for 2008":

There is limited official information available on anti-Semitic hate crimes in the OSCE region.

- Nineteen participating States reported that they collect such data: Austria, Belgium, Canada, Croatia, Czech Republic, France, Germany, Italy, Liechtenstein, Moldova, Netherlands, Poland, Russian Federation, Serbia, Spain, Sweden, Switzerland, United Kingdom, and the United States.
- -But only eight (Austria, Belgium, Czech Republic, France, Germany, Italy, Sweden, and the United Kingdom) submitted figures for 2008 to ODIHR.
- Austria and the Czech Republic reported an increase in incidents compared to 2007. Germany, Italy and the United Kingdom reported a decrease. (The other three countries did not report comparable figures from 2007).
- There are non-governmental sources for data on anti-Semitic crimes in 2008 in many OSCE participating States, including Austria, Belgium, Canada, Czech Republic, Germany, Greece, Italy, Russian Federation, Ukraine, United Kingdom and the United States.
- In only four cases (Austria, Czech Republic, Germany and Italy) were there sufficient 2008 data to enable ODIHR to compare NGO figures with official data from governments. In two cases the unofficial data contained twice the number of anti-Semitic incidents reported in official statistics
- ODIHR collected media reports indicating that anti-Semitic incidents took place in 2008 in Austria, Belarus, Belgium, Canada, Croatia, Czech

261

Republic, Denmark, France, Georgia, Germany, Greece, Hungary, Ireland, Italy, Lithuania, Moldova, Norway, Poland, Romania, Russian Federation, Slovakia, Spain, Sweden, Switzerland, Turkey, Ukraine, United Kingdom, and the United States.

The relevant newsletters and media reported little on the South Caucasus region and on Central Asian countries and, since the participating States did not submit figures regarding anti-Semitic hate crimes, ODIHR has no reliable information concerning these.